Anthropology
A Student's Guide to Theory and Method

What makes this book unique is its attempt to integrate theory and method within a single work. Starting with anthropology's foundations in the late nineteenth century, Stanley R. Barrett brings the reader up to date on such topics as the influence of postmodern and feminist criticism, changes in ethnographic style, and the shift from scientific to humanistic discourse. He discusses the power relationships between anthropologists and their subjects, from the era of colonialism through that of contemporary cultural pluralism. Barrett shows that, in recent decades, a serious gap has emerged between theory and method – a gap that will ultimately have to be addressed by today's students.

STANLEY R. BARRETT is a professor in the Department of Sociology and Anthropology at the University of Guelph. He is author of several books, including *Paradise: Class, Commuters, and Ethnicity in Rural Ontario* and *Is God a Racist? The Right Wing in Canada.*

STANLEY R. BARRETT

Anthropology: A Student's Guide to Theory and Method

UNIVERSITY OF TORONTO PRESS
Toronto Buffalo London

© University of Toronto Press Incorporated 1996
Toronto Buffalo London
Printed in Canada

ISBN 0-8020-0848-8 (cloth)
ISBN 0-8020-7833-8 (paper)

Printed on acid-free paper

Canadian Cataloguing in Publication Data

Barrett, Stanley R., 1938–
    Anthropology

    Includes bibliographical references and index.
    ISBN 0-8020-0848-8 (bound)
    ISBN 0-8020-7833-8 (pbk.)

    1. Anthropology – Philosophy.   2. Anthropology –
    Methodology.   I. Title.

GN33.B37 1996   301'.01   C95-933202-2

University of Toronto Press acknowledges the financial assistance to its
publishing program of the Canada Council and the Ontario Arts Council.

TO PROFESSOR F.G. BAILEY

Contents

Preface

I was seduced by anthropology before I had ever taken a course in the subject. This was back in the 1960s when I taught secondary school for two years in a remote Igbo village in Nigeria under the auspices of CUSO, Canada's equivalent of the Peace Corps. The privilege of getting to know people in a culture different from my own thrilled me, and on return to Canada I switched to anthropology (my undergraduate degree had been in English and philosophy).

I was determined to return to Nigeria, and when I eventually did, this time among the Yoruba, it was as an anthropologist in training. My initial project involved a village that had banned money (and at times marriage), had believed that no member of the community would ever die, and had achieved remarkable economic success with virtually no outside help. Since then I have investigated organized racism and anti-Semitism in Canada, class and ethnicity in rural Ontario, and gender and violence in Corsica. Although it was the romance of anthropology that drew me to the discipline, in the course of conducting these various projects I have had to struggle with theory and method, and to try to prepare my own students for fieldwork. The purpose of this book is to make these tasks easier for others. Most of the book is devoted to an overview of theory and method, with special attention paid to the relationship between them. Towards the end, I also take a crack at clarifying the one part of fieldwork that has defied demystification: the analysis of qualitative data.

In this study the history of anthropology has been divided into three phases: building the scientific foundation of the discipline, patching the cracks that eventually emerged, and demolition and reconstruction – essentially knocking down the original foundation and starting over again. The first phase began in the late part of the nineteenth century and ended in the 1950s, when the colonial world began to disintegrate. The second phase centred around the 1960s, as new theories sprang up and methods were refined in order to cope with doubts that a scientific study of culture had been established, and with the recognition that change and conflict were as prevalent as stability and harmony. The third phase began in the 1970s and continues today, dominated by post-modernism and feminist anthropology. One of my central arguments will be that beginning in phase two, and growing rapidly during phase three, a gap has emerged between our theories and our methods. For most of the history of anthropology, our methods have talked the language of science. In recent decades, however, our theories have repudiated science, in the process pushing us ever closer to the humanities.

I have written this book primarily for students. My hope is that it will provide them with a solid introduction to theory and method, or at least refresh their memories if they are at a more advanced stage in their studies. I shall also be pleased if my colleagues find some value in this study, particularly the organization of the history of the discipline into three phases, and the attempt to deal with theory and method together.

Among those who helped me most with this book, my students come first. I am especially grateful to my graduate students in qualitative methods, and my undergraduate students in theory, methods, and introductory social anthropology. Many of the ideas in this study were tried out on audiences at Edith Cowan University, Curtin University, and the University of Western Australia. I am indebted to Dr Chris Griffin and his colleagues at Edith Cowan University for their invitation and hospitality. Elvi Whittaker, Fred Eidlin, and Marta Rohatynskyj provided useful critical comments and encouragement, as did the three generous and knowledgeable readers arranged by the publisher. Last but not least, Kaye once again gave her unreserved support for my urge to write, and my regular tennis and squash partners (all of them young at heart) not only kept me sane while working on this book, but also reminded me – as hard as it is to believe – that there might be more to life than theory and method!

STANLEY R. BARRETT

ANTHROPOLOGY: A STUDENT'S GUIDE TO THEORY AND METHOD

1

Unleashing the Anthropologist: A Historical Overview

Anthropologists were 'unleashed' at a particular period in history: the age of exploration, when Europeans began to encounter 'the primitive.' This momentous point of contact pushed to the forefront a fundamental intellectual problem: were human beings everywhere essentially the same, or did widespread cultural and physical diversity mean that there was no such thing as the unity of humankind? (see Jarvie 1986). Anthropology led the search for an answer to this problem, but under circumstances in which the balance of power between field worker and 'native' was very much one-sided. Anthropologists were armed with a sense of moral, intellectual, cultural, and military superiority. They possessed an unquestioned mandate to intrude into the lives of non-Europeans, and put them under a microscope. In employing the provocative term 'unleashed,' I certainly do not want to claim that the early anthropologists were like mad dogs, or that they were necessarily insensitive to the welfare of 'the natives'; nor do I mean to cast doubt on the high quality of some of the early studies. What I do want to convey is a picture of the anthropologist in hot pursuit of 'the primitive,' who was a captive specimen in a scholarly exercise.

At that point in history, the idea of natives studying Europeans would probably have been considered an absurdity; for all intents and purposes, anthropology emerged as the scholarly discipline in which Europeans shaped and controlled the image of non-Western peoples, its mandate to do so having only been effectively challenged in recent years. What, then, is anthropology, and how did it develop as a field of study?

Anthropology usually has been defined as the study of other cultures, employing the technique of participant observation, and collecting qualitative (not quantitative) data. Like all the social sciences, anthropology was never discovered but simply professionalized, which among other things meant that its practitioners eventually found a home in the university community. In 1883 E.B. Tylor, an early giant in British anthropology, had been appointed as Keeper of the University Museum at Oxford University. Before the end of the decade, professorships in anthropology had been established at Harvard University and the University of Pennsylvania. By the last quarter of the nineteenth century, thus, it was evident that a specialized academic focus on non-Western or primitive societies had taken root.

This was the era of 'armchair anthropology,' guided by an evolutionary perspective. There was a tendency to assume that every custom that differed from European ones was somehow flawed; in other words, ethnocentrism ran rampant. The leading scholars speculated about the primitive world in relation to European society, and erected grand evolutionary schemes without ever having left the cocoons of their libraries and museums, delegating that tiresome task to travellers, traders and missionaries. A case in point concerns Sir James Frazer, who was appointed to a chair in anthropology at Liverpool University in 1908, and was the author of a famous work called *The Golden Bough* (1958). When asked if he would actually like to visit the natives on their own turf, whose customs he had so cleverly analysed, he reportedly cried: 'God forbid!'

The turning point came in the early part of the twentieth century when anthropologists, no longer satisfied to leave the collection of data to untrained amateurs, began to embark on expeditions to the colonies. This marked the first stage of the fieldwork enterprise – actually meeting the natives face to face, and in later years living in their communities – which has probably been the outstanding feature of the discipline. The assumption behind it was that only if one lived with the people who were being studied, and attempted to behave and think like them, could one truly understand a different society. It is customary to trace the fieldwork orientation to Bronislaw Malinowski (1884–1942), a heroic figure in British anthropology. During much of the First World War, Malinowski lived on the Trobriand Islands in the South Pacific which were controlled at the time by Australia, and set the standard for participant observation. Even a generation earlier, however, other anthropologists, some of them equally eminent such as Franz Boas (1858–1942), the renowned founder of American anthropology, had already embarked on first-hand, face-to-face research.

In summary, the significance of fieldwork, which usually meant living with people in what is now commonly known as the Third World or developing societies, can hardly be overestimated. It was this eyewitness account of the practices and beliefs prevailing in other cultures that provided the discipline with an enviable stature in the academic world, and sometimes among lay people as well. Yet if fieldwork in what unfortunately have often been labelled exotic societies (exotic from whose point of view?) was the main strength of the discipline, it also was the main weakness, because it implied fundamental questions about morality (how does a privileged Westerner have the *right* to describe and interpret the lives of non-Westerners?) and epistemology (how is a person of one culture *capable* of interpreting someone else's culture?). Such questions were barely articulated during the early years of anthropology, but for the past decade or so they have emerged with such force as to almost paralyse the discipline.

General Anthropology

This is the name given to anthropology in the United States, where the discipline is defined very broadly to mean the study of humankind. General anthropology embraces both biological and cultural systems, the scope of which makes it unique, and is composed of four main branches.

1. PHYSICAL ANTHROPOLOGY

In the public's eye, this is probably what anthropology is all about, conjuring up as it does images of prehistoric skulls and skeletons. Physical anthropologists, many of whom prefer nowadays to be called human biologists, study the evolution of the genus *Homo*, using fossils to reconstruct the past (a focus that is labelled human paleontology). Some physical anthropologists specialize in comparing *Homo sapiens* and earlier hominids to other primates (a focus called primatology), while yet other scholars focus on human variation within a genetic framework.

For much of the history of physical anthropology, at least up to the Second World War, the basic concept was race, defined in biological terms. An attempt was made to classify the population of the world into phenotypes (for example, Negroid, Mongoloid, Australoid, and Caucasoid), employing observable criteria such as skin colour and hair type. A great deal of mischief was done by these attempts, leading to the assumption that people could be slotted into distinct races in the biological sense, and that these races varied in terms of intelligence, morality, and so on. Today most physical anthropologists have abandoned classifications based on phenotype, and recognize that all contemporary human beings belong to a single species, *Homo sapiens* (the conventional definition of a species is that of a breeding population: if a male and female member of a single species mate, they are capable of producing fertile offspring).

Physical anthropologists now draw from genetics, population biology, and epidemiology. With genetics, they explore inherited human traits, and highlight the concept 'genotype' rather than 'phenotype.' With population biology, they examine the interaction between environment and population characteristics. With epidemiology, they study the manner in which diseases vary with different populations. Here, too, there is a danger of overestimating the significance of biology and underestimating that of environment, thus encouraging the assumption that certain races are vulnerable to certain diseases. Let us consider, for example, sickle-cell anemia (an abnormality of the red blood cells). It used to be thought that sickle-cell anemia mainly affected people of African descent. But then researchers discovered that it was widespread also in Turkey, Greece, and India. The most probable explanation is that sickle-cell anemia provides protection against malaria, regardless of the race of those afflicted.[1]

2. ARCHAEOLOGY

Whenever people learn that I am an anthropologist, they usually assume that I am a physical anthropologist, playing around with teeth and bones, or an archaeologist, patiently searching for arrow heads and pottery in a peaceful setting of unsurpassed beauty, far from the frantic pace of modern life. Archaeology, in other words, is assumed to be the romantic branch of the discipline.

Archaeology is often described as a special branch of history, focusing on societies without written records. But that is only one type of archaeology, which we call prehistoric archaeology. There is also historic archaeology which studies past societies that have left written

---

1 It should be added that many physical anthropologists do forensic work, identifying deceased persons, which at times throws them into the centre of contemporary human tragedies, such as those in Rwanda and Bosnia.

records. Some archaeologists, indeed, specialize in the immediate past, wading through the debris of demolished buildings in order to put together a picture of the development of industrial society, or rooting through garbage in order to throw light on the cultural patterns of living people. Archaeologists, it should be added, also have contributed to the understanding of marginalized peoples, such as African Americans during slavery, who left little historical record because of the oppressive circumstances of their lives.

3. LINGUISTICS

Although linguistics today enjoys the status of an autonomous discipline, it is still regarded as an important focus within general anthropology. Anthropologists became interested in linguistics because in the early days their research usually involved societies with no written languages. Another reason was the presumed wider significance of language. It often has been thought that learning a language and learning a culture are much the same thing, because culture is reflected in language. Moreover, language is considered to be one of the key dimensions (if not *the* key dimension) that separates *Homo sapiens* from other primates. Many anthropologists would argue, indeed, that it is because of the language capacity of human beings, and the fact that we live in a symbolic universe of metaphor and consciousness, that the social sciences are distinct from the natural sciences, and perhaps require a different scholarly approach. Sometimes anthropologists are only interested in how language is used in speech, reflecting culture, class, and gender – a focus which is called sociolinguistics or ethnolinguistics. At other times, especially if it is assumed that social life consists mainly of rules of conduct, meaning, and interpretation, language is regarded as a model or paradigm for all human interaction. There even is a specialized discipline for this approach; it is called semiology (see Manning 1987).

4. CULTURAL ANTHROPOLOGY

Culture is the fundamental concept in American anthropology, the focus that stamps the American school as unique. Studies typically operate at a very high level of generality, alluding, for example, to Zuni culture, Yoruba culture, Japanese culture, or American culture. Ironically, culture is an exceptionally vague concept, with little agreement on how to define it or what exactly it explains. Is culture a master concept, one that captures the entire way of life of a people, including belief system, social organization, technology and environment? Or should it be restricted to beliefs, values, and ideas – to mentalist data – while excluding behaviour? Is there a meaningful distinction between culture and society, between belief system and social system, and perhaps worldview? Does culture contain its own explanation? That is, by arguing that people think and act the way they do because 'it is their culture,' have we actually clarified anything? Or is it more appropriate to assign culture ideological status, to portray it as a dependent variable, the product of underlying factors such as technology and environment, and possibly even our biological make-up?

I shall consider these questions in some detail below. For the moment, however, I merely want to emphasize that cultural anthropology has for several decades been a most significant branch of general anthropology. Among the early giants of cultural anthropology were Franz Boas, his student Alfred Kroeber, plus the British scholar Edward Tylor. Probably the most famous definition of culture was provided by Tylor: 'That complex whole which includes knowledge, belief, art, morals, law, custom and any other capabilities and habits acquired by man as a member of society' (1871:1). According to Kroeber, culture consists of 'the mass of learned and transmitted motor reactions, habits, techniques, ideas and values – and the behaviour they induce' (1963:8). More recently, Murphy has written: 'Culture means the total body of tradition borne by a society and transmitted from generation to generation' (1986:14).

Social Anthropology

This is the name given to anthropology in Britain. Social anthropology is defined much more narrowly than general anthropology. In fact, social anthropology is almost identical to one branch of general anthropology, cultural anthropology, but is even more restricted in scope than that branch. The British school focuses on social structure and its substructures such as family, religion, economy, and political system. Social anthropology is very similar to sociology, the main difference being that social anthropologists have concentrated on other cultures, mostly in the Third World, while sociologists have studied their own societies, usually industrialized ones in the Western world.

Just as the concept of culture is ambiguous, the same is true about social structure. What is the difference between social structure and society, between social structure and social organization? Is social structure a real thing? Is it concrete or merely an abstraction? In other words, is there a social structure out there to discover, or does the investigator simply impose a structure on the data in order to simplify chaos? Does social structure consist of institutions, roles, and behaviour, or does it include beliefs and values as well? Is the narrow focus on social structure and its substructures fruitful, or is the entire framework a meaningless tautology, a useless attempt to explain something in terms of itself, ignoring the variables that according to many American anthropologists have provided fundamental shape to social life such as technology and environment?

What can be stated is that no other type or branch of anthropology has enjoyed the high reputation and stature accorded to British social anthropology, at least until recently, the success of which has been largely due to its narrow, specialized focus. This no longer is the case today. Since the mid-1980s, American cultural anthropology has soared ahead of its British counterpart, fuelled by a renewed interest in cultural studies, and by a switch in emphasis from social structure to 'meaning' – all of which are part of a new perspective known as postmodernism which will be described in detail in chapter six.

Curiously, if we go back far enough in time we find that general anthropology actually was practised in Britain as well. Mair (1972:5) indicates that when the Royal Anthropological Institute was founded in Britain in 1843, all four branches of anthropology were prominent. According to Lewis (1985), it was not until several years later that social anthropology began to emerge as a separate and distinct discipline. Penniman (1986) too states that British anthropology was originally as broad as the American school, and he regretted the eventual dominance of social anthropology, with its narrow focus on social structure. Clearly, there was an intellectual revolution in British anthropology, in which scholars such as Tylor were left behind, excommunicated by the new prophets such as Malinowski and Radcliffe-Brown (1881–1955).

Many prominent anthropologists, among them the late Robert Murphy (1986:6), see little purpose in separating social and cultural anthropology. That is my own position as well, and throughout this book I shall use the terms social and cultural anthropology interchangeably, or simply socio-cultural. For stylistic reasons, I shall also at times employ the term anthropology, but it will refer to sociocultural phenomena, not physical anthropology, archaeology, or linguistics, unless indicated otherwise.

Finally, a couple of further distinctions. Ethnography is a term applied to raw data (is there such a thing?), to a descriptive account of a people. Often we refer to our books which describe a community or society as ethnographies, and we call fieldworkers who produce such books ethnographers. An ethnology, in contrast, is a comparative and theoretical work, a synthesis of two or more ethnographies which attempts not merely to describe but to arrive at general explanations. An ethnologist, thus, is a person interested in building theory. Note, however, that on the European continent the term ethnology has had the different connotation of the scientific search for the origins of cultural traits.

Basic Concepts

1. NATURE VERSUS CULTURE

Or biology versus culture, race versus culture, heredity versus culture, heredity versus environment, and gene versus symbol.

Whereas general anthropology combines both nature and culture in its conceptual framework, social and cultural anthropologists like myself are concerned with human beliefs and behaviour that are *not* explicable in terms of biology. The basic assumption in socio-cultural anthropology is that the range of variation in human belief and behaviour cannot be explained by or reduced to biology. This does not mean that we deny that biology has any influence on social life; to do so would be ridiculous. What it does mean is that we treat our biological make-up as a constant, and attempt to explain the range of social and cultural variation that is not reducible to biology. Consider the family and marriage. We know that there are several different types of family (for example, the nuclear family and the extended family), and several types of marriage (for example, monogamy, polyandry, and polygyny). The argument in socio-cultural anthropology is that such variation cannot be explained by biology. Actually, this merely confirms the importance of a fundamental principle of logic: a constant cannot explain variation, the constant in this case being biology.

Once again, let me emphasize that to argue that human social and cultural life cannot be reduced to a biological explanation is not tantamount to claiming that biology has no impact on how we live and behave. The point is that biology is no more important for socio-cultural anthropology than it is for sociology, economics, political science, psychology, geography or history; to argue otherwise, I believe, is implicitly racist, the hidden assumption being that there is something about those Third World people (previously labelled savages or primitives) that requires a biological twist in order to explain them, whereas the moderns of the Western world, who are studied by sociologists, do not. By contending that human social life cannot be reduced to a biological basis, but allowing that biology constitutes a parameter which limits the range of human cultural variation (for example, food preferences vary immensely cross-culturally, but all humans must eat), I am adopting a rather moderate position. You should be aware, however, that in the history of anthropology extreme viewpoints have sometimes been taken. For example, there is the assumption that culture explains everything, that biology (and psychology) can be ignored entirely. This sometimes is labelled culturology, and is often erroneously traced to Boas, and to his students Ruth Benedict and Margaret Mead.[2] There is also the theoretical orientation known as sociobiology, made popular in recent years by E.O. Wilson (1978). Sociobiology is the flip side of culturology. The basic assumption is that social and cultural life can be reduced to and explained by a biological framework, which means that disciplines such as sociology and socio-cultural anthropology should be regarded as divisions within sociobiology.

One of the most polemical books in recent history was Derek Freeman's restudy (1983) of Margaret Mead's Samoa. Mead (1973; original 1928) had argued that, unlike in America, adolescence in Samoa was admirably free of tension, and her pioneering study was taken as proof of the remarkable plasticity of human culture, unbounded by biology. Freeman, however, uncovered a world of strain, conflict, competition, and hierarchy, and sought the explanation at the level of biological conditions, stamped by human nature. In the end, however, perhaps the least important element is the different kind of data marshalled by each author, because the simple fact is that competition and strain are just as readily encompassed by a cultural framework as are harmony and order. What really counts here are the quite incompatible starting points of the two authors, Mead's in culture, Freeman's in sociobiology. Put otherwise, Mead and Freeman, each wed to a different theoretical per-

---

2 Erroneously, because a central assumption in the works of Boas and his students (Benedict, Mead, Goldenweiser, Radin, and Sapir) was that culture does not completely determine personality; instead, the individual has a creative capacity. As we shall see in the next chapter, culturology more accurately applies to the works of Kroeber and White.

spective, were talking past each other, which for all intents and purposes takes the wind out of Freeman's controversial attack.

2. CULTURE VERSUS SOCIETY

Or culture versus social structure, culture versus social system, and culture versus social organization.

The distinction between culture and society supposedly corresponds to that between cultural and social anthropology. Cultural anthropology is usually thought to embrace beliefs and values and social organization, sometimes conditioned by the level of technology in a society and its environmental conditions. Social anthropology supposedly focuses on social structure, which includes institutions, roles and social relations. Thus Ember and Ember define culture as 'the set of learned values, behaviour, and beliefs that are characteristic of a particular society or population.' Society, they suggest, refers to 'a territorial population speaking a language not generally understood by neighbouring territorial populations' (1988:527,537). These definitions, which appear in the glossary at the end of their textbook, are quite confusing. To illustrate: whereas it usually is thought that French Canadians have a somewhat different culture to English Canadians, it would seem that the definition of society provided by Ember and Ember is more useful to distinguish the two groups than the definition of culture, especially because they include language under society. Yet why should it be placed there rather than under culture? Just to add to the confusion, early in their textbook (p. 8) they do in fact place language within culture.

Consider, as well, the definition of culture offered by Lewis: 'For our purposes, culture is simply a convenient term to describe the sum of *learned* knowledge and skills – including religion and language – that distinguishes one community from another and which, subject to the vagaries of innovation and change, passes on in a recognizable form from generation to generation' (1985:17). There is nothing particularly grating about this definition. In fact, it strikes me as being eminently clearer than many others. The problem arises as Lewis continues, for he goes on to voice the party line that while cultural anthropology focuses on culture, social anthropology deals with social relations. This will not do. Certainly it is true that social anthropology has embraced a much narrower framework than cultural anthropology. But it is misleading in the extreme to assume that, unlike cultural anthropology, the British school does not focus on beliefs and values. It would simply be impossible to analyse roles and institutions without simultaneously considering beliefs and values, and in fact social anthropologists have always done both in their ethnographies. If a focus on beliefs and values, then, defines one's approach as cultural anthropology, social anthropologists are cultural anthropologists too. In this context, it is instructive to bear in mind that one of the most influential textbooks in social anthropology since the Second World War (Beattie 1964) was called *Other Cultures*, not *Other Societies*.

Just as culture served to separate anthropology in America from an emphasis on biology, and thus to break away from an intellectual climate in which race was front and centre, it also may be interpreted as a conceptual tool by which to distance anthropology from sociology, thus assuring its autonomy. As time went on, the distinction between cultural anthropology and social anthropology took on national significance. The Americans had culture, the British had social structure. Trite as it may seem, it appears that the supposed differences between cultural and social anthropology rest at least as heavily on the micro politics of academia as they do on solid scholarly arguments.

3. BELIEF SYSTEM VERSUS SOCIAL SYSTEM

Sometimes culture is defined narrowly to mean belief system, which sets it apart from society and social system. Once again, this is not a satisfactory distinction between disciplines, because it is only an analytic one. In real life, all human interaction involves both beliefs and behaviour. Thus, religion can be analysed as a set of beliefs and values or as a system of roles in an organization. Similarly, the family can be analysed in terms of its role structure or in terms of the ideas and values associated with it.

Of course, an anthropologist may emphasize either primarily beliefs and values, or roles and institutions, but the decision to do so is arbitrary. Having said that, I must add that the relative importance of beliefs and meaning as distinct from roles and behaviour sometimes varies in degree from one institution to another. For example, while religion certainly can be analysed as an organization, it would make little sense not to concentrate on its belief system. Similarly, while the family can be approached in terms of its associated beliefs, values, and ideology, it would be foolish to ignore its role structure. Lévi-Strauss, the great French anthropologist, introduced the terms 'thought-of orders' and 'lived-in orders.' The first includes mythology and other belief systems, the second kinship and other institutions. Such a distinction is useful, as long as it is remembered that it is merely analytical, and that all human interaction expresses both beliefs and behaviour simultaneously. At this juncture, it is instructive to point out that unlike hypotheses, definitions are neither valid nor invalid; they simply are useful or not useful.

4. BELIEF SYSTEM VERSUS WORLDVIEW

By worldview is meant the most general interpretation of life embraced by a people, or by a category of people, one's cognitive map of the world in which one lives. Usually we speak of the worldview of people in a particular culture, such as the Yoruba in Nigeria; but in a looser sense we could speak of the worldview in pre-industrial versus industrial society, or in the Occident and the Orient. We could also, if we wished, talk about the worldview of scientists, the worldview of rural people, or the worldview of university students. In his 1965 article 'Peasant Society and the Image of the Limited Good,' Foster attempts to spell out the worldview of peasants: everything is in short supply – riches, love, health, blood, manliness, status, and friendship. It makes little sense for a person to attempt to improve her or his economic welfare by working harder, because ultimately it is fate that calls the tune. Moreover, if one person is getting richer or attracting new friends, that person risks attack, because it is believed that there is only a finite amount of good things in life; if someone is getting more, others must consequently be getting less. Foster argues that the image of the limited good explains the high degree of individualism in peasant society, the unwillingness to cooperate in joint ventures, the underlying conservatism and opposition to change, and the great emphasis placed on buried treasures and lotteries as sources of upward status mobility – sources thought to be external to the limited goods within peasant society, and gifts of luck and fate rather than labour.

Sometimes belief system is presented as a less inclusive concept than worldview. For example, we often speak of the religious belief system. But once again, all definitions are either useful or not useful, rather than right or wrong, and it seems to me that there is little reason not to regard worldview and belief system as crude synonyms.

5. CULTURE VERSUS CLASS

There is a tendency in anthropology to treat culture as an independent variable. That is, culture constitutes an 'explanation' of how people think and behave. Thus, if an identifiable group of people occupying a specific territory, and embracing a unique set of customs, such as the Igbo in Nigeria or the Ashanti in Ghana, are known to be especially industrious or respectful of authority, the anthropologist may explain all this by stating that 'it is their culture.' In my opinion, such an explanation is inadequate; in fact, it is redundant. It amounts to stating that people practise certain customs because it is their custom to do so. We know, of course, that social life is partly based on habit and tradition, which means that to some degree it is legitimate to claim that people think and act in the way they do because they have always done so (it is their culture). However, social life is not based on habit and tradition alone. It is also shaped by the environment, level of technology, rationality, irrationality, emotion, political forces in the international arena, and ideas and practices diffused from neighbouring societies. To offer culture as an explanation is tantamount to ignoring these other factors. This point is especially relevant today in relation to social class. Where in the world can we find any group of people – even the most remote population – unaffected by capitalism, and the division of labour it entails, and its artifacts such as the Coca-Cola bottle? Anytime we do a cultural analysis, we must also do a class analysis. In today's world, culture and class are not autonomous. (Just as in pre-class societies, such as among hunters and gatherers, it was always relevant to think in terms of culture and some other variable, such as environment.) Instead, culture and class are reciprocal: they need each other analytically.

If culture is treated as autonomous, it begins to resemble ideology in the pejorative sense, which means it rationalizes or justifies behaviour, and obscures rather than illuminates social life. A pertinent example is ethnicity, which conventionally is said to have its roots in culture. That is, people in a particular ethnic group are thought to share a common cultural origin. However, an analysis of ethnic conflict does not penetrate very deeply if we merely evoke the different cultural backgrounds of the ethnic groups in question. Such differences are not irrelevant. But a more sophisticated explanation would also entertain the role played by competition for scarce resources, and the jockeying for power and privilege among ethnic groups, including, of course, those which are dominant in a society, and which enjoy the ultimate privilege of not being perceived as ethnic groups (such as North Americans of British origin). In other words, an adequate analysis of ethnic conflict requires a synthesis of culture and class. Some anthropologists, especially those of a Marxist persuasion such as Wolf (1969), would take this argument even further, portraying culture as a product of class, or, to use the jargon, assigning it epiphenomenal status, a mere shadow on the walls of the cave. I am quite sympathetic to this position, especially if the alternative is that empty slogan, 'it is their culture.'

6. THE EXPLANATORY LIMITS OF CULTURE

In implying that there are limits to what culture can explain, I do not mean to suggest that it is a meaningless concept. In fact, most anthropologists, including social anthropologists, would probably agree that what distinguishes *Homo sapiens* from other primates is culture. They also would probably accept that culture is learned, shared, and transmitted by socialization from one generation to the next. Leslie White, a prominent American anthropologist, has suggested that human beings are the only living species with culture. The essential dimension of culture for White was 'symboling,' or bestowing meaning on a thing. For example, he observed that humans are the single species capable of distinguishing holy water from ordinary water.[3] At this highly abstract level, culture does mean something, and indeed it would be easy to marshall numerous examples to illustrate the significance of culture in the most elementary human conventions. Consider the following:

Distance

How close does a person get to another person when they talk? Do they stand nose to nose, or do they put three or four feet between them? Anthropologists are perfectly aware that the distance may vary from one culture to another.

Touching

Does one habitually touch another person, or avoid all physical contact? The varied way in which people shake hands from one culture to another is relevant here. Must the handshake be firm as in North America, limp as in France, or elaborate as among the Yoruba in Nigeria? Do people shake hands every time they meet during the day, or at least the

---

3 An analysis of White's contribution to anthropology appears in chapter two.

first time they meet, or hardly at all? Do men and women hold hands in public, or men and men and women and women? These comments are intended to be devoid of a sexual connotation; obviously, heterosexuality versus homosexuality would change the meaning.

Emotional Expression

Does one remain aloof and stoical, or does one wear one's emotions on one's sleeves? The Igbo in Nigeria among whom I lived were very spontaneous and demonstrative. The Yoruba in Nigeria with whom I later dwelled were much more controlled in their emotional expression. The Hausa in Nigeria among whom I travelled extensively seemed to be even more controlled, which apparently was one reason why the British colonizers liked them so much: they were on the same wavelength emotionally.

Speech

Does one talk softly or loudly? Again, there is variation across cultures. I have lived in both Corsica (the island in the Mediterranean which is a French department, or province) and the south of France. In the south of France people sitting in a bar or at a table on the sidewalk usually talk in moderate tones. In Corsica one can be a half-block away from a bar and still hear customers shouting, exclaiming, arguing, and laughing. On a recent trip to Portugal I could not help but be impressed by what at least superficially appeared to be the low key of the culture, the gentleness of the people, their apparent passivity, which was all the more striking in comparison to the more expressive Spanish next door.

There is, however, a danger in this line of analysis, especially the gross generalization it entails. A couple of years ago, on a skiing junket to the United States, I sat by myself in a bar and amusedly observed a half dozen middle-aged people at the next table. Typical Americans, I thought, as I listened to their loud laughter and watched their assertive behaviour. Gradually I realized they were actually Canadians, on holiday like myself. So much for the stereotype! A related danger is that generalizations about emotional expression, speech, or touching tend to flatten out a culture, to portray homogeneity at the expense of difference. This was the Achilles' heel of a long-dead theoretical approach in American anthropology, the culture and personality school (see chapter two), which in its original formulation assumed that in every culture there was a single, dominant personality type (or modal personality).

The importance of culture also is reflected in its tendency to shape the values, attitudes, and behaviour of immigrant groups even into successive generations. A few years ago I did a brief study of ethnic-organized ice hockey leagues in Toronto. In one league body-checking was permitted. In another it was banned. Yet on the basis of observation alone, one would never have been able to guess which of the leagues disallowed body-checking. If anything, the degree of vigorous physical contact was greater in the league that disallowed it. Another difference was the dressing room. In the one league, players quietly packed up minutes after the game and were on their way. In the other league, arena officials had to plead with the players, still joking around and taking refreshments an hour later, to vacate the premises.

In order to appreciate the significance of culture, we only have to reflect on the manner in which baseball is played in Japan, and the dramatic adjustments that have to be made by American players when they join Japanese teams. In the city where I live, there is a large Italian-Canadian population. It is probably the exceptional person among them who does not make wine, or at least share what relatives and friends have produced, and continue to favour Italian delicacies: prosciutto, good salami, and aromatic cheeses. Then there is the intriguing phenomenon in which elderly immigrants, such as Dutch Canadians and Chinese Canadians in the Toronto area, enter residential complexes that cater specifically to their own ethnic group. Yet in these several examples it must not be forgotten that these people are also Canadians; their ethnic origins are only one part of their identity.

This leads to a potentially critical observation. A century or two ago, when people lived more isolated lives in pockets around the globe, it may have made more sense to evoke culture as the explanatory tool. In today's world, however, the pace of geographical mobility and the impact of mass communications have eroded the integrity of individual cultures, and thrown people of various ethnic backgrounds together as never before. In this situation, culture continues to play a role, but it does not tell the whole story. My argument is that it quite possibly never did, because it simply is too crude and it attempts to explain too much. This is precisely the point made by Tyler: 'Culture, conceived as the totality of human behaviour, ideas, history, institutions and artifacts has never been particularly useful as a meaningful method of explaining ethnographic facts. Such a conception merely asserts that culture is equivalent to the whole of human knowledge. As a device which purports to explain all of man's learned behaviour, motivations, prehistoric record, ecological adaptations, biological limitations, and evolution it attempts too much' (1969:14).

7. OTHER ISSUES

A few final observations are in order. First, social systems are older than cultural systems. Other species did not patiently wait for the genus *Homo* to attain a capacity for symbolic communication, for culture, before permitting themselves social organization. Second, there does seem to be one essential difference between belief systems and social systems. Belief systems tend to be neat and orderly, giving the impression that life is purposeful and predictable. Social systems or behaviour systems (how people actually live their lives, their actions) are inclined to be messy, semi-chaotic. One of the important functions of belief systems appears to be to conceal the degree of disorder in our lives. Belief systems, in other words, may constitute a monumental deception, a basic lie, but without them we might all go crazy. Third, it is much easier to sketch out the institutional framework of a society, including its role structure and complexes of beliefs and values, than to interpret its symbolic content. This, of course, holds true for all of the social sciences, but anthropology's cross-cultural perspective makes the interpretive quest even more daunting. Prominent among the difficult issues that face the discipline are the following:

Meaning and Interpretation

Any analysis of belief systems necessarily involves getting at 'meaning,' and interpreting signs and symbols. As an anthropologist, I can enter a society and eventually learn whether monogamy or polygamy is practised or whether witchcraft exists. That is, I can grasp the essentials of the institutional framework of a society. But how do I know what being monogamous or polygamous means to people, let alone witchcraft? How do I get into their heads? Even if research is confined to the anthropologist's own society, the challenge of penetrating meaning, which in many respects reflects the limits of empathy, prevails. How does a middle-class ethnographer interpret what life means to an upper-class or lower-class individual, or cope with meaning across gender, age, and ethnic lines? This is a hot issue today, and not merely in anthropology. For example, can a white novelist legitimately write about Aboriginal people? Can a male novelist focus on female characters, or a female novelist on males?

The Equivalence of Meaning Problem

Because anthropologists have traditionally conducted their research in other cultures, the difficulty of coping with meaning has been compounded. Does the language one speaks shape the way one thinks and behaves? There is a body of literature, centring around what is known as the Whorfian hypothesis, that suggests that language does indeed constrain (but not determine) thought and action. If that is so, the challenge of interpreting one culture in terms of another is formidable, and some distortion would seem to be unavoidable. Previous generations of anthropologists, especially those who opted to focus on social structure and roles, were able to stifle their doubts about these matters by expressing faith in cross-cultural functional equivalents and underlying universal principles (the family may take different forms, but in all societies there must exist some institutional mechanism for the socialization of children). Nowadays we are less confident that such universals exist, and more cautious about asserting that an institution or custom in one culture has its equivalent in other cultures.

Ethnocentrism

Adding to the obstacles that confront anthropologists when doing research abroad is their own cultural baggage. It probably can be claimed that anthropologists have a greater capacity than most people to hold their cultural backgrounds at bay; that is a central part of their training. Yet the very fact that they have been socialized into a particular culture, a culture which encompasses specific values and institutions and occupies a particular moral and political niche in the world order, inevitably suggests, without even considering the individual anthropologist's personality, that some amount of ethnocentrism must always creep in. Sometimes anthropologists joke, at least in private, that our ethnographies consist partly of cultural projection and personal confession, reflecting our own vision of the world, rather than the vision of people who are studied. Although that observation, in the current political climate, may seem less outrageous than ever before, it would be difficult to point to any other discipline engaged in cross-cultural studies that has done the job better.

Relativism

The time-honoured way in which anthropologists have attempted to avoid ethnocentrism is relativism. It has generally been assumed that there are no good or bad cultures or cultural practices. This approach carries with it the danger of slipping into the more radical position of amoral relativism, in which there are no standards whatever. In other words, under the guise of culture, anything goes, because moral judgment is ruled out. This seems to be one of those problems incapable of rational solution. If we criticize someone else's cultural practice, such as clitoridectomy (female circumcision), we would seem to be guilty of ethnocentrism; but if we fail to do so, where do we draw the line? The obvious way around this dilemma is to articulate a set of universal values, but that is easier said than done. Actually, few anthropologists have been amoral relativists, nor have they been value-neutral. Driven by relativistic principles, more often than not they have criticized their own cultural values and celebrated those elsewhere, to the point of romanticizing them.

Manifest versus Latent Functions

Consider, for example, the rain dance. Do we take seriously people's beliefs that its purpose is to produce rain? Or do we look for hidden or latent functions, such as the increase in social solidarity brought about by getting everyone together and evoking a transcendental force beyond the empirical world? Anthropologists have generally preferred the second alternative, reducing belief systems to sociological principles. Religion, for example, the anthropological study of which has been dominated by agnostics and atheists, has been explained as an expression of alienation, compensation for weak personalities, an illusion, or sheer error. Only in recent years has the obvious been recognized: rather than being an irksome feature to be pushed aside, people's beliefs in spiritual beings is the fundamental element in religion, and must be treated as such. This does not mean that the anthropologist must personally accept beliefs as valid, but merely realize that when one analyses belief systems there can be little difference between appearance and reality. Put otherwise, if people believe in spiritual beings, their beliefs have sociological implications. At the very least, then, the analysis of belief systems must include both the actor's and the observer's viewpoints. Failure to include the former violates a central goal of anthropology: to see the world through the subject's eyes.

Intended versus Unintended Consequences

How much of our actions is intentional, deliberate, conscious, and how much is habitual and unintentional? It would appear that a great deal of social life is not only habitual but also shaped by unintended consequences, such as the impact of the Protestant Reformation on the development of capitalism, at least as argued by Weber (1958). Yet if that is so, there are grave implications for anthropological methods. What sense does it make to focus on the actor's point of view, to ask people what they believe or think or do, and why, if their conscious motivation only plays a secondary role? Some anthropologists would gleefully answer that it makes no sense at all. Their argument would be that attitudes, beliefs, and social norms are merely mentalist data, ultimately resting on the hard core of political and economic organization. Other anthropologists would surely regard that conception of the discipline as unacceptably narrow, and might even claim a trained capacity to penetrate the unconscious world of the actor.

Ideal versus Actual Beliefs

It is conventional anthropological wisdom that a discrepancy almost always exists between ideal behaviour and actual behaviour, or between the rules that ought to govern our lives and how we actually live. Take, for example, marriage. In some societies, one ideally marries one's cross cousin. This means that a man will preferably marry his mother's brother's daughter or his father's sister's daughter. In other societies, marriage is preferred between parallel cousins. Here a man selects his mother's sister's daughter or his father's brother's daughter, or a woman her mother's sister's son or her father's brother's son. Yet studies often reveal that as little as 10 per cent of existing marriages in such societies represent the cousin type. In other words, we do not get very far if we only analyse the ideal rules that supposedly guide a society. It is understandable, therefore, why anthropologists try to get to the backstage, so to speak, where the rules are relaxed or discarded. But this is the easy way out, and it is costly as well, because most of what is significant about human existence is located in those turbulent waters between the shores of the ideal and the actual. Put otherwise, it is the tension between the ideal and the actual which generates anthropological puzzles (see Murphy 1971).

Not only is there usually a discrepancy between rules and behaviour, but there also often is at least informal (and sometimes formal) tolerance for such discrepancy. For example, in South Africa in the past Japanese people were defined as nonwhite. A few years ago, the South African government redefined them as white in order to increase trade between the two countries (see van den Berghe 1965:58). A second example can be taken from my research on organized racism and anti-Semitism in Canada. Organizations such as the Western Guard and the Ku Klux Klan were adamantly opposed to homosexuality. However, not only were there a handful of gay members, but they were tolerated as long as they did not publicly flaunt their sexual orientation, contributed funds, and were good 'soldiers' in the organizations. I should add, however, that whenever a reputed homosexual in the far right fell out of favour – perhaps because he or she no longer was as dedicated to the cause, or stole funds from the treasury, or whatever – almost always the accusation that they were gay was also held against them. In other words, homosexuality amounted to a residual sin, to be broadcast when a person got into trouble.

Criteria for Ethnographic Quality

In view of these difficulties, how do we judge the quality of an anthropologist's work? Two suggestions:

   (i) *The good anthropologist is able to write a set of rules about a society that would enable a stranger to operate effectively in it.*

I think that this is an interesting way to measure an anthropologist's grasp of a society, but I have serious doubts that many of us ever achieve this level of sophistication.

   (ii) *The good anthropologist knows the difference between the ideal and the actual in a society; in other words, the good anthropologist knows what to take seriously.*

This is similar to, but somewhat less demanding than, the previous criterion, and in my judgment it is a useful measure of an anthropologist's knowledge and understanding. Take, for example, etiquette connected to eating. Keesing (1976) describes a situation in which an Asian student was invited to dinner by a Bulgarian woman. After the first course, the Bulgarian, out of the politeness that was expected in her culture, asked her guest if he would like a second helping. The student, responding to the rules of politeness in his own culture, said yes. The same thing happened when asked if he would like a third helping. Then a fourth helping. Finally, the student collapsed at the dinner table. But in his mind he had done the right thing, for to refuse his host's offerings would in his own culture have been insulting. Had this young man, however, understood the distinction between the ideal and the actual, between the formalized invitation and the expectation, he would not have made himself sick!

A similar situation faced me almost daily in the Yoruba village in Nigeria where I conducted research. Whenever one passed by people who were eating (and they often did so on their verandahs), one would be asked: 'Come and eat.' The expected reply was: 'Thank you, I am already satisfied.' It would have been a serious blunder had I accepted these invitations. In fact, had I done so I would have been ridiculed as a child who did not know any better; or worse, as an imbecile, which is often the way in which anthropologists are regarded in their initial months of fieldwork, as they stumble around trying to figure out how they are supposed to behave.[4]

Colonialism: the Critical Dimension

Probably nothing has had a greater impact on anthropology, not only in the past but even today, than colonialism. Anthropology has been correctly described as the child of imperialism. The emergence and development of anthropology as a profession in Britain and Western Europe was intrinsically linked to the colonization of what eventually became labelled the Third World (Asad 1973). Until the colonial empires began to disintegrate during the 1950s and 1960s, giving birth to independent nations such as Fiji and Kenya, most anthropologists did research in

4 Peter Stephenson (personal communication) has suggested a third criterion: if the anthropologist can compose a joke that makes people laugh, he or she probably has a deep grasp of the culture.

colonial societies, often supported financially by grants provided by their own nation's colonial office. It was also not unusual for colonial administrators themselves to be trained in at least the rudiments of anthropology (one of my own teachers in England was a retired colonial officer). It may be thought that the starting point in American anthropology was quite different, because America did not possess a colonial empire and research was focused on Native Indians and the Inuit. Yet the Aboriginal population was also under the colonial yoke, although the form it took was internal colonialism.

It sometimes has been suggested that anthropologists helped to soften the impact of colonialism by making its bureaucracies more sensitive to the social organization and beliefs of indigenous societies, and more humane in the treatment of people. On balance, however, it seems to me that anthropologists did more to prop up the colonial regimes than to undermine them. The assumption then was that their research was objective and value-neutral, which conveniently relieved them from worrying too much about the effect of their studies or the moral basis of the regimes in which they worked. It must also be pointed out that while animated attacks on colonialism were mounted by anthropologists such as Berreman (1968) and Gough (1968), some of the most pungent criticisms came from scholars in other disciplines with less vested interests in the colonial world (Frank 1970, Rodney 1972, Said 1979). Of course, the majority of anthropologists in those days apparently did not see themselves as appendages of the colonial empire; human beings are marvellous rationalizers, and the early anthropologists readily justified their activities. One argument was that an investigator could only be objective if she or he did fieldwork in other cultures. Another was that when studying other cultures, one enjoyed 'stranger value.' That is, people would confide in the foreign anthropologist and reveal information that they would conceal from indigenous scholars. A third argument was simply that no one else was doing research in such societies, which meant that anthropologists enjoyed a wide-open field.

The concept of culture emerged as a counterweight to biological explanations of social life, and to the prevailing racial theories of the times (in British social anthropology, social structure eventually served a similar purpose). Yet it would be a mistake to assume that academic racism – what we call scientific racism – abruptly disappeared. Tylor, for example, not only thought that there were different biological races, but also that they varied in terms of innate capacity (see Hatch 1973:32). Boas, the man who contributed so much to combating scientific racism and to promoting the concept culture, assumed that the races of Africa, Melanesia, and Australia were to a certain degree inferior to the races of Asia, Europe, and America, with the latter having larger brains and greater intelligence (see Fried 1972:61). Even Malinowski, renowned for setting the standard for modern fieldwork, for his warm and intimate participation with 'the natives,' especially in his Trobriand research, exposed a different side in his diary (Malinowski 1967). Much to the consternation of contemporary anthropologists, he referred to the Trobrianders as 'niggers.' This leads to a highly complicated question. Should such racist lapses be interpreted as contaminating the entire writings of these pioneering scholars, or in view of the valiant efforts made by these scholars to challenge racist ideology, can they be dismissed as regrettable but unrepresentative remnants of the scientific racism that previously had flourished?

Let us turn to the outlook of anthropologists today. The vast majority of anthropologists whom I have known have been decidedly liberal in their attitudes. Nevertheless, one may not always appreciate the deeper implications of one's activities. In Willis's opinion (1972), anthropology amounts to a kind of tourism, providing entertainment for white people; the fieldwork process itself, he contends, is shot through with racism, as white scholars from the West impose their interpretations on the lives of people of colour. Quite apart from the possibility that this image of the discipline may be obsolete, reflecting the growing tendency to do fieldwork at home, many anthropologists would dismiss these assertions as unfair and even outlandish, arguing that the sociocultural framework constitutes a massive repudiation of racist worldviews. That probably is correct, but the rejection of racism in this sense is only indirect. Very few anthropologists have launched *direct* assaults by actually conducting ethnographic studies of racism. While most textbooks in cultural anthropology include at least a short section on racism, they rarely move beyond the obligatory statement that all human beings belong to a single species, that there is no scientific basis for ranking different population groups on a scale of superiority and inferiority. Furthermore, it is my impression that racist incidents that anthropologists do uncover during fieldwork are usually ignored, at least when it comes time to write their books. It is almost as if anthropologists do not know how to handle racist data, and that may not be far from the truth. Could it be that the battle of culture against biology at the turn of the century was all too resoundingly won, ousting race, but leaving anthropologists blind to racism – a cultural phenomenon if ever there was one?

A mild variation on the racist theme, at least in my judgment, is occasionally associated with salvage anthropology – a research focus on disappearing or dying cultures. It would be wrong to assume that salvage anthropology has only emerged relatively recently, prompted by massive global changes since the Second World War. At the turn of the century, Boas in America and Rivers in Britain worried that it was increasingly difficult to locate native societies still in their pristine state, and they urged their students to record the unique features of these societies before it was too late.

In all this, there seems to have been a lament for the passing of traditional (that is, primitive) society, an attitude that persists today. For example, Lévi-Strauss, the most eminent anthropologist in the 1960s and 1970s, decried the extinction of primitive societies, pointing out that anthropologists were losing their very laboratories (see Fried 1972:63). Even the brilliant and sensitive Robert Murphy has remarked: 'Today, most anthropologists do not conduct research in primitive societies, but it is where the discipline was born and where its fascination still lies' (1986:11). Anthropology's major contribution, Murphy reasonably speculates, has been the documentation of the wide range of cultural variation that existed prior to industrialization. What might grate is one of his other comments: 'The penetration of Western society into every recess of the planet has doomed primitive cultures' (p. 13). Doomed. While Murphy's attitude probably reflects a deep sympathy towards peoples whose cultures have undergone destruction, one might wonder whether citizens of the Third World would draw a different conclusion; namely, that anthropologists would like their societies to remain frozen in time, the intellectual and romantic toys of Western academics.

One might also wonder about the reaction of indigenous peoples to the typical textbook in anthropology. In virtually every one that I have examined (see, for example, Fried 1972:34, Cohen and Eames 1982:20, Lewis 1985:21 and 26, and Peacock and Kirsch 1980:4, 60–1) developing societies are referred to as exotic societies. If this is not blatant ethnocentrism, I don't know what is. Many textbooks, indeed, concentrate on the primitive past, giving the impression, sometimes reinforced by photographs of naked people, that outside the Western world time has stood still. No wonder anthropology has often been regarded with distaste by Third World intellectuals and political leaders.

Finally, there is the powerful work of Said (1979) on Orientalism. Orientalism consists of a set of ideas, images, generalizations, assumptions, and judgments created in the West (or the Occident). Orientalism was intrinsically connected to colonialism, and indeed began to take shape prior to colonialism, paving the way for imperialist excursions. Orientalism is a kind of representation of 'the other,' largely independent of the realities of the Orient as such, an authoritative program that provides the West with intellectual control and material benefit. What is plausible – and alarming – is Said's contention that virtually every contact or association between the Orient and the Occident, from academic discourses to poetry, novels, trade and politics, has been affected by the ideas contained in Orientalism, fabricated in the West. In other words, Westerners, no matter what their interests and regardless of their personal views – malicious or benign – are incapable of thinking about or acting in the Orient independent of Orientalism. One finishes this illuminating book almost with a sense of despair. Can research in other cultures ever again be regarded as innocent, as morally neutral? Is all scholarship abroad little more than a gigantic con, implicitly contributing to the West's domination?

As the impact of works such as Said's *Orientalism* has sunk home, and as anthropology has come to grips with its colonial past, a number of issues and new directions containing the capacity to overcome past flaws and render the discipline meaningful in today's world have been pushed to the forefront.

1. RESEARCH ABROAD VERSUS RESEARCH AT HOME

Although anthropology took root and matured in the context of colonialism, or other cultures, in recent years the tide of opinion has swung to such a degree that conducting research abroad is now often thought to be immoral. It must be pointed out, however, that many anthropologists still do research in Third World countries, while others have adjusted by switching their focus to the rural areas of European societies, which means they continue to work abroad. Finally, the current preference for research at home may be less an expression of moral sensitivity than sheer rationalization for a state of affairs forced on the discipline. The hard fact is that we no longer have ready access to the new nations that have emerged from the colonial era.

2. ETHICS

For the past couple of decades a great deal of soul-searching has been conducted by anthropologists about the ethics of research, whether at home or abroad. Terms such as deception and informed consent have reflected a new concern for the rights of those who are studied. Yet why did ethics become such a hot issue after anthropologists began to do research at home? Part of the answer may be nothing more complicated than an increased appreciation in society at large of the possible negative effects of research, plus a greater emphasis on the rights of the individual. But this is not the entire answer. When anthropologists did most of their research in colonial societies, they were part of the power structure; when they engage in fieldwork at home, especially if their studies are critical of the status quo, which at times is the case, they potentially pose a threat to the power structure. In this interpretation, the intended beneficiaries of ethical guidelines are not the poor and oppressed, but the powerful and privileged.

3. WHO MAY SPEAK?

As I shall explain in much more detail later, not only has there been a partial shift in anthropology from research in other cultures to research at home, but the very authority of the anthropologist to write, to interpret the lives of others, whether abroad or at home, has been challenged. Contemporary research, it is argued, should be a collaborative affair between researcher and subject, so that the distinction (and power imbalance) between them disappears. Ethnographies, the postmodernists urge, should be 'dialogical' or 'polyvocal,' meaning simply that the voices of the subjects have equal or greater prominence than the voice of the anthropologist. The big question is whether these admirable goals are realistic, or destined to remain empty platitudes. The jury is still out.

4. ANTHROPOLOGY AS MALE INTERPRETATION

Another important theoretical direction that has emerged in recent years is feminist anthropology. Although anthropology has always been unusual in academia in terms of the number of women it has attracted, the discipline nevertheless has been dominated by a male interpretation of the world, one which has privileged male activity. Just as postmodernists challenge the capacity and right of Western anthropologists to represent or interpret the lives of people in other cultures, feminists reject a scholarly bias that devalues women's activities. The assumption is that women have been to men what natives have been to anthropology: dominated, oppressed, and misrepresented.

5. STUDYING UP

Almost all anthropological research in the past, and the vast bulk of it even today, has focused on the poor, the oppressed, and the powerless. As long as it was believed that research was beneficial, that it brought improvement to people's lives, everything was rosy. In recent years, however, it has become more and more difficult to swallow that line without choking. Research might be defended as knowledge for its own sake, but judging by the opposition among deprived people to yet further studies of their plight, research is a luxury they seem quite willing to do without. The case can be put even stronger: research might well be subversive, providing information and explanation which enhance the control of societal elites over the rest of the population. If that indeed is the case, an ethical anthropology has no option but to 'study up.'

It has been a quarter of a century since Laura Nader in 1972 urged us to do just that, but few of us have responded, partly because it is much more difficult to conduct research with powerful and knowledgeable people. Yet the rationale for studying up is undeniably sound. First, it provides a counterbalance to the conventional practice of studying down, thus enriching our stock of data. Even more important, by studying up we are able to penetrate the sources of power and privilege in society. If we merely study down, focusing in isolation on the poor and oppressed, we ignore the wider institutions that generate their conditions, which may be tantamount to blaming the victim.

These remarks are directed specifically at conventional research, in which the goals of analysis and explanation are paramount. In recent years a new approach called participatory research has made its appearance. Like postmodernism, it aims to empower people, to provide them with the analytic tools by which they can comprehend and challenge the conditions that oppress and control them. To the extent that participatory research is effective, it suggests that studying down and ethics are not necessarily contradictory.

Crisis or Opportunity?

All of this suggests that anthropology is now at a crossroad. It is no exaggeration to state that never in its history has it faced such a crisis, with its traditional fieldwork setting transformed and out of reach, its authority challenged, and its future uncertain. Reflecting on this crisis, one might conclude that when sociologists and anthropologists agreed (by historical accident) on a division of labour whereby the former focused on Western societies (and did research at home) and the latter on other cultures (and did research abroad), anthropology unfortunately drew the short straw. Yet I disagree. My argument is that because of anthropology's intrinsic connection to colonialism and other cultures, it has been forced to attempt a revolutionary rebirth, one which has the potential of revitalizing the discipline so that it is in tune with what the pundits label the postmodern world. Other disciplines such as sociology, lacking the same links to colonialism, and employing a methodology (quantitative) that is a great deal less intimate than participant observation and informal interviewing, and by that token potentially less exploitative, have not had to re-examine their theories, methods, and mandates to the same degree, which may mean that they will eventually be left behind.

Science or Art?

It was generally assumed during the early decades of professional anthropology that the discipline was (or could be) a science. Most anthropologists then were empiricists and positivists. By empiricism, it is meant that one's work has to be grounded in data, in facts, in the 'real' or concrete world; by positivism, it is meant that the social world is orderly and patterned, and that the fact-value distinction must exist (that is, one's personal values or beliefs must not influence the outcome of one's research efforts). Another relevant term here is nomothetic inquiry, or the search for regularities and laws, the assumption being that such regularity and laws are characteristic of the social world. Radcliffe-Brown's *A Natural Science of Society* can be taken as representative of the nomothetic quest a generation ago.

By the 1960s, anthropologists were somewhat less confident that a science of society was possible. Writers such as Barnes (1990) began to argue that the discipline, and the social sciences in general, occupied a mid-way position between the natural sciences and the humanities. Barnes suggested that, unlike the humanities, which deal with interpretation and empathy, the social sciences are concerned with explanation and prediction. But, unlike the natural sciences, the social sciences are subjective, and the observer or researcher has an impact on his or her research. Another difference, according to Barnes, is that there are no laws in the social sciences.

During the past couple of decades a remarkable reorientation of anthropology has taken place. In the 1970s Clifford Geertz, probably the most influential living anthropologist, urged us to switch our focus from generalization across ethnographic cases to the deep penetration or 'thick description' of individual cases. The fieldwork scene, in his view, resembled a literary text of meanings which the anthropologist attempted to interpret, as in a novel, rather than explain, as under a laboratory microscope. Eventually the postmodernists, partly influenced by Geertz, gained the limelight, pushing anthropology even more aggressively towards the humanities. Not only is it now contended that anthropology is not a science, but also that science per se is an obsolete mode of investigation, regardless of the discipline. Postmodernists argue that it is meaningless, and even immoral, to search for generalizations, laws, evidence, verification, all of which in their view dehumanize people by objectifying them.

Relationship between Anthropology and Other Disciplines

SOCIOLOGY

Anthropology is similar to but not identical with sociology, at least in terms of how each discipline has developed since the last century. Anthropology has focused on pre-industrial societies, sociology on industrial societies; anthropologists conducted their research in other cultures, employed the technique of participant observation (collecting qualitative data), and advocated comparative (especially cross-cultural) analysis; sociologists did research in their own societies, used questionnaires (collecting quantitative data), and rarely attempted to test their generalizations cross-culturally. Of course, there have been many exceptions to these patterns with the result that sociologists have sometimes resembled anthropologists in their labours, and vice versa.

So far, I have been examining the relationship between anthropology and sociology in terms of how the practitioners of each discipline have actually proceeded over the decades. This is a justifiable way of comparing the disciplines, and the conclusion it leads to is that there are important differences. Indeed, a sociologist and anthropologist engaged in research in the same field – for example, Native studies or rural development – may find it difficult to communicate with each other. There is, however, another way of examining the relationship between disciplines: logic. Here one asks not how two disciplines have proceeded historically, but how they are separated logically. This approach leads to quite a different conclusion: anthropology and sociology are synonymous, for they occupy the same conceptual territory, focus on the same institutions, and rely on the same concepts. Moreover, those differences that have existed, such as the preference in anthropology for research in pre-industrial societies and for participant observation, are basically arbitrary rather than logically justified. Durkheim, whose writings have inspired both anthropologists and sociologists, claimed that comparative sociology is not merely a branch of sociology; it *is* sociology. Radcliffe-Brown, who was a disciple of Durkheim, advocated that social anthropology be renamed comparative sociology. As evidence of the cross-fertilization of the two disciplines, there is now a subfield in sociology called the sociology of culture (Hall and Neitz 1993). Goody, a prominent British social anthropologist, has written: 'a sociological "theory" which is distinct from a "theory" of social anthropology is conceivable only to the extent that zoological theory differs from sheep and goats; the base must be common for both' (1969:10). With all this in mind, an observation made by an American cultural anthropologist, Morton Fried, seems to make a lot of sense. As he pointed out, the top scholars in both anthropology and sociology 'spend very little if any time worrying whether what they are doing is sociology or anthropology' (1972:24–5).

PSYCHOLOGY

British social anthropology has historically been quite opposed to psychology. Another way of stating this is to say that social anthropology has been anti-reductionist, which means opposed to reducing the explanation of social life to other disciplinary levels such as psychology. This perspective can be traced back to Durkheim, who declared that any time a psychological explanation is provided for a social phenomenon we may be certain that it is wrong. American cultural anthropology has been much more receptive to psychology, especially the focus on the individual. Boas had been interested in the relationship between the individual and society, and eventually there was the culture and personality school, with its emphasis on modal personality. In more recent years a distinct approach called psychological anthropology has emerged, with a focus on attitudes and values, and child-rearing practices and adolescence (Bourguignon 1979).

The party line is that anthropology examines the group, psychology the individual. Anthropology specializes in social structure or culture, psychology in the personality system, and in mental processes such as cognition, perception, and learning, and emotions and motives. Anthropologists, especially social anthropologists, take the personality system as a constant, and look for variation in the social structure as the basis of their investigations; psychologists accept the social structure as a constant, and look for variations in the personality system as the basis for their analysis. Just as some types of anthropology, such as general anthropology and studies influenced by sociobiology, bridge culture and biology, some types of psychology, especially the experimental or 'rat' variety, bridge personality and biology.

Although the gap between psychology and anthropology has been especially wide in Britain, the rationale is not very sound. Consider, for example, the assumption that anthropology focuses on the group, not the individual. It is probably correct, as Durkheim and others argued, to assume that the group is greater than the sum of its parts, that it cannot be reduced to individual psychology. But the fact is that the only real entities studied by anthropologists are individual human beings. All other concepts such as institutions, roles, statuses, and norms are abstractions (did you ever see a norm?). Even groups must be regarded partly in the same light. Certainly one can observe four or five people gathered together on a street corner, and reasonably label them a group. Yet that depends on the relationships between them (they may be standing next to each other by sheer accident). Moreover, whether or not, assuming they are a group, their collective behaviour is greater than the sum of the individual parts is not itself amenable to observation, although one may observe their actions and deduce that it expresses group properties.

It is wrong, therefore, to state that anthropologists do not study individuals. What makes them anthropologists rather than psychologists is their attempt to generalize at the level of groups, and to explain collectivities in terms of institutionalized norms and rules, or counter-norms and rules in the case of deviant groups. Such an approach may elucidate group behaviour, but obviously it cannot explain individual variation within the group. In recent years the Durkheimian anti-reductionist stance has become much less popular even among British-trained anthropologists. Bailey (1969), for example, rejected the procedure whereby group interaction and institutionalized norms were considered a sufficient basis to explain social life. His alternative was a more fluid and dynamic model of society, one which viewed the individual as innovative, an active agent helping to shape an ever-changing social structure.

One of the sources of confusion between anthropology and psychology is the assumption that some problems and types of data are 'anthropological,' and others 'psychological.' It is much more useful to regard problems and data as disciplinary-neutral, and to assume that what makes them anthropological or psychological is simply the manner in which they are conceptualized, or the framework in which they are placed. Take, for example, attitudes. Are they psychological or anthropological or sociological? In my viewpoint, they are disciplinary-neutral, but if placed within a psychological framework, they are rendered psychological (or in a similar way, sociological). Consider, also, the focus on child-rearing in psychological anthropology. Surely one's emphasis could be on the social structural influences of child-rearing, or on the personality influences. The point is that they can be made to fit the conceptual territory of either discipline.

In concluding, let me emphasize that for both psychologists and anthropologists the only real entity is the individual human being. Whereas anthropologists abstract and generalize at the level of the social system, psychologists also abstract and generalize, but in their case at the level of the personality system. Finally, the work of some psychologists, anthropologists, and sociologists occupies a common ground, reflecting shared interests in integrating social structure and personality. This field of study is generally called social psychology. Academics being what they are, we shouldn't be surprised that in recent years a subdiscipline within this field has emerged, assigned the label 'sociological social psychology' (MacKinnon 1994). And just as there now is a subfield called the sociology of culture, there also is one called cultural psychology (Cole 1990, Shweder 1990 and 1993).

POLITICAL SCIENCE

Whereas the foundation of anthropology was evolutionism, biology, and the great social theorists such as Marx, Weber, and Durkheim, the foundation of political science was classical philosophy. While anthropology deals with all the subsystems of society, political science focuses on the political system and power. It would be a mistake, however, to assume that anthropology is not concerned with power. Edmund Leach (1965), a prominent British social anthropologist, has argued that power is the most fundamental aspect of all social life, and therefore is central to the anthropological endeavour, and in fact there is an area of specialization in anthropology called political anthropology. My own impression is that a great deal of political science only indirectly deals with power. I would include here one of its central concentrations: public policy and public administration.

ECONOMICS

Like political science, economics focuses on a particular institution, and is concerned about the production, consumption, and distribution of economic goods, and with economic development, prices, trade, and finance. As in the case of political science, there is an area of specialization in anthropology called economic anthropology. Most ethnographies in the past, however, merely included a chapter on economics as one of the several institutions that were investigated.

Economics sometimes is considered the most theoretically advanced discipline among the social sciences, partly due to the rigour of analysis afforded by the fact that economists work with quantitative data, or numbers, and thus can employ mathematical models. Yet many anthropologists consider economics to be ethnocentric, applicable only to Western economies based on market principles. Specialists in economic anthropology have attempted to show that assumptions in Western economics such as rational calculation of profit, maximization, (free) choice, and supply and demand are significantly affected and modified within the context of non-Western social structures. Once again, the academic disease of putting a label on everything is evident here, with those doubting the universality of economic principles called 'substantivists' and the others 'formalists.'

GEOGRAPHY

The central concepts in geography are space and environment. Given its focus on the physical world (or environment) and the social world (as conditioned by space), geography overlaps to a considerable extent with a school in anthropology called cultural ecology (see chapter four). As in the case of economics, political science, and psychology, geography contains many areas of specialization such as land usage and climate that are of only peripheral interest to most anthropologists. Yet except for the more conscious concern with the spatial dimension, a concern shared by many urban anthropologists and urban sociologists, there is considerable overlap between sociocultural anthropology in general and social geography. As in sociology, culture has crept into geography as well, reflected in the specialized approach known as cultural geography (Jackson 1989, Soja 1989, Wagner and Mikesell 1962).

HISTORY

It is conventional to argue that anthropology focuses on the general, history on the particular. It is true that some of the early anthropologists such as Radcliffe-Brown denied that history had any relevance for anthropology, mainly because they thought history dealt with unique events, and that a scientific study of the past was not possible. But in 1950 Evans-Pritchard (1968; original 1950), another remarkably talented social anthropologist, broke with tradition and argued that anthropology was not a generalizing (or nomothetic) discipline, but instead a branch of history. Much earlier Boas (1897), the founder of American anthropology, had included historical inquiry as a central feature of anthropological investigation. In recent years historical anthropology has emerged as a distinct field in its own right.

Today, most anthropologists would probably agree that a historical perspective enriches one's ethnography. Unlike historians, however, anthropologists include history not so much in order to document and explain what happened in the past, but rather to help to understand the present. There also appears to be a difference in styles of research. Whereas historians often seem reluctant to draw even modest generalizations from their data, anthropologists are much less cautious (at least some of them are), and there is more pressure than in history to tie one's ethnography to general theoretical orientations. Yet even this is changing as I write. What we are currently witnessing is a new style of anthropology, one that eschews generalizations and abstractions, and opts instead to dig deeply into individual cases – the approach long preferred by historians.

Let me conclude with two or three observations. First, there is considerably more overlap in these several disciplines than most of their practitioners are prepared to admit. Second, there is a tendency towards what can appropriately be labelled disciplinary imperialism. That is, practitioners of each discipline often make explanatory claims beyond their borders, and contend that their own discipline is the fundamental one, the others merely branches of it. Third, there is nothing sacrosanct about the existing academic division of labour. It would be just as logical to rule such divisions out of existence and focus on research problems from a variety of angles, representing all of the above disciplines, and others where relevant. To some extent it may be argued that this goal has already been attained, reflected, for example, in women's studies. Such programs, however, constitute a slim slice of the university pie. A radical transformation of the entire academic world is improbable, if only because of the vested interests of individual scholars; and there is a related obstacle: universities seem, paradoxically in view of the emphasis on innovative thought, to be no less resistant to change than other social institutions.

How to Learn the Fundamentals of a Discipline

FIVE STEPS, FROM NOVICE TO EXPERT!

1. *Major Writers*

When you take your first couple of courses in a discipline, you will soon recognize from the required reading and the instructor's lectures the names of some of the key figures in the discipline (such as Boas, Mead, Malinowski, and Radcliffe-Brown in anthropology); it is a good idea to read as much as you can about these key figures, especially the founders, and to base your first essays on them in courses with a writing component.

2. *Theoretical Orientations*

In step one you will have gained a rudimentary knowledge of key figures and basic concepts; the next step is to become familiar with the various theoretical orientations or schools within the discipline, such as evolutionism, structural functionalism, cultural ecology, and postmodernism. This is a more sophisticated and demanding task than merely learning about key figures, although often it has been these same scholars who have shaped the central theoretical orientations.

3. *Basic Theoretical and Methodological Problems*

At this stage you attempt to come to grips with the famous problems in the discipline, carrying out your research in the library. Here are a few examples: Does language dictate or at least influence the way people think and behave (the Whorfian-hypothesis question). Is society primarily in harmony or in conflict? Are marriage and the family universal? Why do incest taboos exist? Did institutionalized racism exist before the emergence of capitalism? Has gender inequality been universal, including among hunters and gatherers? The issues that are focused on in this stage are more open-ended and ambiguous than those in the two previous stages, and the demands on the student's imaginative and innovative capacity are correspondingly greater.

4. *The Student's Own Choice of Theoretical or Methodological Problems*

By this stage your studies will probably still be confined to the library, although if you are fortunate you may have an opportunity to get your feet wet in a mini-fieldwork project, usually in conjunction with a qualitative methods course. You will, by now, possess sufficient sophistication to define and select the problems you wish to investigate, reflecting your own academic interests. For example, you might be interested in whether racism in urban areas is greater or lesser than racism in rural areas, and turn to the available literature. Or you might wonder whether multiculturalism disguises class conflict and in this way reinforces the elite's hold on power and privilege. Or you might hypothesize that, concomitant with women's gains, such as an increase in the number of female professors in universities, there is a devaluation of higher education, reflecting a continued stranglehold of patriarchy. Of you might delve into purely theoretical issues, such as whether an anthropology at home will mean that the union of anthropology and sociology is inevitable, whether Marxism and feminism are compatible, and whether quantitative and qualitative analyses can be synthesized. The point is that by this stage you are poised on the periphery of creative scholarship, demanding initiative, sensitivity, judgment, and innovation.

5. *Original Research*

By the time you reach this stage, you will possess a clear view of the conceptual territory occupied by the discipline, a grasp of how that territory varies from one theoretical orientation to another, a sense of the explanatory limits of the discipline, a sophisticated anthropological imagination, and a knowledge of the techniques and methods necessary to conduct research. In other words, you are ready to operate highly independently, and to make an original contribution to the discipline. In anthropology, this usually means embarking on a major fieldwork project, often for one's Ph.D. thesis (occasionally for the M.A. thesis), and once you have done so you can justifiably call yourself a professional anthropologist!

Key Terms

At the risk of putting the reader to sleep, I shall wrap up this opening chapter with some definitions of key terms employed in the book. This task is not as straightforward as it might seem, because each term may vary according to the body of theory or school of thought in which it is used; moreover, the anthropologist's own orientation to the discipline – whether it is seen as science or art, objective or subjective – as well as the anthropologist's personal biases and outlook – whether society is thought to be harmonious or conflict-ridden – will have an impact on one's overall perspective, including how key terms are defined.

THEORY

An explanation of a class of events, usually with an empirical referent, providing insight into how and what is going on, and sometimes explaining why phenomena exist. A theory attempts to solve a puzzle, usually (but not always) in the sense of demonstrating that what lay people think is disorderly and random is actually orderly and systematic.

THEORETICAL ORIENTATION

A distinctive school of thought or scholarly tradition, such as structural functionalism. Other terms often used as substitutes for theoretical orientation are model, conceptual scheme, theoretical system, and paradigm. A theoretical orientation is a highly general and inclusive term. It stipulates the conceptual territory in which the discipline supposedly operates (which actually may vary from one orientation to another); the preferred methodology, including research design, techniques, criteria of verification (if any), and assumptions about the relative balance between science and art; the implicit philosophy of the actor, whether free or determined, rational or emotional, good or evil; and implicit or explicit assumptions regarding possible key explanatory factors such as sexual drive, kinship, religion, or techno-economics.

MODEL

Often employed in two quite different senses. In the one, a model is a substitute for theoretical orientation. Thus, we often refer to structural functionalism as a model of society. In the other, model is used much more narrowly. It constitutes an explanatory system, consisting of logically interdependent variables, built to illuminate a specific problem (or set of problems) in a specific setting. In chapter eight I introduce a model that was constructed in order to explain the central features and dynamics of the community which I investigated in rural Ontario.

A model is usually thought to stand midway between general theory and the empirical universe that is studied, thus articulating or bridging the two. The party line is that while a model is valid or invalid, in the sense of being accurate and illuminating, its validity cannot be directly demonstrated. Instead, one extrapolates hypotheses from the model, subjects them to empirical confirmation (or disconfirmation), and if they survive the testing ordeal, the model then can be accepted as at least tentatively valid.

My own judgment is that this conception of model is rather pretentious, suggesting utopian scientific rigour. Perhaps the more appropriate term is typology, a construct which is similar to a model in the sense of consisting of interdependent concepts and variables representing some class of events; but different in that a typology is deemed useful or not, rather than valid or invalid.

Related terms are hypothesis, correlation, empirical generalization, assumption, proposition, and law. A hypothesis is a formal statement relating two variables, and indicating causal direction (that is, X generates Y). A correlation is a statement of the relationship between two variables without indicating causality, or identifying independent and dependent variables. An empirical generalization summarizes trends in the data. An assumption is a pre-condition which permits analysis to precede. For example, by assuming that human beings are rational and exercise free choice, economists build models explaining how the market works. A proposition is a well-tested hypothesis, or series of hypotheses, generalizable to a wide range of phenomena. A law is a proposition, or series of propositions, potentially universal in scope. My own bias is to regard these several terms, all of which belong to the vocabulary of science, with a certain degree of scepticism. In the ethnographies of most anthropologists, a hypothesis is essentially a hunch, guess, or inspired interpretation, and often an assumption is used as a synonym for hypothesis rather than as a pre-condition. While empirical generalizations are widely employed by anthropologists, and justifiably so, given the largely inductive nature of fieldwork, the same cannot be said about propositions and laws; indeed, most anthropologists would be hard pressed to come up with a dozen propositions in the literature, let alone a single law.

METHODOLOGY

Like model, methodology is also often employed in two senses. In the one, it is an inclusive term consisting of philosophy of knowledge, logic of research, operational definitions, analytic procedures, and research techniques. In the other, it refers more narrowly to the logic of research, including epistemological assumptions (how knowledge is produced and demonstrated) and research design (the strategies used to investigate problems).

METHOD

Refers to the techniques of research, such as participant observation, the questionnaire, and archival methods; and to related issues, such as building rapport and recording field notes.

CONCEPTUAL SCHEME

Sometimes used as a synonym for theoretical orientation, at other times employed more narrowly to mean the key interrelated concepts in one's study. A generation ago, students were taught that there was a difference between a conceptual scheme and a theoretical system, and that until the former was put together, it was futile to attempt to construct the latter.

BASIC CONCEPTS

Earlier in this chapter I discussed a number of basic concepts in the discipline, such as culture, society, belief system, worldview, class, ethnocentrism, and relativism. Basic concepts consist of the minimal vocabulary necessary to understand the perspective of a discipline. Basic concepts all have theoretical implications, in that they represent or allude to persistent, fundamental problems. Related to basic concepts are primitive terms, constructs, and operational definitions. In the philosopher's sense, primitive terms are the fundamental terms in a discipline, the smallest number of terms to which all others can be reduced. They might be thought to be comparable to phonemes (basic sounds) in a language. Constructs are particular kinds of concepts: high-level concepts which enable the researcher to capture and penetrate key dimensions of the universe under investigation. For example, in a study of capitalism, 'alienation' might be considered a construct, just as 'grief' might be in a study of chronic illness. With operational definitions, we plunge full steam into the vocabulary of science. An operational definition specifies the conditions and measurement procedures by which hypotheses are tested empirically. An illustration, I suppose, could be these last pages on key terms. If this section did prove to be soporific, at least we have a measure of its impact!

Organization of the Book

In this opening chapter I have tried to provide the reader with a broad overview of anthropology, and I now turn directly to theory and method. Parts one, two, and three are organized on the basis of the three phases of the discipline that were described in the preface: laying the discipline's foundation, patching the cracks that eventually emerged, and the recent radical trend towards demolition and reconstruction. Phase one corresponds to the early decades of professional anthropology, and here I focus on three theoretical orientations: evolutionism, historical particularism, and structural functionalism. What characterized this era was the great confidence that the discipline was (or could be) a genuine science, although even in those days there were sceptics. In phase two, which emerged after the Second World War and the break-up of colonialism, I shall deal with conflict theory, social action theory, and cultural ecology. By this period serious questions were being raised about the soundness of the previous models of society, and by implication about the dream of a scientific study of other cultures. Yet most anthropologists stifled their doubts and devoted their efforts to firming up the foundation that had been designed by the discipline's early architects. In phase three I examine the most significant theoretical orientations that have emerged during the past two or three decades: structuralism, postmodernism, and feminist anthropology. Whereas the goal in phase one was to build a science of society, and in stage two to keep that dream alive, phase three marks a revolutionary departure from anthropology up to that point, either by reconceptualizing the discipline in a manner that challenges the positivistic approach, or dismissing the quest for a science of society as morally and epistemologically bankrupt.

One of my basic questions has been whether the shifts in theory that occurred have produced corresponding changes in method. What I found was an ever-increasing gap between our theories and our methods as phase one gave away to phases two and three. The trajectory of our theoretical orientations has taken us further and further away from science. The trajectory of our methodological literature has been in exactly the opposite direction. At the very time when doubts about a science of society were being expressed in our theoretical orientations, the textbooks on methods were bent on showing us how to demystify the fieldwork experience, how to become more rigorous and scientific.

Part four takes us in a somewhat different direction. Since the 1960s an enormous amount of literature has appeared on qualitative methods. Pick up virtually any textbook and you will find accounts of how to make entry into the field, how to do participant observation and informal interviews, plus advice on stress and ethics. What you will not find is much that is helpful about how to analyse qualitative data. This is what I call the last frontier in qualitative research, and in chapter eight I try to fill the gap in the methods literature, at least to a modest degree. In the final chapter I cast my eye on the future direction of the discipline. Will postmodernism and feminist anthropology continue to lead the way? Will the gap between our theories and our methods grow even wider, throwing us into yet another crisis, or will extreme positions be abandoned and a middle ground be reached? Forecasting is a risky business, but about at least one thing we can be certain: anthropology will be with us for the foreseeable future. The unique capacity of fieldworkers to observe people in their everyday worlds, to grasp the meaning of their lives, and to encourage communication across class, cultural, ethnic, and gender boundaries – this last issue being possibly more critical than ever before in view of the magnitude of global upheaval – will ensure that happy outcome.

PART ONE: BUILDING THE DISCIPLINE

2

Theory

The early decades of professional anthropology witnessed the discipline's transformation from the armchair to the field. The dominant intellectual perspective in the middle of the nineteenth century was evolutionism, and the fledgling discipline of anthropology did not escape its grip. Eventually evolutionism was overwhelmed by two other orientations, historical particularism and structural functionalism, which derived part of their power from their promotion of first-hand, original field research. Together, evolutionism, historical particularism, and structural functionalism were the most significant theoretical orientations in the discipline for almost one hundred years – indeed, right up to the Second World War.

1. Evolutionism

Evolutionism removed two roadblocks that stood in the way of a scientific investigation of society. The one was the prevailing supernatural and theological version of the origin and development of the universe. The other was the idea that social life, unlike natural life, is spontaneous and free, devoid of regulation and pattern. With its emphasis on struggle, competition, expansion, and historical progress, evolutionary anthropology sought nothing less than to plot and explain the entire sweep of human history, treating sociocultural phenomena as part of nature, subject to its laws.

One of the early controversies was whether all human beings have a common origin and development (monogenesis) or different origins and developments (polygenesis). The monogenisists tended to assume a psychic unity of humankind, the polygenists psychic plurality associated with different races. Much of the theorizing that went on in this era was contaminated by racial prejudice, but the pioneers of anthropology did not invent racism. Earlier writers had paved the way. Blumenbach (1865), for example, had argued that all human beings were born white; the Negroid was said to be merely a degenerative form of the Caucasoid, caused by environmental factors such as climate and diet. Then there was the eighteenth-century notion (see Harris 1968:87) that Negroid skin colour was a form of leprosy. It was during this period, too, that phrenology emerged, with the assumption that the study of the head could explain sociological and psychological patterns. Connected to phrenology was the cephalic index. This was a technique used to classify human populations on the basis of the ratio of head length to head breadth.

BASIC FEATURES

1. *Ethnocentrism.* The early anthropologists tended to evaluate the cultures of the world in terms of the model of Victorian England. The underlying assumption was that evolutionism had culminated in England and Europe, and had been retarded or retrogressive in the primitive world.

2. *Armchair speculation.* The early evolutionary anthropologists did not themselves do field work, especially in the modern sense of intensive participant observation over a long period of time with a limited population. Instead they relied on data supplied by untrained amateurs. At the heart of the evolutionary perspective was the comparative method, with the assumption that societies could be arranged into a taxonomy, and that comparisons across cultures were meaningful.

3. *Unilinear scheme.* The prevailing assumption was that all cultures had gone through the same stages of evolution in the same order.

4. *Inevitable progress.* As sociocultural life evolved, it supposedly got better in the sense of being more civilized, moral, and orderly. Here the influence of the Enlightenment era of the eighteenth century is evident, with its emphasis on progress, order, and rationality.

KEY FIGURES

Edward Tylor (1832–1917)[1]

Tylor was born into a wealthy family in London, England. Although he

---

1 Throughout this book birth and death dates will be provided only for scholars who are no longer living.

never attended university, and indeed quit school at the age of sixteen, he eventually ended up as a don at the University of Oxford. Tylor suffered from poor health as a youth, and led a life of leisure, supported financially by his family. Although he was never to conduct in-depth, original fieldwork, he travelled widely, and it was a trip to Mexico that turned his interests to anthropology. In 1871 he published the highly influential book *Primitive Culture*, with its special focus on and famous definition of religion: a belief in spiritual beings.

Tylor argued that culture evolved from the simple to the complex, and passed through three stages: savagery, barbarism, and civilization. In order to analyse historical development, Tylor relied on the comparative method, and on what he termed 'survivals.' Survivals were 'traces' or a prior evolutionary stage. They consisted of aspects of culture which persisted by force of habit into a higher evolutionary stage. Since the conditions that generated these cultural aspects no longer operated, survivals lacked purpose or usefulness (except, of course, for the anthropologist attempting to reconstruct the past!).

Tylor stressed the rational basis of culture – of all cultures. He placed the emphasis on the human mind. In his scheme, social institutions are driven by reason, and customs which are merely traditional or habitual are bound to eventually disappear, because they lack utility. Those that do not are by definition labelled survivals. Despite his assumption that all peoples, regardless of evolutionary stage, are rational, and all cultures are guided by purpose and usefulness, his scheme is not quite as liberal as it might appear. Primitives, for example, were only said to be rational in the context of their own cultures. That is, given the absence of scientific knowledge, they were thinking as logically as could be expected, but in a manner that might be regarded as irrational in modern society. Tylor's intellectualist perspective has become known pejoratively as the 'if I were a horse' theory – if I were a horse, I'd think like a horse.

Tylor emphasized not only rationality and utility, but also the psychic unity of humankind. Yet as Hatch (1973:32) points out, at the same time he held the contradictory position that different races possessed different degrees of innate ability – a conventional assumption at the time in which he wrote. Although his efforts to establish a scientific, evolutionary study of culture is only of historical interest to most contemporary anthropologists, one part of his writing continues to have some influence; this is his intellectualist approach to the analysis of religion – an approach which has encouraged researchers to pay attention to religion as an explanatory system, one that makes sense of the world to people who embrace religious beliefs.

Louis Henry Morgan (1818–81)

In the United States the outstanding cultural evolutionist was Morgan. He actually was a lawyer by training, and conducted his ethnographic studies, focusing on Native American people, as a hobby. But what a hobby it was! Not only did he do some of his own fieldwork, but he also prepared questionnaires concerning kinship and social organization, and made them available to government officials and others in contact with Native people in order that systematic data would be collected. The end result was an anthropological classic, *Ancient Society* (1877). Like Tylor, Morgan posited three stages of evolution: savagery, barbarism, and civilization, with the first two divided into lower, middle, and upper subtypes. Tied to his scheme were five stages of the development of the family and marriage, three classes of kinship terminology, and an evolutionary portrait of social and political organization ranging from what he referred to as the promiscuous horde to the tribe and finally the modern state.

Morgan's name also is associated, favourably, with the anthropological distinction between classificatory and descriptive kinship terminology. In a classificatory system, the same terms that apply to relatives such as husband and wife may also be applied to a wider range of kin. For example, a woman among the Yoruba in Nigeria might use the term husband (*oko*) when addressing her husband's brothers, her husband's sisters, and her husband's parents. In contemporary Western societies, descriptive terminology predominates, which means that terms such as father or daughter designate a specific and narrow range of individuals characterized by a biological or marital relationship. Yet even there, terms like brother, sister, aunt, uncle, and son sometimes have classificatory overtones, such as in service clubs and political and religious organizations.

The keys to Morgan's evolutionary scheme were techno-economic factors. What caused the shift from a lower to a higher stage, he contended, was the introduction of a significant technological innovation, such as pottery, the plough, or the bow and arrow. Morgan's emphasis on the role played by technology and economy won the admiration of Marx, to the extent that he wanted to dedicate his major work, *Das Kapital*, to him. Morgan, a highly conservative lawyer, was horrified, and declined the honour.

For Morgan, like Tylor, the transition from a lower to a higher stage meant progress, not only in technological sophistication but also in morality. This helps to explain his racist bent. Although he was a staunch defender of American Indians throughout his life, he did not think (see Harris 1968:138–9) they were the equal of the European, and he was manifestly prejudiced against African Americans.

Contemporary scholars attracted to evolutionary models (and there are still some around such as Marvin Harris) continue to draw inspiration from Morgan, recognizing in his scheme, and in particular the attention he gave to technological innovations, a useful framework for constructing the development of human culture. To be sure, they no longer accept many of his specific assertions, such as that the people of lower savagery were only gatherers of fruit and nuts (rather than hunters as well), and they distance themselves from the racist undertones in his work. But even in this respect, their assumption seems to be that the basic integrity of Morgan's evolutionary framework has stood the test of time; all that was required to modernize it was a nimble terminological adjustment so that savages became hunters and gatherers, barbarians became horticulturalists, and civilized peoples became citizens of the modern, stratified state.

Herbert Spencer (1820–1903)

Another central evolutionary writer was Spencer, born in England and the author of numerous books, including *Principles of Sociology* (1876). Spencer posited two stages of evolution: militaristic and industrial, characterized respectively by centralized authority and individual freedom. Spencer thought that society evolved from the simple to the complex, a process involving struggle, adaptation, and progress. He drew a close parallel between biological and social evolution, and tended to treat society as an organism comparable to a biological organism, with one important exception: as society evolves from the militaristic to the industrial stage, the individual human being enjoys a degree of autonomy unknown to other species. In other words, at an advanced stage of evolution the parts of society (individuals) dominate the whole (the state) rather than the reverse.

Spencer remains of great interest to contemporary scholars because some of his key ideas paved the way for Darwin. It was Spencer, for example, not Darwin, who coined the expression 'the survival of the fittest.' In Spencer's view, the development of society was subject to the same natural laws that applied to the non-human world, and he thought this was a good thing; in the long run, society would progress to the point of perfection. This is illustrated by his argument (Harris 1968:127) that intelligence and fertility were inversely related, so that the most intelligent people had the fewest children. Since Spencer assumed that the most intelligent individuals and races were slated for survival, this meant that overpopulation would never become a problem for humankind.

In many respects Spencer's writings bear a remarkable resemblance to the tracts of contemporary right wingers. His evolutionary perspective became an apology for capitalism, private property, and free enterprise, and an onslaught against government intercession, socialism, and communism. In Spencer's view, capitalism and free enterprise were consistent with the laws of nature, while socialism and communism were opposed to them. These laws, according to Spencer, could not be modified by human intervention, by culture; nor should they be, for they were driving *Homo sapiens* to ever-increasing levels of perfection.

EVALUATION

If the goal of anthropology is to establish a scientific study of society (or culture), then evolutionism had its strengths. By assuming that society is subject to the same laws of nature that shape non-human phenomena, such as struggle, competition, adaptation, and directional change from the simple to the complex, the evolutionists had a framework that enhanced nomothetic inquiry. Critics, especially those who do not think that science can cope with the complexity of social and cultural life, might counter that evolutionism was little more than a self-fulfilling ideology. Writers such as Tylor, Morgan, and Spencer, in other words, merely found in the history of humankind the patterns and changes that their theories demanded them to discover. Be that as it may, what can be asserted about early evolutionism, besides its crudeness, is that it was perfectly suited to its times, at least in a political sense. With the emphasis placed on the survival of the fittest and with the assumed superiority of the European, it provided ideological support for imperialism and colonialism.

2. Historical Particularism

The main reaction in American anthropology against evolutionism became known by the somewhat clumsy term, historical particularism. An integral part of historical particularism was diffusionism. The central idea in diffusionism was that an aspect of culture such as the discovery of the wheel, a marital practice, or religious belief tended to spread from one culture to another, eventually becoming integrated into all of the cultures in a given geographical area.

Diffusionism threw a monkey wrench into the evolutionary scheme, for no longer did it make sense to argue that each culture had to evolve through specific stages in a specific order. Diffusionism was also behind one of the most renowned methodological issues in early anthropology: Galton's Problem. At the turn of the century Edward Tylor (1889) presented a paper to the Royal Society in Britain. His thesis was that given the same level of technology and environmental conditions, the residence patterns following marriage will be the same (whether, for example, newlyweds will set up their own household independent of the wife's and husband's parents – neolocal residence – whether they will live with the wife's parents or lineage – matrilocal residence – or whether they will live with the husband's parents or lineage – patrilocal residence). Tylor presented systematic data from neighbouring ethnic groups to illustrate his thesis, and by doing so he appeared firmly to establish the scientific stature of the discipline. But in the audience was the famous scientist, Francis Galton, who also dabbled in anthropology. He apparently asked a question that has plagued the discipline ever since: how did Professor Tylor know if the individual societies for which he had data were truly independent cases, rather than being contaminated by diffusion? In other words, was each of his examples of post-marital residence patterns discrete, or had cultural borrowing muddied the waters?

There were actually three separate schools of diffusionism. One was the Vienna-based *Kulturkreise* School. Writers such as Ratzel, Graebner, and Schmidt tried to explain the development of culture through migration and diffusion. They posited several distinct culture areas or culture circles (the literal meaning of *kulturkreise*), the elements of which over time had spread throughout the world, and thus helped to explain cultural similarities across space. Another school was in Britain, promoted by the influential W.H.R. Rivers at Cambridge University, and by W.J. Perry and G. Elliot Smith. British diffusionism was short-lived, possibly because of its unsophisticated excesses. Smith, for example, made the implausible claim that Egypt was the source of virtually all cultural traits and innovations, which then had diffused to the rest of the planet. The third, and no doubt most significant, school of diffusionism took shape under the guidance of Boas in the United States, and leads us directly to historical particularism.

BASIC FEATURES

1. *Limited historical inquiry*. The American school was opposed to the crude, speculative assumptions of the evolutionists and to the sloppy use of the comparative method, based on data of dubious quality. But it was not anti-historical. It advocated that one's study be limited to a particular culture (or cultural area), and that the history of that culture be reconstructed – hence the label historical particularism.

2. *Diffusion*. Perhaps the basic assumption of the historical particularists was that any particular culture was partly composed of elements diffused from other cultures.

3. *Culture as a shreds and patches*. While each diffused element is reshaped in order to fit its new cultural context, the degree of integration is never complete. Culture, in other words, is a loosely organized entity rather than a tightly fused system.

4. *Culture as unique*. Each particular culture is to some extent unique, the result of the diffusionist process and local needs.

5. *Emic analysis*. Emic and etic analysis are terms taken from linguistics, and refer respectively to the actor's insider (subjective) perspective and the observer's outsider (objective) perspective. Historical particularists give priority to emic analysis and to subjective data such as values, norms, and emotions.

6. *Habit and tradition*. An underlying assumption is that social life is guided by habit and custom. This assumption, along with the emphasis placed on emotion, contrasts sharply with Tylor's view that culture is driven by rationality and utility.

7. *Relativism*. Given that each culture is to some degree unique, it is unacceptable to pass judgment on the beliefs and actions found in other cultures. Such beliefs and actions can only be understood in the cultural context in which they are located.

8. *Cautious generalization*. The factor of uniqueness also means that any attempt to generalize across cultures must be undertaken with utmost care, and only when sufficient data are available.

9. *Fieldwork*. By emphasizing original fieldwork, the historical particularists rectified one of the most glaring weaknesses among the evolutionists. It might be said that the historical particularists embraced an almost puritanical approach to fieldwork, hesitating to generalize until masses of data had been collected, and cautious about making general observations even within a particular culture whose history had been reconstructed.

10. *Inductive procedure*. Finally, the historical particularists supposedly went about their business without preconceived theories. Explanation, to the extent that it emerged at all, grew naturally out of the masses of data that had been collected.

KEY FIGURES

Franz Boas (1858–1942)

The outstanding individual associated with historical particularism was Franz Boas. Indeed, the basic features that I have just outlined represent the Boasian version of anthropological inquiry.

Boas was born and educated in Germany where he studied physics, geography, and mathematics. In the 1880s he undertook a geographical investigation of the Inuit on Baffin Island. That experience seems to have persuaded him that cultural factors play a greater role than geographical ones, turning him towards anthropology. He was later to concentrate his research efforts on the Native people of the west coast of British Columbia. He published a half-dozen books during his career, and, amazingly, more than seven hundred scholarly papers, including descriptive accounts of the potlatch among the Kwakiutl (Boas 1897). The potlatch, which involved a peculiar approach to status competition – the ceremonial destruction of property – undoubtedly ranks as one of the outstanding ethnographic descriptions in the discipline, prompting a debate about its essential irrationality (Benedict 1959; orig. 1934) or rationality (Codere 1950, and Harris 1968, 1974).

Although Boas was a brilliant practitioner of general anthropology, which meant that he was capable of synthesizing the biological and cultural dimensions of human behaviour, he often is credited with (or accused of) promoting culturology, or the argument that culture has a life of its own, and exhausts the explanation of human interaction. Boas has also been criticized as being anti-scientific, but this is quite unfair. It is true that he was opposed to grand theoretical schemes, and dubious that cultural laws would ever be discovered. But he did not contend that culture was devoid of regularities. In fact, it could be argued that in his own way Boas was exceptionally scientific-oriented. The standards that he demanded for fieldwork were rigorous – some would say unattainable – which may have reflected his early grounding in the hard sciences. He also was an inductivist, which meant that only after masses of solid data had been collected could stabs at explanation and generalization be made, and only then about the culture on which the investigation had been based. Boas, I should add, also led the way in insisting that the fieldworker collect native texts, vernacular accounts of aspects of culture. Such caution, such emphasis on data rather than theory, flies in the face of the deductive procedure, in which one tests hypotheses derived from general theory – supposedly the most elegant representation of the scientific method. Yet the Boasian approach was a healthy counterpoint to the grand schemes of the evolutionists, and indeed may be the procedure most appropriate to the social sciences.

Boas's impact on American anthropology was not limited to his publications, prodigous as they were. From 1896 to 1937 he taught at Columbia University, and trained a remarkable number of talented anthropologists, some of whom are described below.

Alfred Lewis Kroeber (1876–1960)

Boas's first student to receive a Ph.D. was Kroeber, a remarkably productive scholar who spent most of his career at Berkeley. Kroeber accepted much of his mentor's conception of historical particularism, especially the emphasis on historical reconstruction, the key role played by diffusion, and the inductive procedure. Yet in some important respects Kroeber parted company from Boas and introduced his own version of historical particularism. Boas had become increasingly interested in the individual, and the relationship between the individual and culture. Kroeber, in contrast, assigned overwhelming priority to culture, which he termed the superorganic, asserting that the individual is completely subordinate to culture, and therefore irrelevant from the point of view of anthropology. Kroeber was also not satisfied with the Boasian conception of culture as a shreds and patches. In Kroeber's scheme, culture became a highly integrated entity, its elements tightly interwoven and mutually consistent.

Kroeber divided culture into basic and secondary features, or what he also labelled reality culture and value culture. Basic culture concerned practical issues, like making a living and producing food, which Kroeber thought were conditioned by technological and environmental factors. Secondary culture dealt with the creative side of human beings, such as artistic endeavours and crafts, and were ends in themselves, relatively independent of technology and environment. Perhaps Kroeber's best-known example of secondary culture was the changing patterns of fashion in dress (Kroeber and Richardson 1940).

What is curious is that a scholar would concentrate his efforts on what he himself saw as the secondary rather than basic, fundamental features of social life. I suppose this was largely a matter of personal taste and interest (Kroeber had studied English before turning to anthropology), but it also reflected his perspective on the discipline. Kroeber was sceptical of (but not completely opposed to) the scientific study of culture; he saw more value in the historical method, and regarded anthropology as a branch of the humanities. In contrast, one of Boas's other renowned students, Robert Lowie, who actually coined the 'shreds and patches' phrase, shared his teacher's doubts that laws of cultures existed, but at the same time insisted that there were cultural regularities, the discovery of which demanded scientific rigour.

Ruth Benedict (1887–1948)

Benedict was also trained by Boas, and became one of the best-known anthropologists in the world, notably for her popular book *Patterns of Culture* (1934). Benedict also was a poet, writing under the pseudonym Anne Singleton. She shared with Kroeber the assumption that anthropology had more in common with the humanities than the sciences, and that culture was not the untidy entity dreamed up by Boas, but instead highly integrated and coherent. Each culture, she accepted, consisted of the fortuitous interaction of elements diffused from elsewhere, but these elements became welded into a consistent whole. Where she diverged sharply from Kroeber, and remained faithful to Boas, was in the emphasis that she placed on the individual.

Benedict became a leading figure in what became known as the culture and personality school, an offshoot of historical particularism. Boas had speculated about the relationship between the individual and her or his culture, but left the theme essentially uninvestigated. Benedict filled the gap. She thought that each culture promoted a distinct personality type, and that there was a high degree of consistency between cultural type and patterns of emotion. In fact, she coined the expression 'culture is personality writ large.' *Patterns of Culture* provided a clear example of her approach. In this book the Zuni are described as Apollonian: moderate in temperament and oriented to group or collective behaviour. In contrast, the Kwakiutl were said to possess a personality labelled Dionysian: intemperate and characterized by excessive individualism. Each culture was thought to be unique, with its own personality or 'configuration.' What this meant was that cultures such as the Zuni and

Kwakiutl could be compared and contrasted, but generalization across cultures was not meaningful. In other words, Benedict took anthropology much further away from nomothetic inquiry than Boas had advocated, whose own attitude towards a science of culture could be described as cautious rather than hostile.

While the pioneers in the culture and personality school such as Benedict tended to claim that in each culture there was a basic personality type shared by all of its members, it should be noted that later writers backed away from this extreme position, suggesting instead that in each culture there was a modal personality, a statistically most prominent personality which left room for other types. Eventually the view emerged that in each culture there were several modal personalities. By that time, however, the culture and personality school had begun to fade from the academic scene and it is tempting to conclude that it left little of value as its legacy. Contemporary anthropologists, it is correct to say, probably would have little patience for the crude generalization implied in the concept of the modal personality. Yet some of the central interests of the culture and personality school remain very much alive today, notably the relationship between the individual and society (or culture), the focus on the individual as innovator rather than cultural puppet, the emphasis on subjectivity and emotion, and scepticism towards cross-cultural generalizations.

Margaret Mead (1901–78)

Mead was a student of both Boas and Benedict. She became famous early in her career after publishing *Coming of Age in Samoa* (1928), *Growing Up in New Guinea* (1930), and *Sex and Temperament in Three Primitive Societies* (1935). Under the influence of Boas, she selected Samoa as a test case to demonstrate the overwhelming importance of culture, focusing on teenage Samoan girls. She concluded that unlike in the United States, adolescence in Samoa is tension-free, the product of culture, the implication being that biology played only a secondary role in human interaction.

Mead also contributed to the culture and personality school, which led her to search for typical personalities and national character. She has been criticized, notably by Freeman, not only for promoting an exaggerated picture of the role played by culture, but also for the implicit claim of being able to get inside the heads of her informants in order to comprehend their emotions and attitudes. Yet in a methodological appendix to *Coming of Age in Samoa*, she suggested that anthropological analysis has more in common with the work of a physician (or psychiatrist) than with a physicist. The former probes deeply into each individual case, with the hope that insight and illumination will emerge; the latter, in contrast, aims for proof and verification, and attempts to generalize across cases. As we shall later see, Mead's characterization of the anthropological endeavour is remarkably consistent with the viewpoint of contemporary writers such as Geertz.

In her later years Mead achieved the status of an intellectual guru, in high demand on the lecture circuit, not least because her prolific research and publications, focusing on women and sexuality in a cross-cultural perspective, made a major contribution to a field of inquiry that was only later to come into its own: gender studies.

EVALUATION

During the past few decades it has become almost a ritual to dismiss historical particularism as a backward step in anthropology. Certainly, with its emphasis on the emotional side of human beings, and the untidy shreds and patches image of culture, plus the more or less presumed uniqueness of each society, leading to doubts about cross-cultural generalization and the discovery of laws, historical particularism did not match up to the goal of nomothetic inquiry embraced by the evolutionists. Yet in many respects historical particularism, especially as represented by Boas rather than by his students, resonates clearly with the most recent directions taken by the discipline under the guidance of postmodernism. Relevant here is Boas's emphasis on subjectivity, his insistence on collecting original texts (emic inquiry at its pinnacle), and his distrust of grand theoretical schemes, not to mention his promotion of relativism. Historical particularism, in other words, was not merely a healthy reaction to evolutionism. To some extent it has been reborn in postmodernism.[2]

3. Structural Functionalism

As in the United States, the initial reaction in British anthropology against evolutionism took the form of diffusionism. Unlike in America, the British school of diffusionism, led by Rivers at Cambridge Univer-

2 For an overview of postmodernism, see chapter six.

sity, quickly petered out. Radcliffe-Brown, a student of Rivers, had begun his career as a diffusionist, but he soon discovered Durkheim, and with the help of others such as Malinowski he turned the discipline in the narrow direction of social anthropology, guided by what became known as the structural functional model. For nearly half a century, right up to the 1950s and early 1960s, structural functionalism reigned supreme in British anthropology, and achieved much the same stature in sociology. Such was the clout of structural functionalism that Kingsley Davis (1959) was moved to argue that it was not merely a special approach in the discipline: it *was* the sociological model.

BASIC FEATURES

1. *Organic analogy*. Society is supposedly like a biological organism, with structures and functions comparable to the heart, lungs, and blood. It is in this context that the structural functional model sometimes is known humorously as the Big Animal Theory of Society.

2. *A natural science orientation*. Structural functionalists were thoroughly committed to a natural science model of society. Social life was deemed to be empirical, orderly, and patterned, and therefore amenable to rigorous, positivistic, scientific study.

3. *Narrow conceptual territory*. For the most part, structural functionalists shared the viewpoint that their investigations should be restricted to the social structure (or society) and its subsystems such as the family, the economy, the polity, and worldviews or beliefs. Unlike American anthropologists, their British counterparts rarely paid much attention to art, language, child-rearing, and ideology, or to the individual and technological and environmental factors.

4. *Functional unity, indispensibility, and universality*. In the cruder versions, it was assumed that all the institutions and roles of society meshed neatly together, that existing structures and institutions in any particular society contained indispensable functions without which the society would fall apart, and that these structures and functions or their equivalents were found in all healthy societies.

5. *Anti-reductionism*. Consistent with the assumption that the discipline's conceptual territory should be narrowly defined, and in this way manageable, the British school was generally opposed to explanations drawn from other disciplines, notably psychology. The underlying premise was that social anthropology provided a type of explanation, concerned explicitly and solely with social structure, that no other disci-

pline dealt with. Theoretical progress depended on the careful and cautious exploration of the exact properties of the social structure, and the relationships among its substructures.

6. *The significance of kinship and the family.* It was assumed that in pre-industrial societies, where most British anthropologists did their fieldwork, one subsystem or institution had greater impact than any other. This was the kinship system. Pre-industrial people supposedly organized their economic, political, and even religious and ritual activities at least partly in terms of their kin relations, clan, or lineage. To illustrate the significance of family and kinship, anthropologists sometimes refer to the following distinction: when strangers in industrial societies meet, one of the first questions asked is what do you do? When strangers in pre-industrial societies cross paths, there is a different query: what is your family name or clan affiliation?

7. *Equilibrium.* Society was not only thought to be highly patterned, but also in a state of equilibrium, characterized by harmony, a central value system, and internal consistency. When disruptions did occur, there existed re-equilibriating mechanisms to return society to an even keel.

8. *Static analysis.* Given the assumption about equilibrium, it followed that society exhibited long-term stability. In other words, it invited a static (and conservative) analysis rather than a dynamic one.

9. *Anti-historical.* Partly because of the presumed equilibrium and stability, and partly because of the assumption that the past is unknowable in societies without written records, structural functionalism did not encourage an historical perspective.

10. *Fieldwork orientation.* Perhaps even more so than in the case of historical particularism, structural functionalists were totally devoted to first-hand, participant observational research. In fact, it used to be joked that if a person actually went to some distant land, survived the ordeal, and wrote it up, the Ph.D. degree was automatic. During the early years in British social anthropology, more emphasis was placed on the high quality of the data than on theoretical innovation, which sometimes earned the British school the reputation of being merely descriptive. However, there certainly was an implicit theoretical framework in the structural functional school, with agreed-on assumptions about the role of social structure, the interaction of its parts, and epistemological issues having to do with evidence and proof. As in the case of Boas and his students, the structural functionalists were inductivists, strongly opposed to commencing research with preconceived theories or ideas. It is argu-

able, of course, just how open-minded and unbiased one can be, especially since both the American and British anthropologists conducted their research under the guidance of identifiable frameworks: historical particularism and structural functionalism.

Emile Durkheim (1858–1917)

Born in France and trained in philosophy, Durkheim joined the Department of Philosophy at the University of Bordeaux in 1887. A decade later he was appointed to the first professorship in the social sciences in France. By then he had published several outstanding works, including *The Division of Labour* (1933; orig. 1893), *The Rules of Sociological Method* (1938; orig. 1895), and *Suicide* (1951; orig. 1897). Durkheim was totally committed to building a natural science of society. He believed that social phenomena were as real as natural or physical phenomena, in the sense that a person can no more will away a marital practice or religious belief than he can a stick or stone. Like Boas, he argued that social life is driven by emotion and sentiment, not reason and utility; yet at the same time he was vehemently opposed to psychological explanations, in which the individual was entertained as a causal agent. In Durkheim's view, the individual's beliefs, emotions, sentiments, and actions were a product of the social structure, or what he labelled the collective conscience.

The controlling role of society over the individual was expressed in his concept 'social fact.' Social facts were external to the individual, coercive over the individual, and general throughout society. The most inclusive social fact was the collective conscience, which in contemporary social science might be labelled the central value system. Durkheim argued that group behaviour was greater than the sum of its parts (that is, of the individuals who compose it) because the very fact of interacting in a group transformed the emotions and sentiments of each of the participants in a unified direction. The implication, again, was that the sociological investigator got nowhere by focusing on the individual in isolation from the social structure.

While the collective conscience was Durkheim's most general social fact, it was broken down into two subtypes: mechanical and organic solidarity. The first predominated in pre-industrial societies, and was based on homogeneity, a tendency towards group interaction, and the absence of individual choice. The second made its appearance as society began to industrialize and become more complex, and was based on heterogeneity, an emphasis on individualism and choice. What must be stressed is that even the elements of individualism and choice in Durkheim's scheme were products of the social structure, rather than the free expressions of the actor's will.

Durkheim's most elaborate illustration of his theoretical position concerned suicide, which he selected as a topic of investigation largely to demonstrate that what appeared to be an individualistic phenomenon was in actuality a social phenomenon. His two main types of suicide were altruistic and egoistic (a third type, anomic, which prevails when social order breaks down, will not be dealt with here, since Durkheim treated it as atypical). Altruistic suicide occurred when there was too much solidarity in society, or insufficient individualism, especially in mechanically organized societies. Egoistic suicide occurred when there was too little social solidarity, notably in organically organized societies. In mounting his argument, Durkheim used statistics and the comparative method, and indeed contended that the comparative method was not a special procedure in sociology: it *was* the sociological method.

A.R. Radcliffe-Brown (1881–1955)

Although Durkheim did do some original empirical work, especially in *Suicide*, he was essentially an armchair scholar. Nevertheless, he had an enormous influence on social anthropology, primarily via his disciple, Radcliffe-Brown. Born in England, Radcliffe-Brown undertook fieldwork from 1906 to 1908 in the Andaman Islands, located west of Thailand. His flair, however, was for theory.

Like Durkheim, Radcliffe-Brown was anti-reductionist, and committed to promoting a natural science of society. He identified three stages of scientific investigation: observation (collecting the data), taxonomy (classifying the data), and generalization (theoretical excursions). He regarded the comparative method as the anthropologist's alternative to the controlled laboratory experiment and, unlike Benedict, assumed that cross-cultural comparisons and generalizations were not only possible, but indeed essential to the anthropological enterprise. Writing in a style that could be described as clean and cold as ice (and reputedly capable of the same bare-bone logic in his oral seminar presentations), Radcliffe-Brown made an outstanding contribution to classical anthropological topics such as joking relations (ritualistic verbal exchange between people in potentially hostile relations, such as in-laws), and the significance of the mother's brother (who usurps some of the responsibilities of a person's biological father in matrilineal societies where descent is traced through one's mother's lineage). Yet his constant harangues for a nomothetic, natural science approach to the discipline, dismissed long ago by Lowie (1937:222) as mere 'confessions of faith,' were more impressive in the classroom and on the lecture circuit than in the ethnographer's laboratory – that is, the societies that they studied. As the fieldwork enterprise blossomed, to the extent of becoming a rite of passage for aspiring anthropologists, it became increasingly evident that the natural science model of society, at least Radcliffe-Brown's version, was unable to cope with the complexities of social life, and that perhaps a more subtle model was required – one which recognized the methodological difficulties in trying to grasp and make sense of subjectivity and meaning in an ever-changing universe.

Bronislaw Malinowski (1884–1942)

Radcliffe-Brown's rival for the leadership of social anthropology was Malinowski, who was born in Poland but taught for most of his career at the London School of Economics. Whereas Radcliffe-Brown was renowned as a powerful theoretician, Malinowski was lauded as an exceptionally gifted fieldworker. Indeed, many anthropologists would credit him for establishing modern fieldwork, with its emphasis on long-term participant observation in a small community, enabling the heroic researcher to understand life from the native's perspective. Ironically, Malinowski's much admired example of how to conduct ethnographic research came about partly by accident. At the outbreak of the First World War, he found himself poised to do research in the Trobriand Islands, located to the east of New Guinea, which were controlled at the time by Australia. He was granted permission by the Australian authorities, despite being a Polish national and thus an enemy alien, to engage in research among the Trobrianders, and he remained there off and on for four years, setting the standard for future fieldwork.

Malinowski, like Boas, introduced one of anthropology's major ethnographic examples: the kula ring. Necklaces were exchanged clockwise from one Trobriand island to another, and armshells were exchanged counter-clockwise. The exchange was ceremonial, for neither the necklaces nor the armbands were intrinsically valuable. Yet the exchanges increased the level of interaction and decreased the degree of hostility among the people of the various islands, and made possible *gimwali*: a bartering activity that did involve valuable economic goods such as fish, pottery, and building materials. An important element in the kula ring was that people who exchanged necklaces and armbands with each other were not permitted to engage in bartering activity involving valuable goods such as fish, although they could freely do so with others. This ensured that the distinct ceremonial and economic transactions would not be confused, thus protecting the former's contribution to social solidarity from potential squabbles over who got the best in a business exchange.

Although both Malinowski and Radcliffe-Brown were structural functionalists, their theoretical approaches were by no means identical. Malinowski placed the emphasis more on function than structure – what institutions actually contributed to a society – and was less sensitive than Radcliffe-Brown to the potential flaws in structural functionalism, such as the assumptions of functional unity, universality, and indispensability. Radcliffe-Brown gave priority to social structure, and denied that a functionalist school, which became associated with Malinowski's approach, even existed. Malinowski argued that the function of institutions was to satisfy biological needs. Radcliffe-Brown saw their function as fulfilling the mechanical needs of society. Malinowski advocated a very general framework, the causal lines of which ran from basic biological and psychological needs to social organization. Radcliffe-Brown, like Durkheim, was defiantly anti-reductionist. Malinowski defined the discipline as the study of culture, not social structure, which was Radcliffe-Brown's preferred label. Malinowski focused at times on personality, exploring the cross-cultural applicability of Freud's Oedipus complex. And, like Boas, he stressed the importance of gathering native texts, or accounts of beliefs and behaviour in the native's own words – all of which caused Radcliffe-Brown to throw a fit.

Despite these apparent differences, the approaches of Malinowski and Radcliffe-Brown had a great deal in common. In fact, it is tempting to dismiss some of their disagreements as little more than a power struggle for the position of top dog in the discipline. Consider, for example, Malinowski's definition of culture: 'Culture is an integral composed of partly autonomous, partly coordinated institutions' (1944:41). He goes on to define anthropology as the theoretical analysis of institutions. Yet Radcliffe-Brown also identified the discipline as the study of institutions, which he thought were coterminous with social structure. Then, too, on his appointment to the London School of Economics, Malinowski urged that the discipline as practised there be called social (not cultural) anthropology. Indeed, Malinowski sometimes has been accused of cannibalizing culture by portraying human beings as self-interested manipulators, thereby highlighting individual motivation rather than culture.

EVALUATION

Structural functionalism provided anthropology with a coherent and tidy framework, one moreover that was manageable in the fieldwork setting. Boiled down to its essence, the procedure only required ethnographers to identify patterns of action and belief, and specify their functions. Yet the costs of such a relatively simple approach were considerable. Structural functionalism downplayed conflict and almost ignored social change. Just as evolutionism provided ideological support for European colonial expansion, structural functionalism was equally suited to maintaining the colonial empires once they had been established. After all, if society is harmonious, in a state of equilibrium, and every pattern of action has its purpose, why attempt to change things? Anthropology, as I indicated in chapter one, has often been accused of propping up colonialism. The ideology of structural functionalism helps to explain its culpability.[3]

Conclusion

Throughout phase one of anthropology there was a general commitment to establishing a scientific study of culture or society. The evolutionists certainly were devoted to this goal. Historical particularism and structural functionalism were healthy reactions to the grand schemes and unfounded speculations of evolutionism, not least because they shifted the discipline from the library to the field. But they were not anti-scientific. In including historical particularism in this claim, I am making the assumption that its outstanding proponent was Boas, not his students who pushed the discipline towards the humanities. While it might be said that historical particularism and structural functionalism represent weak and strong versions of science respectively, in my judgment historical particularism in Boas's capable hands was scientific nevertheless. As I have pointed out, Boas's standards of research were

---

3 In the next chapter, however, I shall point out that towards the end of his career Malinowski was urging anthropologists to expose the evils of colonialism.

exceptionally high, and his opposition was not to science, but merely to sloppy work unsupported by the data.

It is also clear that neither historical particularism nor structural functionalism were uniform theoretical perspectives. Kroeber redefined Boas's conception of untidy culture as a highly integrated, consistent whole, within which the individual swung back and forth like a puppet, much the same as in Durkheim's social structural framework; and Benedict fashioned aspects of historical particularism into what became known as the culture and personality school. As for structural functionalism, we already have seen that differences existed between Radcliffe-Brown and Malinowski.

Over the years, British anthropologists such as Firth (1964a, 1964b) attempted to deal with the criticism that structural functionalism was incapable of coping with social change. Firth distinguished between social structure and social organization. The first was static, consisting of persistent patterns of action. The second was dynamic, tied to actual behaviour as it unfolded, and focused on the individual's capacity to make choices, a fundamental source of social change. Yet except for the emphasis given to the individual, Firth's distinction was merely a re-run of concepts introduced earlier by his teacher, Radcliffe-Brown. The earlier writer, who explicitly stated that society is dynamic rather than static (1952), separated structural form and actual structure. The first, which was static, was offered as the observer's analytic model; the second, which was dynamic, represented empirical reality. In fact, Radcliffe-Brown also introduced the exact distinction later drawn by Firth: social structure versus social organization.

Although the onslaught against evolutionism by the historical particularists and the structural functionalists was vigorous, not everyone would agree that it was justified. In separate works, Harris (1968), and Kaplan and Manners (1972) have contended that the purported flaws in early evolutionism have been exaggerated, especially the charge of unilinear development. What is curious, and important, is that many of the writers most opposed to evolutionism, such as Durkheim, embraced an implicit evolutionary framework. We merely have to recall his distinction between mechanical and organic solidarity, found respectively in pre-industrial and industrial societies. Moreover, in their mature years both Radcliffe-Brown and Malinowski expressed a renewed interest in evolutionary studies, and as we shall see in the chapter four, a revived version of evolutionism emerged on the scholarly scene around the period of the Second World War.

Finally, what has been the fate of historical particularism and structural functionalism? Few anthropologists today would be pleased to be identified by either of these labels. The approach taken by Radcliffe-Brown, with its emphasis on nomothetic inquiry, has been especially harshly dealt with. In contrast, Boas and Malinowski, with their less elegant perspectives, seem to be more in tune with contemporary interests and orientations. Could this be because they were also the more committed and gifted fieldworkers?

3

Method

My aim in this book is to sketch out the history of theory and methodology in anthropology, and to examine the changing relationship between them over time. This task, however, is not quite as simple as it might appear. One reason is that it involves not two but three distinct components: the theoretical literature, the methods literature, and the fieldwork situation – what anthropologists have actually been doing. Another reason is that a theoretical orientation includes a lot of things. It contains an explanatory system such as the functions of institutions and the interdependence of subsystems in structural functionalism. It also stipulates methodological principles regarding research design and the choice of techniques. Not least of all, it embraces implicit assumptions about how knowledge is produced and demonstrated, and about human nature – whether, for example, people exercise choice or are cultural and biological puppets.

This leads us to a very important clarification. In a discipline such as anthropology there are, in a sense, three separate statements about theory. There are the various theoretical orientations themselves, the implications and assumptions intrinsic to the methods literature, and the type of explanation that is produced by fieldworkers in their ethnographies. Similarly, there are three separate statements about methodology. There is the specialized methods literature, the methodological principles embedded in theoretical orientations, and the methodological approaches employed in research.[1]

In the best possible world, the theoretical orientations, methods liter-

---

1 See Menzies (1982) for a somewhat similar distinction between what he labels theoretician's theory and research theory.

ature, and actual research speak the same language. In other words, there is between them a great deal of consistency. This was essentially the case during phase one in the discipline.

The Methods Literature

One of the great misconceptions in anthropology is that before 1960 almost nothing had been written about fieldwork methods. It is true that methods courses, both at the undergraduate and graduate levels, were virtually unheard of until the 1960s and 1970s, but this does not mean that a substantial literature was not available. I have more than one hundred references to articles and books (or sections of books) on methods published before 1960, about half of them before 1950. Some indication of the wide range of techniques and issues covered in this literature is reflected as follows: general discussions of fieldwork methods (Kahn and Cannell 1957, Lowie 1937, Madge 1953, Selltiz et al. 1959); participant observation (Kluckhohn 1940); informants (Nadel 1939, Tremblay 1957); interviewing (S. Harvey 1938, Merton and Kendall 1946, Nadel 1939); the genealogical method (Barnes 1947, Rivers 1900 and 1910); life histories (Dollard 1935); personal documents (Allport 1942); census collection (Richards 1938); surveys (Fortes et al. 1947, Leach 1958, Marwick 1956, Streib 1952, Vidich and Schapiro 1955); statistics (A.T. and G.M. Culwick 1938, Driver 1953, Fortes 1938, Hunter 1934, Kroeber and Driver 1932, Siegel 1956); learning native languages (J. Henry 1940, Lowie 1940, Mead 1939); community study methods (Arensberg 1954, Warner 1949); methods for the investigation of culture contact (Malinowski 1938 and 1945, Schapera 1935); the use of psychological techniques in fieldwork (Henry and Spiro 1953); psychological studies of anthropologists (Roe 1952); sampling (J. and I. Honigmann 1955); notetaking (Paul 1953, Sturtevant 1959); reliability and validity (Arensberg 1954, Dean and Whyte 1958, Vidich and Bensman 1954); analysis and interpretation (Becker 1958, Vidich 1955); fieldwork as personal experience (Bowen 1954); research design and selection of topics and themes (Hunter 1938, Mead 1933 and 1938:147–52, Spindler and Goldschmidt 1952; also *Notes and Queries*, first published in 1874).

Both American and British anthropologists contributed to the early methods literature. Although this often amounted to little more than a few pages in a monograph (Evans-Pritchard 1940, Firth 1957, Kuper 1947, Malinowski 1922, Mead 1938), some of the discussions were extensive (Kroeber 1953, Nadel 1951, Warner 1949), and in a few cases entire books were devoted to methodological issues. The earliest, and perhaps best known, of these was *Notes and Queries*. Published initially by the British Association for the Advancement of Science in 1874, the era before anthropologists had begun to collect their own data, it provided a guide to amateurs, highlighting the themes and categories on which they should focus their inquiries.

Another early publication was the edited work by Bartlett et al. (1939). Perhaps the outstanding article in this collection was Audrey Richards's 'The Development of Fieldwork Methods in Social Anthropology.' In this wide-ranging piece, she discussed selection of community, entry into the field, building rapport, formal interviews, the collection of autobiographies and native texts, and observational roles. These are the same issues that are at the heart of current textbooks in qualitative methodology, and at one point Richards made a statement that very much has a modern ring to it: 'in a sense the informant becomes himself an anthropologist' (p. 300). In this same volume, however, we find Nadel's article, 'The Interview Technique in Social Anthropology.' Nadel reasonably argued that interviews should always be combined with direct observation, so that what people say can be measured against what they do. What grates is his advice on how to get reluctant informants to cooperate, especially when probing 'secret and forbidden topics.' The anthropologist, he suggested, should employ a 'bullying' technique, purposefully belittling and angering informants with the hope that they will be stimulated to open up and reveal all (p. 323). Although the methods literature in the 1950s and earlier did cover most of the issues that interest us today, very little attention except for passing remarks (Mead et al. 1949, Paul 1953) was paid to ethics. Certainly, Nadel's advice about bullying techniques dates his approach to the discipline.

Also of interest is *Methods of Study of Culture Contact in Africa* (1938).[2] This collection of articles also contains statements that resonate with more recent issues, such as the suggestion by both the Culwicks and by Fortes that anthropologists should focus on the individual as innovator, a central theme in the social action perspective that emerged in the 1960s (see chapter four). Once again, the most impressive article was by Audrey Richards, who stated: 'Any anthropologist working in Africa at the moment is really experimenting with a new technique' (p. 46). In the

---

2 This full-length book on methods was originally published in volumes 7, 8, and 9 of the journal *Africa*. No author or editor is indicated, although Malinowski's long introduction is partly devoted to a commentary on the several articles contained in the book.

Trobriand and Andaman Islands of Malinowskian and Radcliffe-Brownian fame, where people lived in small, isolated communities, participant observation may have done the trick. But Africa, with its large tribes, European presence, and rapid cultural change, presented a different challenge. In order to cope with the complexity, Richards relied on a battery of techniques, including questionnaires, genealogies, maps of settlement patterns, and individual case histories.

Malinowski not only enjoyed a tremendous reputation as a gifted fieldworker, but also contributed to the emerging literature on fieldwork methods. In the opening pages of *Argonauts of the Western Pacific* (1961:1–25; orig. 1922), possibly the most famous statement of the fieldwork enterprise in that era, he advocated the collection of three kinds of data: on institutions, customs, and patterns of activities; on the 'imponderabilia' of everyday life, with special attention paid to the difference between the rules of behaviour embedded in customs and institutions and actual behaviour; and on native texts – typical speech patterns, narratives, myths and folklore.

The image of Malinowski that we have inherited, however, appears to be somewhat distorted, and this may be a good place to put the record straight. For one thing, Malinowski is often portrayed by contemporary writers as having been an incorrigible functionalist, a man who promoted social stability and ignored conflict and change. Yet towards the end of his life, in his introduction to *Methods of Study of Culture Contact in Africa*, he urged anthropologists to concentrate primarily on social change, expressed deep concern about the evils of colonialism, and promoted applied anthropology. He also criticized anthropologists for staying on the sidelines, rather than bravely addressing colonialism and racism. The functional method, he observed, was meant for the analysis of societies in equilibrium, not the dynamic, complex societies of Africa. In Malinowski's words, 'The anthropologist is now faced with the tragic situation which has often been bewailed in lecture-rooms ... Just as we have reached a certain academic status and developed our methods and theories, our subject-matter threatens to disappear' (p. xii).

If Malinowski's reputation as an inflexible functionalist is undeserved, the same may be true about his extraordinary capacity for fieldwork. Our image of Malinowski is that of a person who could penetrate into the heart of primitive culture, isolating himself from the outside world, living like the natives, depending on them for human psychological needs, becoming in fact one of them, thereby allowing him to grasp the native's point of view. His famous (or infamous) posthumous *Diary*

(1967) provides quite a different picture. He apparently paid his assistants and informants, and often arranged for them to visit him in his hut instead of going to theirs; and rather than relying on the natives for human contact and comfort, he spent a remarkable amount of time with European traders and missionaries. Few anthropologists, it might be retorted, have done any better than Malinowski, or portrayed the personal side of fieldwork with such honesty. But that is not the point. Malinowski supposedly set the standard against which the rest of us are measured.

Finally, there is the image of Malinowski as the brilliant inductivist, whose ethnographic insights emerged entirely from the fieldwork situation, unguided and uncontaminated by preconceived theories and problems. Brilliant he was, but as Thornton and Skalnik (1993) have recently shown, Malinowski's ethnographic efforts were massively informed and directed by theoretical positions and problems that he had grappled with before he had ever got to the field. What is especially intriguing is the apparent degree to which his fieldwork was shaped by theoretical and philosophical issues emanating from his native Poland. This is hardly surprising. Indeed, one might observe that the preoccupation of social anthropologists with structure, role, position, order and stability amounted to a projection of British society and values onto the fieldwork setting abroad.

The Fieldwork Situation

In the late 1800s there was a division of labour between the professional anthropologist and the amateur fieldworker, with the former remaining in the comfort of the library and museum, and the latter travelling to remote parts of the world collecting materials. By the early part of the twentieth century anthropologists themselves began to do fieldwork. At first, the emphasis was an observation rather than participation. That is, anthropologists followed the practice of natural scientists, observing people in their natural settings as if they were the equivalent of flora and fauna. During this early period anthropologists often joined scholars from other disciplines on large expeditions, mapping the cultures of peoples over a broad geographical area on the basis of quick forays into accessible villages and settlements. However, by the time the 1913 edition of *Notes and Queries* was published, Rivers (see Stocking 1983: 92) had argued for intensive participant observation studies, to be carried out by a sole researcher in a small population over a period of at least a year.

This was the beginning of modern fieldwork, and what is interesting is that it put an end to a systematic, quantitative drift in the discipline that had begun to emerge. There was, for example, Morgan's questionnaire in the 1850s on kinship terminology, made available to non-specialists in contact with North American Indians and indigenous peoples around the globe. In 1884 in Britain, Tylor had helped establish the Committee on the North-Western Tribes of Canada. A general survey instrument was provided to government officials, missionaries, and travellers so that systematic data could be gathered. None other than Franz Boas, the force behind early American anthropology, was hired as the committee's principal fieldworker.

BASIC ASSUMPTIONS

As the fieldwork tradition, dominated by participant observation and the native's point of view, emerged in anthropology, a number of assumptions crystallized:

1. Research in other cultures was preferred over research at home in order to enhance objectivity and benefit from stranger value.

2. The social world, just as much as the natural world, was governed by underlying order, and patient fieldwork would reveal the patterns.

3. Rules of behaviour (norms) and behaviour itself (acts) were closely correlated. The individual investigator might give causal priority to either of them, but the bottom line was that if the one was known, the other was too.

4. The small community was the appropriate unit of investigation because it presumably represented the entire culture, implying simplistic homogeneity.

5. The data 'shone in the dark' in the sense of being intrinsically explanatory, independent of the investigator's interpretations.

6. The patterns in the data discovered by the researcher were social facts, as real as sticks and stones; this was implied in the very language used by researchers – *collecting* and *gathering* data, as if they were sitting there like apples waiting to be picked and sorted.

7. Anthropology was assumed to be a positivistic science. Even after fieldwork emerged as a rite of passage for aspiring anthropologists, some quantitative data continued to be 'collected.' The overwhelming emphasis, however, was on qualitative data. This did not mean that anthropology was not positivistic. It is often erroneously assumed that positivism implies quantitative techniques and phenomenology qualita-

tive techniques. Yet what counts in positivism are the underlying assumptions of order in the universe, the fact-value distinction, and the notion that every event has a cause, all of which were accepted by anthropologists at the time.[3]

8. There were methodological short cuts available to the anthropologist. Rivers, for example, thought that the kinship terminology revealed by the genealogical method threw light on the entire social structure. Durkheim argued that one well-executed experiment was the basis for universal proof.

BASIC TECHNIQUES AND RELATED ELEMENTS

1. Participant observation (the defining feature of anthropological methods).

2. Reliance on informants (who were sometimes paid assistants and interpreters).

3. The interview (usually unstructured).

4. Genealogies and life histories.

5. Collecting census material and using a schedule: the unit of the census was usually either the household or the domestic group; a schedule differs from a questionnaire in that it is not distributed to people and returned on completion; instead, the questions are asked verbally by the investigator, who fills in the answers. Not all ethnographic data, as the census and schedule imply, were qualitative.

6. Long period of fieldwork (at least a year, in order to observe the annual cycle of events and behaviour).

7. Learning the indigenous language.

8. Emphasis on the actor's point of view (emic rather than etic data).

9. Emphasis on informal rather than formal structure, or the back rather than the front stage.

10. Emphasis on validity rather than reliability: validity implies 'truth,' whereas reliability simply means that repeat studies will produce the same results (since it is dubious that reliability can be demonstrated in any rigorous manner in qualitative research, it is not surprising that validity was privileged).

11. Limit on the size of population. Because random samples rarely

---

3 As Bryman has observed: 'The suggestion that participant observers are carrying out research which is outside the positivistic mainstream often seems highly farfetched when their research monographs are examined closely' (1984:88).

were employed, the unit of investigation had to be small enough for the researcher to get to know every individual, which was hardly feasible in a community larger than five hundred people.

12. The comparative (especially cross-cultural) method as the alternative to the controlled laboratory experiment. The cross-cultural method had been prominent in the early days of anthropology, before first-hand fieldwork emerged as the accepted approach. While lip service continued to be paid to the comparative method, from the time of Malinowski onwards most studies only were 'comparative' by virtue of having been conducted in other cultures. The reason was clear: the time and effort required simply to produce a sound ethnography of a single community.

13. An inductive (not deductive) research design; most anthropologists had an area or a tribe to study, not a problem, and without a problem it made no sense to attempt to erect a model, extrapolate hypotheses, and test them in the field – sometimes regarded as the purest positivistic procedure. Probably most anthropologists were (and continue to be) opposed to a deductive approach on the grounds that problems and themes should emerge from the fieldwork setting, rather than being imposed by the investigator.

14. Search for virgin territory. There was a tendency among anthropologists to speak of 'their people,' to claim some sort of ownership over 'their natives.' It was considered poor taste to venture into another fieldworker's territory, and replication studies were almost unknown.

15. Exaggeration of the degree of cultural uniqueness. Kudos were given for putting a previously unexamined culture under the microscope, and for demonstrating that it was in some way distinctive. This was the stuff out of which reputations were made, and it would hardly be surprising if ethnographers were tempted to emphasize difference rather than similarity, even if by doing so they undermined the common ground necessary for the cross-cultural method. Even today, as we approach the twenty-first century, there is a lingering attraction to those dwindling pockets of pre-industrial existence, the more exotic the better.

16. The Bongo-Bongo or Panga-Panga principle. The name itself is not important (I prefer to call it the Fergus-Fergus principle, in honour of a town in the part of the world where I live). What counts is the in-joke: that one's research site should be as far away and isolated as possible so that no other anthropologist will ever bother to check up on one's ethnographic findings.

17. The fieldworker personality. It was assumed that not everyone

was cut out to do ethnographic research. The fieldworker had to be extremely flexible and perceptive, possess a sense of humour, have a strong constitution, and be a good listener. Individuals who were self-centred, or had an urge to talk all the time, or a need to walk around with answers rather than questions, were out of luck. While this may well have been a personality profile of the successful fieldworker, it must be stated that it is exceedingly difficult to predict just who will shine in the field. It is well known, for example, that some individuals who would appear to be ill-suited for the job turn out to be stars, partly by projecting among strangers the personality that they would *like* to have, and behaving in a manner that would stun their friends back home.

I might add that it is sometimes suggested that individuals who have experienced some kind of trauma in their teens, such as the break-up of their families and perhaps a move to a new community, are especially attracted to the social sciences. The assumption is that such an experience makes them somewhat marginal, and encourages them to be analytical.

18. The genius syndrome. The early anthropologists, especially those who belonged to the sink or swim school, which included most of them, sometimes gave the impression that successful fieldwork was a matter of sheer brilliance; either one had it or one didn't. Let me clearly state that the accomplishments of people such as Malinowski, Boas, Richards, and Mead were nothing short of remarkable. What often is overlooked, however, is the hard work that is involved in fieldwork. If students realized that in addition to personality and intelligence, success in the field is dependent on their willingness and determination to put their noses to the grindstone day after day, month after month, they might be less anxious about the looseness of qualitative methods.

19. Sustained disbelief. Ingrained into the discipline of anthropology, and possibly into social science in general, was an attitude of sustained doubt – doubt about what people said, about their explanations for their beliefs and behaviour. The prevailing assumption (or paranoia) was that people attempted to conceal their true motives and actions, or at least were unaware of them. The anthropologist's job, then, was to take what people said with a grain of salt, and try to trick them into revealing the truth. The alleged gap between what people said and what they did, between the front and back stages, undeniably existed, and still does today. In no small measure, however, the anthropological stance of ingrained disbelief is the basis of much of the hostility towards the disci-

pline among contemporary research subjects, who demand respect rather than scepticism.

HUMAN RELATIONS AREA FILES (HRAF)

This overview of the fieldwork situation, including basic assumptions and techniques, probably fits early social anthropology better than it does early cultural anthropology. Cultural anthropologists focused on a wider range of topics and a broader conceptual territory, from child-rearing practices to native texts, life histories, and socio-linguistics. American anthropologists also were more inclined to use formal research techniques, such as Rorschach tests, and it was an American anthropologist, George Murdock, who developed the Human Relations Area Files (HRAF) in 1949.[4] Initially called the Cross-Cultural Survey, the HRAF provided systematic data on more than 250 cultures. They were intended to elevate cross-cultural analysis to a fully scientific exercise, one amenable to quantitative analysis, and towards this end Murdock introduced the World Ethnographic Sample in 1957.[5] Although the HRAF became available in numerous North American universities, they were virtually ignored in Britain. Even in the United States, only a small number of anthropologists used them.[6] While this may have been because of the uneven quality of the data in the Files, an equally important reason probably was the bias against library research in the discipline, and for original fieldwork studies.

REDFIELD-LEWIS CONTROVERSY

American anthropologists also have been involved in the few replication studies that have been done. Undoubtedly the most famous of these is the Redfield-Lewis controversy. During 1926–27 Robert Redfield carried out fieldwork in a Mexican village. In *Tepoztlan: A Mexican Village* (1930), he wrote about the good life in the community, emphasizing the coherent framework of the society and the happy, fulfilled life enjoyed by the people. Seventeen years later, in 1943, Oscar Lewis began field-

4 See Murdock (1949) for a statement of his approach.
5 Throughout this study I have concentrated on qualitative methods and analysis, simply because they have dominated anthropology, but it should be noted that a quantitative thrust (albeit less prominent) has almost always been present as well.
6 Stanley Udy (1959) produced one of the best-known studies based on the HRAF.

work in the same village. In *Life in a Mexican Village, Tepoztlan Restudied* (1951), he wrote about the bad life in the community, highlighting the numerous quarrels, homicides, jealousies, and rampant crime.[7] As Lewis pointed out Redfield portrayed Tepoztlan as 'a relatively homogeneous, isolated and well-integrated society made up of contented and well-adjusted people.' In contrast, his own account stressed 'underlying individualism ... the lack of cooperation, the tensions between villages ... and the pervading quality of fear, envy, and distrust in inter-personal relations' (pp. 428–9).

Both Redfield and Lewis were highly accomplished and respected scholars. How, then, can their radically different portraits of Tepoztlan be explained? One possibility was that during the span of seventeen years the village had drastically changed. But neither of the authors thought that was the case (see Redfield 1960:132–6). Instead they concluded that what made the difference was their personal perspectives. Redfield explained that he was interested in what pleased the Mexican villagers about their lives, while Lewis was interested in what displeased them.

It is now accepted that Redfield portrayed the ideal or formal belief system, and Lewis the actual or informal system – what went on in the back stage. Although there is a tendency to regard back stage material as more real than front stage material, it could be argued that both versions of the village were valid, but at the same time incomplete. The implication is that the two studies merely complemented each other, for the benefit of the discipline at large. That may well be true, but it is difficult to overlook the degree to which the fieldworker's personal outlook and interests (and theoretical inclinations and biases) shape what is found in the field, and all that this means for a discipline with scientific aspirations.[8]

Conclusion

Because there was no such thing as a single, uniform theory during the

---

7 Lewis also published *Tepoztlan* (1960), a shorter version of his earlier book, with a new chapter based on data collected in 1956.

8 For a less well-known, but equally significant, replication study, see Goodenough (1956) and Fischer (1958), whose studies of residence patterns of the same community produced quite different results. Interestingly, in neither the Redfield-Lewis nor the Goodenough-Fischer case did the authors purposefully set out to do a replication study. Of course, the other famous replication study is Freeman's restudy of Mead's Samoa.

early decades of professional anthropology, but rather several theoretical perspectives of quite different character, it is difficult to measure the fit that existed then between theory and method. However, if we assume that modern anthropology began with the emergence of the fieldwork tradition – that is, after the evolutionary perspective faded from the scene – the situation becomes much clearer. Despite the differences between historical particularism and structural functionalism, writers such as Boas, Malinowski, and Radcliffe-Brown assumed that the discipline was an empirical one, and that explanations based on rigorous, scientific investigation were the goal. In other words, at this stage of anthropological work, the aims and procedures of theory and method were generally consistent.

PART TWO: PATCHING THE FOUNDATION

4

Theory

Historical particularism in America and structural functionalism in Britain proved to be remarkably robust theoretical approaches, dominating the discipline up to the Second World War. By the 1950s and 1960s, however, it was clear that anthropology's theoretical landscape had changed. In this chapter I shall focus on three orientations: cultural ecology, conflict theory, and social action. The first was primarily associated with American anthropology, the other two with British anthropology.[1] Each orientation, in quite different ways, attempted to keep the dream of a scientific study of society alive by patching the cracks that had begun to weaken historical particularism and structural functionalism.

1. Cultural Ecology (and Neo-Evolutionism)

Although renowned as the founder of American anthropology, Boas had originally been trained in geography, and never completely lost his interest in the influence of environment on culture. Yet it was left to others such as Julian Steward to develop the environmental factor into a full-fledged theoretical orientation. This became known as cultural ecology. What was intriguing was that cultural ecology eventually was grafted onto a revitalized version of evolutionism. In other words, the theoretical approach which had been attacked so vigorously by the historical particularists and the structural functionalists as inappropriate, misleading, and almost unethical in its assumptions was dusted off and marched back on stage.

---

1 As it will be shown, conflict theory also emerged in American sociology.

BASIC FEATURES

1. *Impact of environment.* Culture is shaped by environmental conditions.

2. *Impact of technology.* Techno-economic factors combine with envi-ronment to influence the character of social organization and ideology.

3. *Focus on adaptation.* Human populations continuously adapt to techno-economic-environmental conditions. 'Culture' is the mechanism that makes adaptation possible.

4. *Reciprocal links between culture and ecology.* While techno-economic-environmental factors shape culture, the converse is also true. This blurs the distinction between the former and the latter, and underlines the complexity and dynamism intrinsic to the perspective of cultural ecology.

5. *Emphasis on etic rather than emic data.* The objective conditions of existence – environment and technology – not subjective conditions – values, norms, meaning and individual motivation – explain human interaction. In cultural ecology, subjectivity is dependent on the objective conditions of existence, meaning is a product of social structure, and priority in research is given to the 'hard' dimension of human interaction, to etic rather than emic data.

6. *Culture perceived as practical and useful.* Unlike Boas, but like Tylor, cultural ecologists assume that culture is purposeful and functional, not accidental or irrational.

7. *De-emphasis of individual.* The privileged position assigned to the individual by Boas, Benedict, and Mead is deemed inappropriate by the cultural ecologists. Social structure, social groups, ecological and technological factors explain culture. The individual as a component in the explanatory system is quite expendable.

8. *Nomothetic inquiry.* With the emphasis on etic data, anthropology is considered to be thoroughly scientific, solidly empirical, capable of producing causal explanations and laws.

9. *Evolutionary context.* Not only are ecological and technological factors the driving forces in human interaction, they are fundamental to the historical development of society, and indeed can be fruitfully tied to an evolutionary perspective.

KEY FIGURES

Julian Steward (1902–72)

Steward was taught by Kroeber, who had been taught by Boas. I suppose, then, that we could call Steward the intellectual grandson of Boas, but his approach was remarkably different. Steward began using the term ecology as far back as the 1930s, but it was not until the publication of *Theory of Culture Change* in 1955 that he fully elaborated the concept. By ecology, he meant the adaptation of culture to environmental and technological factors.

Steward theorized that the less developed the level of technology in a society, the greater the influence of the environment. For example, hunting and gathering societies were at the whim of their environments. Both social organization and population size were dictated by the environment. People in these societies had to live in small groups, and had to be egalitarian, because there was no economic surplus to permit stratification. The same harsh environmental conditions, coupled with a low level of technology, meant that people were forced to migrate periodically in search of new sources of food supply. In chapter six Steward illustrated this theory in relation to the Shoshonean peoples in the western United States. Arid conditions and a hunting and gathering economy restricted the size of their population, and fostered the small nuclear family consisting of parents and offspring.

As the level of technology in a society improves, there is greater control over the environment, increased economic surplus and population density, and a shift from egalitarianism to class stratification. Much to his credit, given his commitment to the cultural ecology framework, Steward argues that in highly advanced technological societies the environment ceases to be a controlling force, and thus cultural ecology loses its explanatory clout. This does not mean, however, that human beings become freer. What happens, Steward speculates, is that the determinism of the environment is replaced by the determinism of culture, defined in this context as ideology.[2]

Steward contended not only that environmental conditions shaped culture, but also that each culture constituted a thoroughly practical and useful adaptation to its environment. This was to such an extent, he thought, that if a foreign culture consisting, for example, of agriculturalists and possessing a different social organization was suddenly plopped into the ecological zone occupied by hunters and gatherers, the alien culture, if its members were to survive, would be forced to adapt

2 One's ideas can become dated quickly; the notion that the environment loses its significance in advanced technological societies will strike readers today, concerned with the effects of pollution and deforestation, as curious, to put it mildly.

the social organization and values characteristic of hunters and gatherers. Only if the level of technology was capable of overcoming the impact of the hunting and gathering environment by producing an economic surplus could that outcome be avoided.

Steward divided culture into core and periphery. The core consists of the enduring and causal features of culture, the periphery of fortuitous or accidental features. The core includes social organization, politics, and possibly religion. The periphery includes artistic patterns, fads, and idiosyncratic behaviour. The core cannot escape the impact of techno-environmental factors. The periphery is largely independent of the techno-environmental base, and subject to a wider range of social change, partly influenced by diffusion and individual innovation. In many respects, core and periphery are comparable to Kroeber's basic and secondary culture, although Steward, it must be noted, did not follow Kroeber's lead by placing priority on the periphery.

Finally, we come to the connection between ecology and evolutionism. By the early 1950s Steward had begun to identify himself as an evolutionist. Yet he saw his approach as quite different than the works of the early evolutionists such as Tylor, Morgan, and Spencer. One reason was simply his emphasis on the critical role of environment in the evolutionary scheme, which was largely ignored by the early writers. A second reason was that he rejected out of hand the notion of unilinear development. In Steward's words, 'particular cultures diverge significantly from one another and do not pass through unilineal stages' (p. 28). His argument was that while evolutionism as a framework is viable and significant, there has been no single, all-embracing line of evolutionary development. Instead, cultures have evolved along several different lines, at different rates, and rather than assuming one grand scheme, with specific stages, it is the researcher's task to work out the exact direction taken by particular cultures. To distance his approach from that taken by Morgan, Tylor, and Spencer, Steward coined the term 'multi-linear evolutionism,' implying a more complex and less rigid framework. Today, anthropologists who play around with an evolutionary framework are usually labelled neo-evolutionists.

Leslie White (1900–75)

Steward was not the only prominent American anthropologist to point the discipline back towards evolutionism. Leslie White's life work was devoted to that goal. Like Steward, White repudiated many of the central assumptions in Boasian historical particularism. He emphasized the etic rather than the emic, saw culture as a highly integrated entity rather than a loose bundle of traits, and assigned causal priority to techno-economic factors, while dismissing the individual and personality as irrelevant to the anthropological endeavour. He also shared Steward's view that culture is highly practical and useful (or utilitarian) in the sense of providing the necessary material conditions of life (food, shelter, defence), rather than merely habitual or expressive. In White's scheme, culture is composed of four sectors: technological (tools and food production), social structural (institutions and roles), ideological (beliefs and values), and attitudinal (sentiments and emotions). While he assumed that technology is normally the driving force in culture, he did allow the possibility that under certain conditions, and in the short run, any of the other three sectors could achieve prominence.

Yet there were significant differences between the evolutionary frameworks espoused by White and Steward. White (1949, 1959) tended to view culture as a reality in itself, shaped primarily by one of its parts – technoeconomics – but nevertheless self-contained. Steward, obviously, took a quite different approach, because in his scheme culture ultimately rested on an extraneous factor: the environment. In other words, while White certainly was an evolutionist, he was not a cultural ecologist. Furthermore, whereas Steward dissociated his approach from the unilinear evolution of the nineteenth century, White contended that his own brand of evolutionism was essentially identical to the works of Morgan and Tylor. White did depart sharply from Spencer's biological reductionism. In fact, White has been an eloquent spokesperson for the contemporary evolutionary assumption that the symbol has replaced the gene in importance as an explanatory tool. Which is to say, we live today in a symbolic universe, guided more by culture than heredity.

In this context, it should be pointed out that White draws an important distinction (see Kaplan and Manners 1972:44) between signs and symbols. The meaning of signs is inherent in things; the meaning of symbols in things is arbitrary. White contends that while sign behaviour is characteristic of all of the higher animals, only human beings practise both sign and symbolling behaviour. The character of symbols is reflected in language, where the relationship between the sound of a word and its referent or meaning is arbitrary. A well-known example is green for go and red for stop.

Sahlins (1960) has portrayed the difference between White and Steward in terms of general and specific evolution. White was attracted to the grand sweep of history, to 'culture' writ large. Steward focused on the evolution of particular cultures, and was concerned with middle-range theory.

The majority of neo-evolutionists, including Steward, rejected the old assumption that evolution equals progress. Not so Leslie White. He argued that evolution was directional and progressive, and could be precisely measured: culture advances according to the increase in the amount of energy per capita per year, or according to the efficiency by which energy is utilized (Kaplan and Manners 1972:45). White's famous formula was $E \times T = C$; E represents energy, T the efficiency of tools, and C culture. The amount of energy varies across cultures. The simplest societies rely completely on human energy, the more advanced on animate and non-animate energy, such as camels, horses, steam, and the atom. Concomitant with the increase in energy, or the advancement of culture, is greater human control over nature. It would be a mistake, however, to interpret this to mean that White paid much attention to individual human capacity and personality. To the contrary, in White's scheme human beings are essentially 'cultural dopes,' responding robot-like to the cultural framework that encapsulates them.

Marvin Harris

Harris has possibly been the most eminent figure in recent years among those who continue to dream of a general anthropology, in which physical anthropology, cultural anthropology, linguistics, and archaeology are unified within a single framework. Essentially an armchair anthropologist rather than a fieldworker, his fame rests largely on his highly scholarly and authoritative textbooks. *The Rise of Anthropological Theory* (1968), for example, is encyclopedic in range, and is noteworthy for its sophisticated and extensive treatment of race and racism. Harris regards his approach as being very similar to Steward's. In the preface to one of his textbooks he wrote: 'I should also like this book to please Julian Steward since the theoretical orientation employed throughout has been inspired by his interest in causality, evolution and ecology' (1971:x). Yet Harris does not think that his approach, which he labels cultural materialism, is exactly the same as Steward's. Cultural ecology, he indicates (1968:658), is a subcase of cultural materialism.

According to Harris (1991:23), cultural materialism focuses on and assigns causal priority to the material conditions of life, such as food and shelter. The underlying assumption, echoing Karl Marx, is that before there can be poetry and philosophy, people must eat and be protected from the elements.[3] Materialism in this context has nothing in common with its more popular connotation: the greedy accumulation of expensive objects. Human activity organized to satisfy the material conditions of life is affected and limited by our biological make-up, the level of technology, and the nature of the environment, which in turn generate ideological and social organizational responses. In Harris's scheme, these various components of cultural materialism form the analytic basis with which to depict the evolutionary trajectory of culture and civilization.

Like Steward and White, Harris downplays the importance of emic data. People's consciousness, their subjective dispositions, perspectives, interpretations, ideas, attitudes, and emotions, never explain their actions (Harris 1975:6 and 62). He has also been a vocal critic of writers such as Ruth Benedict who have given the impression that human behaviour and culture are irrational, whimsical, inscrutable, devoid of logical design. Perhaps the best-known illustration of his position is that of India's sacred cattle (Harris 1966 and 1975). The refusal of Indians to eat their cattle has often been interpreted as a perfect example of just how irrational cultural practices can be. Supposedly it is the Hindu doctrine of *ahimsa* which compels Indians to worship their cattle rather than eat them, even if they are starving. In other words, spiritual obsession obliterates material welfare. No such thing, Harris counters. His argument is that India's undersized cattle are far less important as a source of food than they are as a source of power and transportation; cow dung, moreover, provides fertilizer for crops and fuel for cooking. Harris concludes that the undersized, undernourished cattle in India are perfectly suited to the difficult environmental conditions which they face. And the sacred cattle complex, rather than being irrational, plays a positive and critical economic role in India. In fact, Harris concludes, 'India makes more efficient use of its cattle than the United States does' (1975:31).

John Bennett and Roy Rappaport

While the ideas and interpretations of armchair scholars such as Harris

---

3 It should be pointed out that while Harris draws heavily on Marx, he has sometimes been criticized as being a vulgar or mechanical materialist (see Friedman 1974). This is because he downplays opposition, contradiction, and dialectics, all of which are central to Marxism.

may be stimulating, the litmus test in anthropology always involves the ethnographer in the fieldwork setting, which brings us to the works of Bennett and Rappaport. In *Northern Plainsmen* (1969), Bennett undertook an ecological investigation of ranchers, farmers, Hutterites, and Plains Cree Indians in a region in southern Saskatchewan which he called Jasper. He drew a sharp distinction between general or natural ecology and human ecology, and argued that the former is not applicable to humans; this is because it cannot accommodate the degree to which humans, qua innovators, are constantly changing the ecosystems in which they live. In other words, Bennett recognized that culture not only adapts to ecological conditions, it also modifies them.

In Bennett's approach the key to cultural ecology is adaptation. But adaptation is not restricted to the reciprocal links between culture and environment. Groups or categories of people like the Hutterites, farmers, ranchers, and Indians in the Jasper region must also adapt to each other, as well as to external factors such as fluctuating prices for their goods and changing patterns of food consumption. By describing the various ways in which these four different groups of people adapted to the same environment. Bennett laid to rest the simplistic notion that for each set of ecological conditions there can only be a single cultural response.

Bennett introduced an important distinction between adaptive strategies and adaptive processes, which correspond to the emic and etic distinction. Adaptive strategies are conscious; they concern decision-making: whether to consume or not, whether to innovate or stick with the old ways, whether to stay on the homestead or migrate. Adaptive processes consist of the long-term trends resulting from adaptive strategies which are observed and analysed by the anthropologist. To Bennett's credit, his study is enriched not only by its historical dimension (his study covers a period of more than half a century), but also by its synthesis of subjective and objective data.[4]

Rappaport's *Pigs for the Ancestors* (1967), celebrated as an illustrious application of the ecological framework, has probably been even more widely read than *Northern Plainsmen*. The study is based on the Tsembaga, a Maring-speaking people in New Guinea. Their economy revolves around agriculture, with rudimentary tools such as the digging stick, steel axe, and knife; hunting, employing bows and arrows, spears, and wooden shields; and pig husbandry.

4 See also his later publications *Of Time and the Enterprise* (1982) and *Human Ecology as Human Behavior* (1993).

Unlike Bennett, Rappaport does not draw a sharp distinction between general ecology and human ecology. To the contrary, he treats the latter as a subcase of the former, and argues 'The study of man the culture-bearer cannot be separated from the study of man as a species among species' (p. 242). In this context, he regards the Tsembega as just another ecological population in the ecosystem.

The centrepiece in *Pigs for the Ancestors* is ritual. According to Rappaport, ritual mediates between the Tsembaga people and their environment. More specifically, ritual regulates competition for scarce resources between people and pigs, redistributes land, facilitates the exchange of economic goods and people in the territory, and even is the guiding hand behind warfare. As the pig population builds up, threatening the equilibrium between people and pigs, warfare with neighbouring groups erupts, decimating the population of both humans and animals, and restoring it to a level compatible with the carrying weight of the ecological niche.

Harris has referred to Rappaport's study (actually to his Ph.D. thesis on which the book was based) as a 'brilliant tour de force' (1968:366). Such high praise is easy to understand. The book is remarkably systematic, replete with quantitative data. In comparison with *Northern Plainsmen*, it deals with an exotic people, and with themes such as primitive warfare that speak to romantic anthropology. Yet in my judgment, Bennett's study may be the more sophisticated. For example, Rappaport distinguishes between operational (etic) models and cognized (emic) models (p. 241), which are comparable to Bennett's adaptive strategies and adaptive processes, but essentially ignores cognized data – the attitudes, beliefs, values, and interpretations of the Tsembaga themselves. There is, moreover, an explicit emphasis in *Pigs for the Ancestors* on equilibrium and system maintenance, rather than on adaptation and change. In Rappaport's words, 'the study has been concerned with regulation, or processes by which systems maintain their structure, rather than adaptation, or processes by which the structure of systems change in response to environmental pressures' (p. 242). Finally, there is the matter of the relationship of cultural or human ecology to natural or general ecology. Reacting to an article by Rappaport and his mentor Andrew Vayda (who wrote a foreword to *Pigs for the Ancestors*), Kaplan and Manners (1972:86) question the soundness of an approach that fails to recognize the unique capacity of humans to manipulate and shape the ecosystem itself. In the end, then, we are left with the old debate as to whether the study of human beings requires procedures and assumptions unnecessary for the study of other species, or whether the effort to do so is nothing more than unfounded romanticism.

EVALUATION

Cultural ecology, with its emphasis on causality and objective conditions, especially technology and the environment, constituted a massive repudiation of historical particularism. Steward did not merely attempt to patch up historical particularism; he leapfrogged back over it and tied cultural ecology to a revitalized version of evolutionism. Cultural ecology and neo-evolutionism certainly aspired to be scientific, but to achieve that status most of the 'soft' data in human interaction such as subjectivity, meaning, emotions, and individual motivation had to be relegated to the sidelines. Anthropologists who are still convinced that anthropology is (or can be) a genuine science would likely applaud the direction taken by cultural ecology and neo-evolutionism. Yet in recent years, as it will be shown in chapter six, it is these same soft data that have increasingly commanded the anthropologist's attention. In this sense alone, cultural ecology and neo-evolutionism are very much out of step with the march of contemporary anthropology.

2. Conflict Theory

Structural functionalism was the dominant theoretical orientation in British social anthropology (and in American sociology also) right up to the 1950s. However, a number of writers began to criticize its central assumptions, namely that the healthy society rested on a unified set of indispensable, universal functions. Even the procedure of explaining the existence of social institutions in terms of the functions they provided was characterized as putting the cart before the horse, comparable to stating that people grow noses in order to have a convenient place to rest their glasses. It was argued that by placing so much emphasis on social integration and by promoting the image of society as that of a stable equilibrium, structural functionalism provided ideological justification for the status quo, and was incapable of coping with social change. Emerging from these criticisms was a new model of society – conflict theory.

BASIC FEATURES

1. Conflict is normal and widespread. The assumptions made here

are exactly the opposite of those found in structural functionalism, in which conflict was viewed as abnormal and rare.

2. Conflict is positive or functional in that it knits society together, creates solidarity, and thus maintains society in a state of equilibrium.

3. Conflict acts as a safety valve. It provides an opportunity for people to let off steam before it builds up and disrupts society.

4. Conflict with an outside group generates internal solidarity. Faced with a common threat from the outside world, people in a group or community rally around each other.

5. Society consists of criss-crossing identifies, loyalties and strains which ultimately nullify each other, resulting in harmony and integration.

6. Societal equilibrium is the product of the balance of oppositions.

7. Conflict is a sociological phenomenon. As in the case of the structural functionalists, the conflict theorists were generally opposed to psychological reductionism.

KEY FIGURES

Max Gluckman (1911–75)

Born in South Africa, and a Rhodes scholar at Oxford in the mid-1930s, Gluckman emerged as the guru in what became internationally celebrated as the Manchester school of anthropology. Just as we described Steward as Boas's intellectual grandson, Gluckman's relationship to Radcliffe-Brown was similar. Although Gluckman sometimes attended Malinowski's seminar at the London School of Economics, two of his teachers, Hoernlé and Schapera, had studied under Radcliffe-Brown, and it was the latter's version of anthropology, and thus Durkheim's too, that shaped Gluckman's work. His debt to Durkheim was clearly acknowledged in his article on the state of anthropology (1968; orig. 1944), and like Durkheim he made it clear that psychological reductionism had no place in his own discipline.

At this juncture, given the leading roles played by Durkheim and Radcliffe-Brown in fashioning the structural functional model, the alert reader might well wonder what exactly is going on here. How did conflict theory emerge from an intellectual tradition that emphasized harmony and cohesion? The short answer is that Gluckman introduced a number of new assumptions which were intended to address the flaws that had been identified in the previous model. For example, he argued that conflict is intrinsic to social interaction, rather than rare and abnormal. Moreover, society does achieve equilibrium, but this is not the result of any intrinsic or natural tendency in social systems; it is the product of nothing less than ubiquitous conflict.

To understand Gluckman's theoretical position, we must turn to *Custom and Conflict in Africa* (1956), which he originally delivered as a series of BBC lectures in 1955. Here Gluckman sets out his thesis with admirable clarity: 'my central argument [is] that conflicts in one set of relationships lead to the establishment of cohesion in a wider set of relationships' (p. 164). To elaborate, people tend to create different sets of loyalties and allegiances which clash with each other. However, these criss-crossing loyalties cancel each other out. For example, two people may belong to opposed associations in one institutional sphere, such as politics, but to the same association in another sphere, such as occupation or religion. As Gluckman put it, 'A man's several loyalties strike at the strength of his loyalty to any one group or set of relationships, which is thus divided. Here the whole system depends on the existence of conflicts in smaller sub-systems' (p. 21). And elsewhere: 'social life breeds conflict, and societies by their customary arrangements ... accentuate conflicts. The conflicts in wider ranges compensate one another to produce social cohesion' (p. 48).

Gluckman illustrated his argument in relation to the Zulu. The Zulu have a king, plus several counties within the kingdom, each with its own leader. Periodically rebellion breaks out as a county tries to make its own leader king. Such conflict, in Gluckman's opinion, is positive. Its effect is to unify the kingdom, because the rest of the counties throw their support behind the ruling monarch. Moreover, the purpose of the rebellion is not to destroy the monarchy but to gain control over it. Gluckman concluded that Zulu society, internally divided into opposed segments, enjoyed overall equilibrium because the different segments balanced each other out, maintaining the integrity of the kingdom (pp. 115–16).

Some scholars seem to have a relatively high capacity for self-criticism. Gluckman is a case in point. In 1963 he published another book, *Order and Rebellion in Tribal Africa*, in which he repudiated the argument that conflict produces integration. His mistake, he explained, was to have relied too much on Radcliffe-Brown's structural functionalism. 'I now abandon altogether the type of organic analogy for a social system with which Radcliffe-Brown worked, and which led me to speak of civil war as being necessary to maintain the system' (pp. 35, 38).

Lewis Coser

There is an old saying in academia that fresh ideas periodically float in the air. That is, circumstances, sometimes prompted by social changes that render long-established models obsolete, produce the potential for a new way of looking at the world, and before we know it several imaginative scholars independent of each other are busy promoting the same novel message. Such was the case of conflict theory. In the same year that *Custom and Conflict in Africa* appeared, an American sociologist, Lewis Coser, published *The Functions of Social Conflict* (1964; orig. 1956). The overlap with Gluckman's study was quite remarkable. Coser, too, portrayed conflict as normal, widespread, and positive, contributing to the integration of society and acting as a safety valve for strains that otherwise might build up and tear society apart. Like Gluckman, he argued that multiple group affiliations and criss-crossing conflicts cancelled each other out, preventing deep social cleavages from developing, and he placed special emphasis on the part played by external conflict in elevating the level of group or community consciousness and cohesion. The overall impression in Coser's work was that conflict had a salutary impact on just about everything that it touched.

To be fair to Coser, he did point out that conflict is not always 'functional' (pp. 92–3). When a society or community is particularly disorganized, conflict with another society or community can produce apathy or even disintegration. Then, too, he recognized that in some cases external conflict is intentionally fostered by societal elites in order to deflect hostility and tension within a community onto an imaginary enemy. By doing so, elites may have won themselves some breathing space, but the flaws in the community that created internal strain remain intact (pp. 155–6).

Coser also distinguished between realistic and nonrealistic conflict. The first arises from frustrations between two or more persons, and zeros in on the source of frustration to achieve a specific and positive solution. The second concerns free-floating frustrations; here the accompanying aggression flies off in all directions, and rather than resolving the frustrations, aggression is an end in itself. Anti-Semitism and racism, Coser suggests (p. 49), are examples of nonrealistic conflict.

Although the models of conflict erected by Coser and Gluckman were almost identical, the sources for their ideas were quite separate. Gluckman was able to draw on a tradition in anthropology that argued that strain expressed in one set of interpersonal relationships was cancelled out in another set, resulting in the overall consistency and harmony of society. Fortes on the Tallensi, Colson on the Tonga, and Evans-Pritchard on the Nuer all had promoted this interpretation. It was not accidental that the Tonga and the Nuer were feuding societies, because the persistent anthropological analysis of feud has been to stress how it contributes to the overall cohesion of a society. Evans-Pritchard (1969:159; orig. 1940), for example, regarded feud as an essential institution among the Nuer, because it maintained a balanced opposition or equilibrium between the different segments of Nuer society. Even the more recent literature on feud has taken a similar line. Black-Michaud's *Cohesive Force* (1975) – the title itself conveys a message – contains the argument that in highly fragmented, amorphous societies lacking central leadership or societal-wide administrative units, feud, by bringing people (enemies, that is) in contact with each other, amounts to a system of communication and establishes social relationships that enhance overall cohesion.

Coser's sources were quite different. Available to him were the works of the early American sociologists such as Small, Park, Cooley, and Ross, all of whom portrayed conflict as intrinsic to society. Even more influential was the work of Max Weber's contemporary in Germany, Georg Simmel, which Gluckman claimed he had never read. Almost every important idea in *The Functions of Social Conflict* was a restatement of Simmel's work, including the distinction between realistic and nonrealistic conflict. There has always been a great deal of cross-fertilization between sociology and social anthropology, and thus it is not surprising that Coser also drew from the anthropological literature. For example, he points out (1964:63) that Malinowski (1941) argued not only that conflict is inherent in face-to-face relationships, but also that the smaller the cooperating group, the greater the degree of aggression. Coser also referred to Radcliffe-Brown's analysis (1952) of joking relationships in which ambivalence (and thus potential hostility) between, for example, in-laws, is smoothed over by ritual.

A decade after *The Functions of Social Conflict* appeared in print, Coser published another treatise on conflict theory, in which he drew attention to the remarkable similarity between his ideas and Gluckman's (1967:5). But whereas Gluckman eventually had second thoughts about the positive functions of conflict, Coser continued to defend his model against the massive criticism that soon was levelled against it. What the critics were saying, in a nutshell, was that the conflict model was essentially a disguised equilibrium model, little different than the structural functional model that it was meant to replace.[5]

Marxian Conflict Theory

Paralleling the Gluckman-Coser model was a markedly different version of conflict, one which drew its inspiration from Marx. Among its basic features was the assumption that society is divided into competing interest groups rather than being characterized by a central value system, that conflict and contradiction are intrinsic to human interaction and are the motors that propel social change, and that a class analysis reflecting the division of labour is the bedrock of scholarly investigation. In sharp contrast to the Gluckman-Coser model, the Marxian model does accommodate change, even revolutionary change. Such change is a product of the dialectical play between contradictions in society, such as the divergent interests of wage-earners and the owners of the means of production in capitalism.

Although there is no single version of Marxism, ranging as it does from Lucacs's phenomenological stance (1971; orig. 1923) to Althusser's 1969 complicated scientific (structuralist) version, and kept alive by what became known as the Frankfurt school of critical theory between the two world wars (Held 1980 and Jay 1974), a Marxian anthropology crystallized around the themes of colonialism (Berreman 1968, Gough 1968), dependency theory (Oxall et al. 1975), development studies (Rhodes 1970), and the political economy perspective (sometimes in conjunction with a Weberian approach, sometimes in opposition to Weber).[6]

Marxism, it should be added, significantly informed what became known as French economic anthropology, its roots traced back to the 1960s. Writers such as Meillassoux (1964), Terray (1969), and Godelier (1972) grappled valiantly with the problem of how to apply Marx (especially the distinction between the superstructure and substructure, or ideological and material forces) to pre-capitalist, kinship-dominated

---

5 See also Beals and Siegel (1966), who distinguish between nondisruptive and disruptive conflict, the first being positive, the second negative.

6 For a recent subtle application of the political economy perspective, informed by a flexible version of Marxism that accommodates subjectivity as well as relations of production, see Smith (1991).

societies in the Third World. While the leading figures in French economic anthropology often disagreed about fundamental issues, such as whether kinship belongs to the superstructure or substructure, they shared the assumption that society is laced with internal contradictions containing the potential for revolutionary change.

In the 1960s and 1970s a Marxian-oriented anthropology thrived. In recent years, however, probably reflecting momentous changes in the former Soviet Union and a turn towards capitalism across the globe, not to speak of a drift towards right-wing politics, its glow has somewhat dimmed. I hasten to add that the discovery of Gramsci's work (1976), with its subtle portrayal of hegemony and rejection of simplistic economic determinism, has done its part to keep alive a Marxian version of conflict theory.

EVALUATION

The initial reception among anthropologists and sociologists to the works of Gluckman and Coser was enthusiastic, and for good reason. During the several decades in which structural functionalism had dominated, conflict and strain had been ignored, or treated as a 'disease.' Gluckman and Coser helped to liberate us from an image of society that was obviously one-sided and misleading. Coser, it must be added, was quite aware that conflict could be dysfunctional, but as he explained in the preface to *The Functions of Social Conflict*, in the wake of structural functionalism it was the positive aspects of conflict that needed to be highlighted at that point in time.

The attack against the Coser-Gluckman model was not long in coming, and it was mounted by both fieldworkers and theoreticians. Lloyd (1968), an expert on the Yoruba in Nigeria, pointed out that despite Gluckman's focus on conflict, he continued to promote the old idea that society was in a state of equilibrium. Dahrendorf (1958 and 1959) criticized Coser for focusing almost entirely on the integrative functions of conflict, which gave the impression that social life is static, and shifted analysis away from social change.[7] Perhaps the most devastating criticism of all came from Lenski. In his only reference to Coser, which was relegated to a footnote, Lenski wrote: 'Labels can sometimes be misleading ... I do not include under the heading of conflict theorists writers

---

7 In his second book, Coser took note of Dahrendorf's criticism, but asserted that it was not justified (1967:5).

such as Lewis Coser, author of *The Functions of Social Conflict*. Though this volume is focused on conflict, its basic purpose is to show how conflict serves society as a whole. In short, the underlying theoretical orientation is functionalist' (1966:16). Genuine conflict theorists, Lenski argued, emphasize interests which divide people in society, not common values that unite them.[8] In other words, the Marxian version of the conflict model is immensely more powerful than the Gluckman-Coser version, a viewpoint to which I readily subscribe.

3. Social Action

When conflict theory, at least the mainstream Gluckman-Coser version, proved to be an inadequate substitute for structural functionalism, British social anthropologists began to tinker with other theoretical approaches. What emerged was a model that was clearly novel, rather than structural functionalism in disguise, and which had the capacity to cope with both social change and conflict. While I prefer to label this new approach 'social action' in order to place it in a theoretical context that dates back to Weber (and Marx too), it is often referred to as the interactional or transactional model.

BASIC FEATURES

1. Society is constantly changing, and social structure is fluid and porous rather than rigid.
2. Norms are ambiguous, even contradictory.
3. There is always a gap between the normative order and actual behaviour, which means rules or norms do not explain behaviour.
4. Human beings are in constant competition for scare goods and rewards.
5. Human beings must constantly choose between alternatives.
6. An emphasis on the individual as a self-interested manipulator and innovator whose actions continually modify the normative and institutional framework of society.
7. An emphasis on reciprocity, exchange, and transaction.
8. A focus on the informal rather than formal structure, or back stage rather than front stage.

---

8 In any functional analysis, I might add, one must always ask: functional for whom? Failure to do so may stamp one's work as an apology for the status quo.

F.G. Bailey

A central message in structural functionalism is that human beings conduct their behaviour in accordance with the rules laid down by society. The central value system in conjunction with the complexes of norms associated with a culture's major institutions define the content of roles and render people's behaviour regular and predictable. There certainly was a seductive simplicity to this approach, but in the minds of a number of anthropologists it did not remotely fit their fieldwork experiences. Social life, they argued, is messy and disjointed. People say one thing but do another thing; and rather than adhering perfectly to the rules of society, they bend, twist, and ignore these rules as self-interest dictates.

An eloquent expression of this alternative way of looking at the world appeared in Bailey's *Stratagems and Spoils* (1969). On one level, this is a study of politics and power, with the argument set in a broad and imaginative comparative framework ranging from rural life in India to state politics in France and England, and even the power struggles that take place in universities. On another level, the book provides a theoretical perspective applicable to the entire discipline. Bailey's starting point is to challenge the assumption that there is a simple, direct relationship between the normative order and actual behaviour. Such an assumption, Bailey argues, fails to take into account the degree to which individuals manipulate the world around them, including the normative order. In everyday life, Bailey observes, most of us, guided by self-interest, thread our way between the norms, seeking the most advantageous route. He does not deny that altruistic behaviour exists, but argues that its price can be calculated on a scale of costs and benefits for the individuals involved. As Bailey put it, 'One of the great gaps in anthropology is that we have been too much interested in the "system" and although we know that people live half their lives finding ways to "beat the system" we tend to take serious notice of them only when they are caught out, brought to trial and punished' (p. 87).

Bailey distinguishes between normative and pragmatic rules of behaviour. Normative rules are general guides to conduct; they make up the public, formal, or ideal rules of society. Pragmatic rules are deviations from the ideal rules; they consist of the tactics and stratagems that individuals resort to in order effectively to achieve their goals. Bailey treats the ratio of normative to pragmatic rules as an index of potential social change. When pragmatic rules dramatically increase, the normative order, or ideals of society, must be rebuilt to fit current realities. Bailey's assumption is that pragmatic rules more closely correspond to how people actually behave, and not surprisingly these are the type of rules on which he focuses.

Stratagems and Spoils was an innovative work, and one of its most significant achievements was to introduce a novel theoretical perspective. The people portrayed on Bailey's canvas are not puppets controlled by the institutional framework; they are active, choice-making agents locked in competitive struggle. Nor is the social structure unified and static; rather, it is a dynamic entity, continuously being reshaped by the shifting allegiances, coalitions, and conflicts that characterize human interaction. Some critics might complain that this is an unjustifiably cynical image of *Homo sapiens*, but one thing is beyond debate: unlike conflict theory, the social action model represents a genuine alternative to structural functionalism.

Bailey's further achievement was to demonstrate the advantage of introducing a more subtle conceptual scheme into the discipline, reflected in the distinction between normative and pragmatic rules. In *Stratagems and Spoils* political life is deconstructed into a rich array of concepts including mediators, middlemen, factions, brokers, cores, and transactions. Bailey, in other words, not only sketched out the fundamentals of a new theoretical orientation, but also provided a vocabulary with which to articulate it.

Jeremy Boissevain

Five years after the publication of *Stratagems and Spoils*, Boissevain brought out *Friends of Friends* (1974). The very title is suggestive: social life unfolds in the informal arena, where what counts is one's contacts – who one knows rather than what one is qualified to do. Boissevain opens with an energetic critique of structural functionalism. Within that framework people supposedly behave according to the rules of society and attempt to do what is best for society at large. But in reality they do what is best for themselves. Structural functionalism, in Boissevain's opinion, merely documents how people are *supposed* to behave, not how they *actually* behave. In his words, 'Instead of looking at man as a member of groups and institutional complexes passively obedient to their norms and pressures, it is important to try to see him as an entrepreneur who tries to manipulate norms and relationships for his own social and psychological benefit' (p. 7).

Like Bailey, Boissevain employed a language foreign to the structural functionalists: patrons, brokers, strategies, factions, coalitions, cliques, and transactions. Everyday life, he thought, is acted out in an arena of competition and conflict, and social change rather than stability is the normal state of affairs. Ungenerously, one might observe that in terms of the social action framework, most of what is valuable in *Friends of Friends* had already been said in *Stratagems and Spoils*. Let me hasten to add that Boissevain's study did contain some unique features. First, it provided a highly intricate application of the approach, employing both his own original ethnographic data in Malta and Sicily and the ethnographies of other writers. Second, it attempted to render social action theory more systematic and rigorous by grafting onto it a technical procedure known as network analysis. Network analysis, pioneered by Elizabeth Bott (1957), was intended to fill a gap formerly occupied by kinship analysis in a world where the family no longer dominates the entire social structure. Networks consist of relationships between people – friends of friends – of transactions and coalitions that occupy the social space between the individual's family and the state. One of the criticisms against network analysis, to some extent exemplified in *Friends of Friends*, is that it bogs anthropologists down in technical detail, and conveys the unfortunate implication that methodological rigour equals theoretical insight.

Fredrik Barth

Barth, a Norwegian anthropologist, whose influence was acknowledged by both Bailey and Boissevain, is another important figure in the social action school. In his study of political leadership in Pakistan (1959) he describes the relationship between leaders and followers as a form of transaction. The leaders provide protection, the followers allegiance. But the moment that leaders grow soft and no longer fulfil their side of the contract, off go the people below them to a leader who can do the job.

In 1966 Barth published a thin but elegant volume that soon became widely known: *Models of Social Organization*. Embedding his analysis in the ethnography of a Norwegian fishing boat, he covered the same conceptual ground later explored by Bailey and Boissevain: self-interested individuals manipulating values and norms to their own advantage, choosing between alternative strategies, and establishing relationships and alliances governed by reciprocity, with the whole process feeding back on and transforming the value system and social organization.

In one sense, however, Barth's study was even more ambitious than the works of Bailey and Boissevain. He attempted to formalize social action theory. Rather than focusing on structural form (or social structure or patterns of action), he advocated a focus on the processes that produce structural form. Central to these processes is the capacity of people to make choices. Such choices are constrained by existing values and norms, reflect the incentives and goals embraced by individuals, and are modified by the transactions into which they enter. The end products are patterns of behaviour which are formed and reformed over time. Barth labels this procedure the search for generative models, because what the investigator does is attempt to generate the principles conditioned by constraints and incentives that result in structural form.

Barth certainly provided interaction theory with a clear, promising, and unique procedure, yet over the years it seems fair to say that his generative models have been more admired than followed. Perhaps his successors have simply not been talented enough to match the level of theoretical sophistication demanded by his generative models. An alternative explanation is that the attempt to systematize the social action approach contradicts the underlying assumption that social life is inherently complex, messy, and unsystematic.

Victor Turner

While Turner is renowned for his highly innovative writings on ritual (1967, 1969, 1974), it is his earlier work, *Schism and Continuity in an African Society* (1957), that interests us here. On one level this book is a study of conflict in the tradition of Max Gluckman, under whom Turner studied. On another level it amounts to an exploratory statement of the social action model.

Turner analyses three types of conflict: that between principles of social organization, that between individuals and cliques striving for power, prestige and wealth, and that internal to the individual personality as it is pulled between egoism and altruism (or selfish and social motives). His main focus is on the first type of conflict. Occasionally his interpretations seem to be little different than Gluckman's. For example, he writes: 'Conflict is endemic in the social structure but a set of mechanisms exists whereby conflict itself is pressed into the service of offering group unity' (p. 129). This fails, however, to capture the subtlety of

Turner's approach. He focuses on social dramas, which are crises generated by quarrels between people, ultimately reflecting contradictions embedded in the social structure. The Ndembu people, on which he based his analysis, attempt to resolve a crisis by turning to the divination of sorcery for explanation, and by arriving at a ritual reconciliation between the quarrelling parties. However, the harmony thus achieved is short-lived, and inevitably new crises erupt, sometimes creating shifts in power and alliance because the contradictions in society remain intact.

Another theme in this book revolves around the second type of conflict, that between individuals competing for scarce goods, and here Turner's work overlaps more clearly with social action theory. The normative order itself, he observes, is neither uniform nor coherent. Inconsistent, even contradictory, norms exist side by side. That is necessarily so because norms must express the opposite sides of the contradictions rooted in society. This presents individuals with an opportunity, as they select and discard the norms most advantageous to their interests, and manipulate their relationships and cliques through a mine field of opposition and change.

Schism and Continuity in an African Society contains an early expression of social action, but it does differ from the works of Bailey, Boissevain, and Barth. These other authors certainly paid attention to conflict, but treated it as just another condition associated with social action. In Turner's study, the emphasis is reversed, with conflict and ritual occupying the centre of the stage.

EVALUATION

The social action or transactional model can be traced back to the Manchester school of anthropology presided over by Gluckman, under whom Bailey, Boissevain and Turner all received their training. But its roots were much older. Malinowski today is often remembered as a simple functionalist, but that devalues the richness of his perspective. Not only did he portray human beings, including the Trobrianders, as self-interested manipulators, welded to the larger community by the grace of reciprocity, but he also emphasized the huge gap between what people say and what they do, or between the rules of behaviour and actual behaviour. Leach, who studied under Malinowski, kept these themes alive and eventually passed them on to his own student, Fredrik Barth.

Social action succeeded where conflict theory failed largely because it constituted a genuine alternative to the oversocialized model of the actor embraced by the structural functionalists, and because it incorpo-rated conflict into its framework. Today, a quarter of a century after the publication of Bailey's *Stratagems and Spoils*, the transactional model continues to have its share of followers. Indeed, some anthropologists would argue that it is the fieldworker's model par excellence, made to measure for investigating the informal realm of society, where the real action unfolds. This does not mean that the perspective has escaped all criticism. One objection (see Silverman 1974–5) is that by concentrating on the intricate and complex manoeuvres of individuals and coalitions, its exponents have lost sight of the larger social structural context in which choice and manipulation operate. Another objection (see Albera 1988) is that people such as Bailey have been so concerned with the observation of everyday life as it unfolds before them that they have failed to take history into account, and the degree to which it explains the present. Both criticisms are variations on what is known as the macro-micro dilemma, which has plagued virtually all anthropological perspectives: how to achieve a sensitive and detailed analysis of the local situation while simultaneously bringing into play the wider struc-tural-historical context.

Conclusion

There was more going on in terms of theory in the 1960s and 1970s, of course, then represented by the three orientations in this chapter.[9] In America, psychological anthropology, with a focus on the comparative study of child-rearing, was gathering steam (see Bourguignon 1979), as was cognitive and linguistic anthropology. Cognitive anthropology, which involves specialized techniques for analysing mentalist data (Tyler 1969), will be more appropriately dealt with when we turn to methodology. As for linguistic anthropology, Dell Hymes (1964) has left his mark, and Noam Chomsky (1973) shook the very foundations of the study of language. His approach, which became known as transforma-tional linguistics or generative grammar, focused on the deep structure of language, on the unconscious patterns of rules that produce (surface

---

9 Perhaps this is a convenient place to clarify another issue. While I have organized anthropological theory into three separate chronological phases, to some extent this has been a stylistic device. Specific orientations such as conflict theory, social action, and cultural ecology, although they crystallized in phase two, were foreshadowed in phase one and in different degrees persisted into phase three.

level) speech, and on the relationship between meaning and sound. There were also a host of short-lived approaches, such as McClelland's *n* Achievement theory (1967), which advanced the dubious assumption that the principle obstacle to development facing Third World people was in their minds: if only they would learn to think and dream like middle-class Westerners, economic growth would dazzle them.

In Britain, some anthropologists took the attack on the rigid, deterministic model of society so dear to the structural functionalists even further than social action theory, introducing concepts such as quasi-groups (Mayer 1966, Boissevain 1971) and even non-groups (Boissevain 1968). As ethnicity emerged as an increasingly significant focus of research, a theoretical approach called pluralism took shape, its roots traced back to a Dutch writer, Furnivall (1939). At the same time British scholars such as Banton (1967) and Rex (1970) had begun to develop a sophisticated analysis of racism, to which Fredrik Barth (1969) contributed. The switch in focus to 'talk' and 'meaning,' to 'things said, not done,' currently so central to postmodernism, had already been anticipated by Bailey and his students in their ethnographies of the villages of western Europe. In France, as I have indicated, economic anthropology was given a Marxist twist (Godelier 1972, Meillassoux 1964, and Terray 1969), and on both sides of the Atlantic Marx was the inspiration for a critical anthropology aimed at colonialism and capitalism, with Berreman (1968), Gough (1968), and Worsley (1964) leading the way.

In chapter two I made a distinction between strong and weak versions of science, and pointed out that the first was represented by British structural functionalism, the second by American historical particularism. Following the Second World War the situation had reversed. The strong version more aptly described the American school, dominated by cultural ecology and neo-evolutionism, while the weak version captured the character of social action theory. Men such as Julian Steward and Marvin Harris obviously regarded their work as scientific, but the same thing, it must be stressed, was true for the conflict and social action writers. Gluckman certainly thought he was doing science, and Bailey wrote: 'The purpose of any scientific endeavour is to suggest verifiable propositions about relations between variables' (1969:8). In Boissevain's *Friends of Friends* we find expressions such as 'the proposition was verified,' and Barth went on at length about falsifying hypotheses. Clearly, then, while the nature of anthropological theory changed dramatically from phase one to phase two, the pursuit of science remained much the same.

5

Method

Although cultural ecology, social action theory, and conflict theory were all regarded by the writers who created them as models that kept scientific anthropology alive, the last two, by introducing a greater degree of complexity than had characterized structural functionalism, unintentionally made the goal of science more difficult to achieve. Conflict theoreticians rejected the tidy assumption of a unified central value system, and social action writers promoted the image of the choice-making, manipulative actor, and the porous, shifting social structure. Ironically, when all of this was going on, there emerged a concerted effort to create a qualitative methods literature that would put an end to the frustrating mysteries of the fieldwork endeavour. In other words, phase two witnessed the first signs of a gap between theory and method.

The Methods Literature

In the 1960s a minor rebellion took place within anthropology, mounted mainly by young scholars just beginning their careers. As graduate students, they had been desperate for direction on how to do research, but when they had sought help from their teachers, the majority of whom belonged to the sink or swim school, they were assured that if they were up to scratch all would become clear once they got into the field. Rather than being provided with a set of techniques, they were advised to take lots of paper and pens, keep their running shoes dry, and not have sex with the natives.

Dissatisfied and frustrated, the young Turks began to write about their own fieldwork experiences and triggered off an explosion of publications on ethnographic methods that continued to expand in the 1970s.

The slogan of the day was demystification. Virtually every conceivable aspect of qualitative research, from entry into the field, building rapport, choosing informants, becoming a participant observer, and ethical issues, was held up to inspection. The aim was to render open and public what previously had been closed and mysterious.

So vast was the literature that I cannot hope to give a blow-by-blow account of it. All that I can do is to indicate some of its principal features. There were 'how to' textbooks and anthologies, most of them committed to the goal of rendering fieldwork more rigorous and scientific (Brim and Spain 1974, Crane and Angrosino 1974, Denzin 1970, Epstein 1967, Filstead 1970, J.M. Johnson 1975, Jongmans and Gutkind 1967, Junker 1960, Moore 1961, Naroll and Cohen 1970, Pelto 1970, Schatzman and Strauss 1973, Spradley 1979, R. Wax 1971). There were sober, retrospective works in which anthropologists reconstructed the methodology that had guided their own projects (Beattie 1965, Chagnon 1974, Friedlich 1970, Middleton 1970, Spindler 1970, Williams 1967). There were confessional, experiential books, which 'let it all hang out,' or what might be labelled 'I was there' testimonials (Malinowski 1967, Maybury-Lewis 1965, W.E. Mitchell 1978, Rabinow 1977). There were some critical, philosophical works (Bruyn 1966, Cicourel 1964, Lévi-Strauss 1974, Phillips 1971). In addition, books and articles appeared on a wide range of specific techniques and issues: the use of photography in the field (Collier 1967), the life history approach (Langness 1965), coping with stress in the field (Henry and Saberwal 1969), learning an unwritten language (Gudschinsky 1967), methods for studying kinship (Schusky 1965), unobtrusive techniques (Webb et al. 1966), informants (Berreman 1962, Casagrande 1960), the politics of fieldwork (Berreman 1968, Diamond 1964, Gough 1968), women in the field (Golde 1970), historical methods (Pitt 1972, Trigger 1968), team ethnography (Price 1973), analysis, validity and reliability (Becker and Geer 1960, Killworth and Russell 1976, Lofland 1971, McEwen 1963, Salamone 1977, Young and Young 1961), surveys (McClintock et al. 1979, Myers 1977, O'Barr et al. 1973), statistics and quantification in fieldwork (Johnson 1978, Kay 1971, Thomas 1976), and ethics (Barnes 1967, Beals 1967, Erikson 1967, Fabian 1971, Jarvie 1969, M. Wax 1977).

During the 1960s and 1970s, then, qualitative methods had become a growth industry in the publishing world, and courses on fieldwork sprang up not only in anthropology but also in neighbouring disciplines such as sociology. Much of the literature was produced by American anthropologists, and one series in particular made a major contribution:

the Holt, Rinehart and Winston monographs on anthropological method edited by George and Louise Spindler.

When anthropologists started to write about their fieldwork methods in the 1960s and 1970s I was a true believer. My own efforts in my Ph.D. thesis and first book to include appendices and comments on methods had not gone down well with the old guard. One prominent anthropologist thought it curious that anyone would bother to include a blurb on methods. Another eminent figure dismissed my comments as 'methodological autobiography.' Although cut to the bone at the time by such criticisms, as the years went by I became less and less impressed by the burst of publications on methods in the 1960s and 1970s.

One reason was the discovery, much to my surprise, that a large and relevant body of literature on fieldwork methods had existed prior to the 1960s. It is true that this literature had been more often than not ignored by practising anthropologists, and that courses on field techniques had been virtually unheard of. Curiously, this did not stamp the discipline as unscientific. As Kuhn (1962) has pointed out, a relative disinterest in methodological issues is characteristic of the hard sciences. Students learn methods by actually doing research, which was essentially the attitude of the early anthropologists.

Stocking (1983:8) has acknowledged that some discussion of methodological issues existed in the decades prior to the 1960s, but stated that little attention was given to epistemology, ethics, and the psychological aspects of fieldwork. This is correct, but the older literature did deal with the same basic issues that dominated the literature of the 1960s and 1970s: entry, rapport, observational roles, informants, and interviewing. Moreover, this newer literature had little to say about epistemology; that perplexing topic was sidestepped until the structuralists, postmodernists, and feminist anthropologists came into the limelight.

It is tempting to conclude that the major difference in the literature on methods in the 1960s and 1970s, compared to the literature that predated it, was simply that there was so much more of it. Certainly, had anthropologists in the 1940s and 1950s known the available literature adequately, they could have mounted sophisticated courses on methods. This does not mean that the explosion of books and articles on methods since then has lacked purpose. It no doubt sharpened our understanding of old issues, and highlighted techniques, especially quantitative ones, that rarely had been relied on previously. Then, too, some of the older writings on methods had been buried in monographs or published in obscure journals; the newer literature was immensely more accessible.

Finally, the sheer bulk of the literature in the 1960s and 1970s served a political purpose: it profiled qualitative methods as a distinctive research approach, and provided them with a degree of legitimacy.

A second reason for losing my faith in the methods literature concerns its value for both the neophyte and the experienced ethnographer. In my judgment, speaking as a practising fieldworker as well as a teacher, this literature is more interesting and valuable after one has done fieldwork than before. Before one gets one's feet wet in the field, the methods literature serves as a security blanket; after, one reads it in a different light – it is transformed into data, theory, and epistemology. What I am suggesting is that neither the professional anthropologist nor the beginning student learns much from the how-to books on qualitative methods, or the confessionals for that matter, except for those sections devoted to techniques more closely associated with quantitative methods such as types of samples, coding procedures, scales, and statistics. Indeed, I would put the case even more forcibly: individuals who do not possess the sensitivity, flexibility, and subtlety demanded in fieldwork before taking a course on qualitative methods or embarking on an original project possibly are unsuited for this type of research. What I am saying here, I realize, may upset students, many of whom expect a methods course to provide a straightforward set of rules and techniques that can be followed almost blindly. Yet it is only after students go to the field that the methods textbooks begin to make sense to them. This is why the most important part of a methods course is the student's own original fieldwork project.[1]

A third reason for my disillusionment is that there seems to be a basic contradiction between the methods literature and the fieldwork enterprise. Demystification in the literature has meant providing fieldwork with a set of shared, communicable, public, rigorous, and systematic procedures that can be passed on from one generation of researchers to another. Yet this does not remotely describe the fieldwork situation. Rather than being a linear activity, with each stage unfolding in logical sequence, fieldwork is a nonlinear activity. It is governed by unexpected shifts in focus, accident, good and bad luck, false starts, sudden insights, and personal, subjective experiences unique to the fieldworker. Cer-

---

1 In this context, I cannot help commenting on an unfortunate trend in courses on qualitative methods, especially at the undergraduate level. As they have become more popular, with larger enrolments, there has been a tendency to turn them into lecture courses, and to minimize the student's opportunity to do an original project.

tainly one can attempt to follow a systematic model of fieldwork, but a slavish devotion to it is likely to promote the culture of science at the expense of insight and explanation.

A fourth reason for my scepticism is that too much of what is portrayed in the literature as new and improved methods amount to little more than rationalizations which have been forced on ethnographers by changes in the research setting beyond their control. Here we might include the supposed superiority of the interview over participant observation or talk over behaviour. In recent years both Agar (1980) and McCracken (1988) have espoused the interview and talk. Yet their reasons for doing so seem to relate less to defensible methodological arguments than to their own research experiences. Rather than conducting a community study – the traditional unit of anthropological investigation – they have focused on the elderly in their individual homes and junkies on the street corner.

I applaud the trend among ethnographers to move into research areas previously considered 'non-anthropological,' and recognize the necessary adjustment in methods. These changes, however, have not been inspired by the discovery of new and improved techniques. They are the result of the transformation of the research enterprise, from a sole focus on pre-industrial, small-scale societies, which erroneously were regarded as homogeneous, to complex, large-scale societies at home and abroad, including those in the Third World. Also relevant is the changing nature of the small community. In today's world it makes little sense to speak of community as a self-sufficient entity where people identify with each other and think and act in a unique manner. Not only has the distinction between urban and rural been reduced to the point of insignificance, but the very notion of community as a distinctive territorial unit has become obsolete. It is the changes in the fieldwork setting, then, and not the supposed superiority of the interview and talk, that have caused fieldworkers to turn their backs on participant observation.

Even if the shift in methods is therefore understandable, this does not mean that the discipline has been strengthened. It will be recalled that long ago Nadel argued that the interview must always be complemented by observation, in order to measure the correspondence between things said and things done. Arensberg, in his influential article 'The Community-Study Method' (1954), pointed out that in anthropology the focus can never be solely on what people say; instead, it is on the relationship between norm and act, attitude and behaviour. Several years ago Phillips (1971) voiced his dissatisfaction with studies restricted to people's reports about their behaviour – the typical procedure in survey research. In my judgment, especially in light of the shift to the interview and talk, his misgivings ring just as true today.

One might also include the switch in emphasis from research abroad to research at home as a rationalization. Certainly, there are sound epistemological and ethical arguments for the change in direction, but sometimes the reason for doing so is nothing more complicated than the ages of one's children and respect for one's spouse. Indeed, my guess is that if it were still possible to conduct research in the Third World without hassles, most of us still would be there. This observation, I quickly add, probably holds more for seasoned professionals than for their graduate students, who have been raised in a different intellectual atmosphere.

To sum up, the scientific direction of the methods literature in the 1960s and 1970s certainly was consistent with Steward's cultural ecology, but much less so with regard to the British perspectives of conflict and social action. Even on the American scene, however, not all was what it appeared to be. The purpose of the methods literature was to demystify the fieldwork process, to render it more scientific. Yet not all of the literature had that effect. Berreman's famous piece 'Behind Many Masks' (1962), for example, illustrated the tremendous degree to which one's data and interpretations are shaped by one's informants, to the extent that two different informants can result in two radically different ethnographies; it also underlined the part played by chance and accident in fieldwork. Put otherwise, an unintended consequence of at least some of the methods literature was to cast doubt on anthropology as a science, rather than showing us how to attain it.

The Fieldwork Situation

Most of the basic assumptions and elements of research that existed in phase one continued into phase two, but there were some modifications. Fieldwork as a rite of passage came under attack. The joke that one's Ph.D. was guaranteed if one managed to survive in the field for a couple of years had begun to wear thin. Greater emphasis was placed on theory, and fieldwork became shorter. Students were urged to narrow the focus of their inquiries, and to concentrate on a limited number of sharply defined problems rather than trying to cover everything.

The vast majority of studies were probably still conducted in small communities. But it was not quite business as usual. The notion of the isolated community was replaced by the recognition that outside social and historical forces always penetrate and shape the small community, and must be taken into account. During this period there was at least some recognition that the cultures being studied were no longer primitive. Development studies proliferated, and there was a greater willingness to consult literature dealing with modern issues. For example, Fallers (1965) drew on Weber's bureaucratic theory in order to illuminate the social organization of the Basoga people in Uganda.

As I pointed out earlier, not only did the interview (usually unstructured) emerge as a principal technique, but the questionnaire and the survey also found their way into the discipline (see Cohen 1969). Unlike sociology, however, they were not usually pre-tested in a pilot study; in most ethnographic projects, that was not feasible, mainly because it was only after the anthropologist had completed several months of research that it was possible to know what questions to ask. In addition, it takes a long time to build up sufficient rapport to use an instrument such as a questionnaire, and most fieldworkers would probably cringe at the idea of doing a trial run with a target group in a neighbouring community.

There was an increased emphasis on the ethics of fieldwork at this time, with the recognition that the anthropologist did not have a God-given right to intrude into people's lives, and that knowledge for its own sake may be sufficient motivation for the researcher, but fall short for those being investigated. There was a demand for research to be useful, for fieldworkers to make their research goals explicit, and to seek permission from and respect the privacy of people. This greater sensitivity to ethical issues, I must point out, might also be described as a rationalization, rather than a sign of a moral awakening in the discipline. The hard reality was that the political context of new nations left anthropologists little choice in the matter.

SOME NEW RULES OF THUMB

1. Use multi-methods, not just participant observation and informants; in other words, to employ the jargon, 'triangulate.'
2. Keep a daily diary on methods, recording impressions of rapport, commenting on your role as participant observer, on the strengths, weaknesses, and peculiarities of informants, and on various projects and techniques that might be tried in later stages of the project.
3. Include an appendix on methods in your report, thesis, or book; the diary will form the basis for the appendix, which should provide suffi-

cient information for the reader to understand your methodological approach, and thus to be in a better position to evaluate the quality of your data and the validity of your arguments.

4. In your fieldwork notes, keep separate the data themselves, the actor's interpretations of the data, and the observer's interpretations (your interpretations) of the data; this may sound like a logical thing to do, but it is highly dubious whether there is any such animal as data in themselves, 'raw' data, uncontaminated by interpretation; moreover, by the time one writes up the data, the distinction between the actor's and the observer's interpretation is usually blurred, unless a major effort has been made to collect and include long stretches of native texts.

5. In your report, thesis, or book, clearly identify native analytic concepts and observer analytic concepts, so that the reader is in a better position to evaluate the theoretical framework; for example, if investigating power and authority in a Yoruba village in Nigeria, what are the indigenous concepts and connotations, how do they jibe (if at all) with these concepts in the theoretical literature, and what do they indicate about hierarchy and equality, and about Yoruba conceptions of free will and fate? A widespread assumption in anthropology has been that before one can entertain the implications of one's data for broader theoretical issues, one must first understand the indigenous explanatory system. In recent years, under the influence of postmodernism and feminist anthropology, there has been a tendency to regard native theory as the only possible legitimate theory.

6. Select your research project on the basis of a problem to be solved, rather than an area or tribe to investigate. In the decades leading up to the Second World War, anthropologists looked for virgin territory, untouched by previous ethnographers. Since so little research had been done, there may have been some justification to this approach. Although even today it is probable that many anthropologists decide to do research in a specific part of the world because they are attracted to it, by the 1960s there was a growing notion that in order to advance the discipline's body of theory, one's problem should dictate the choice of research site. Margaret Mead, incidentally, was one of the few scholars before the Second World War to do just that; she chose Samoa as a propitious setting in which to investigate cross-cultural variation in adolescent behaviour.

7. Let the research problem dictate your choice of methods. This is the standard message in virtually all textbooks, and while it makes sense logically, few ethnographers take it seriously. Instead, research projects

are selected in terms of their suitability for participant observation, interviewing, etc. Of course, it is not only anthropologists who allow the methodological tail to wag the dog. The same holds true for quantitative-oriented sociologists. So much for logic!

Methods are also supposed to be chosen on the basis of their prospects for replication. Yet this principle too cuts little ice with anthropologists. How is it possible to replicate studies based on participant observation and informants? As the works of Redfield and Lewis suggest, any attempt to do so is likely to produce embarrassment rather than reliability.

8. Learn to count; anthropologists had always peppered their monographs with expressions such as 'more, less, a lot, or a little.' In the 1960s, driven by the goal of science, they were urged to clean up their act and provide, where possible, quantitative data. This was simple stuff, and in my judgment it made a lot of sense, especially if the counting was confined to objective factors such as the number of canoes and radios in a community. Most fieldworkers, fortunately, did not attempt to gather quantitative data on what people thought and felt, on values and attitudes; nor did they get carried away with fancy statistical tests of association and probability, the playground of sociologists.[2]

There also has been some effort made to improve the analysis of qualitative data, but as I shall argue in chapter eight most of it has been a dismal failure. Many anthropologists would defend their overwhelming concentration on data collection by arguing that that is exactly what is required in qualitative research. In this context it is interesting to reflect on the fact that the sociologist's research assistant, who is often assigned the job of administering questionnaires and conducting telephone surveys, is almost unknown in anthropology. Because of the personal

---

2 At this juncture it may help to clarify a general difference between anthropological and sociological work. The research process consists of research design (the logical steps in executing a project, such as the case study and before and after studies), data collection, and data analysis. Sociologists usually have done a much better job with the first and third stages than with the second; my impression, in fact, is that the collection of data has been regarded at times as the least important step, something that can be put in the hands of hired research assistants. Anthropologists, in contrast, have focused most of their efforts on the second stage, but have slipped blithely over the other two. In the 1960s and 1970s this began to change, at least in the textbooks if not in the field, as writers such as Brim and Spain (1974) and Pelto (1970) concentrated on research design.

dimension involved in collecting qualitative data, the vast majority of ethnographers believe they must do their own research.

9. Provide universities in countries where research is conducted with copies of one's publications. This was part of the new ethical stance in anthropology, a response to the charge of data imperialism. The view also emerged that copies should be made available to the communities in which research was conducted. It is dubious, however, that this was often done, mainly because the tendency of ethnographers to be critical of the public image and to muck around in the back stage mitigated against a warm reception.

10. Assure that informants represent all sectors of a community. There has been a tendency among fieldworkers to rely tremendously on the assistance and views of one or two individuals, often their landlord and landlady. As the image of society as homogeneous and harmonious gave way to heterogeneity, conflict, and divided interests, it was realized that unless informants were representative of the various divisions, their data would be unacceptably limited and biased.

11. Take a good break midway through a project. This gives the residents of a community a breather from your presence and constant questions. It also allows you an opportunity to spend a few weeks revving up your motor, taking stock of what you have accomplished, and getting a clearer view of what the end product will look like. Some fieldworkers find it valuable to use the break as an opportunity to write a paper or two on their project, and solicit feedback from colleagues. Another advantage of an extended break is that people are usually genuinely pleased to see the researcher again on return, and the data often flood in then at a rapid rate.

12. Get psychoanalysed or join a drama club. I doubt that many anthropologists have done either, but the rationale behind this idea makes sense. The more fieldworkers are comfortable with and know themselves, the less the probability that their personal quirks and anxieties will interfere with the fieldwork exercise, which undoubtedly is a highly personal undertaking. As for drama, not only must fieldworkers be sensitive to the roles that people play, but they themselves are on stage all the time, and the audience is often a demanding one. Psychoanalysis and drama may be two areas in which students with borderline aptitudes for qualitative research can learn something valuable before embarking on fieldwork.

13. Do research both abroad and at home. The day has passed when anthropology was defined solely as the study of other cultures. As far back as the 1960s the occasional scholar such as André Gunder Frank

urged anthropologists to give up research away from home entirely. In the years since, an increasing number of anthropologists have done research both at home and abroad, and that is a good thing. Without fieldwork experience abroad, one avoids the painful process (and the joys) of learning what it is like to live in and grapple with the meaning of a different culture. With such cross-cultural experience, one brings a deeper perspective to one's own culture.

FORMAL ANALYSIS

While these various rules of thumb were equally applicable to cultural and social anthropology, in the American school there was an even greater effort to introduce more systematic research procedures, which had also been the case in phase one. Julian Steward (1955:22), for example, thought that the most challenging methodological problem facing anthropologists was to establish a sophisticated taxonomy of cultural phenomena. His solution was a taxonomy of different levels of socio-cultural integration, from the nuclear family to the folk society (associated with peasantry) and the modern state. Such a taxonomy, he assumed, was critical to the cross-cultural method.

American anthropologists were also the force behind what has been variably labelled formal analysis, cognitive anthropology, ethnoscience, componential analysis, and the new ethnography. Formal analysis supposedly was able to provide a scientific explanation of mentalist data. As Tyler stated, 'Cognitive anthropology is based on the assumption that its data are mental phenomena which can be analysed by formal methods similar to those of mathematics and logic' (1969:14). Claiming a capacity to get inside people's heads, to get at people's folk categories and taxonomies, the formalists supposedly presented culture as it was perceived and experienced by people themselves (see Harris 1968: chapter twenty). Not everyone was convinced. In fact, formal analysis can be written off as a brief blip on the anthropological record with few followers and even fewer successes. Geertz probably spoke for the majority of anthropologists when he described componential analysis as 'extreme subjectivism ... married to extreme formalism' (1973:11). Hocus-pocus is how Burling (1964) characterized the approach. As Kaplan and Manners (1972:185) observed, none of us has direct access to the human mind, which means that the cognitive maps, codes, and rules spelled out by the formalists were mere inferences rather than cognitive reality per se.

Not a single prominent British social anthropologist, Kuper (1975: 223) pointed out, was converted to the American school of formal analysis, mainly because of its pseudo-scientific pretensions. However, social anthropologists introduced their own version of the technical quick-fix. This was network analysis (see Barnes 1968, 1969a, 1969b, 1972, Boissevain 1974, Bott 1957, Mitchell 1969). Network analysis did what it implied. It traced a person's connections to others in her or his environment, identifying cliques and teams, specifying instrumental and expressive relationships. Network analysis, as I stated earlier, was intended as a successor to kinship analysis, which had been undermined by social changes that had transformed the family from the backbone of pre-industrial cultures to just another institution. Network analysis, too, failed to live up to its advanced billing, mainly because what was in essence a modest technical operation was touted as an explanatory system on the par with structural functionalism or cultural ecology.

Case Study One: A West African Utopia

In order to convey more vividly what it is like to do fieldwork, I shall compare the methodology in two of my own projects. The first project, an example of research abroad, involved a wealthy theocracy in Nigeria (Barrett 1974 and 1977). The second project, an example of research at home, focused on organized racism and anti-Semitism in Canada (Barrett 1984a and 1987). The Nigerian community, located in an isolated part of the Niger delta, accessible only by boat and canoe, and built on stilts because the region was almost entirely under water during the wet season, was founded in 1947 by a group of fishermen who had been inspired by God. Their religious practices were a mixture of Christianity and indigenous Yoruba beliefs, and they thought that God had blessed them with the reward of immortality – not in Heaven, but on earth. They did not have a burial ground, because they believed that no member of the community (the population was about twelve hundred) would die.

The Holy Apostles, as they called themselves, also believed that God wanted them to live completely communally. Towards this end, all money and financial transactions within the village were banned. People worked for the common good, with basic necessities provided to them, including food, housing, and clothing. Profits from fishing and other industries that were eventually established went to the community treasury, to be reinvested by the *oba* (king) in the economic infrastructure. The communal system also affected social organization. The family was banned, and at different periods marriage too, and the village was divided into female and male sectors. Within a few years Olowo, as I call the community, became a remarkable success story, wealthier by far than any of the dozens of villages that surrounded it.

CHOOSING THE PROJECT

Because of its utopian features and economic success, Olowo enjoyed a degree of fame in Nigeria, and I had visited it while teaching with the Canadian University Service Overseas (CUSO). When I switched to anthropology, my major interest was in development studies, and I became intrigued with the possibility that Olowo might serve as a model of economic progress for other small communities.

RESEARCH DESIGN

As a graduate student in the 1960s, I was impatient with what I regarded as the haphazard, unscientific manner in which fieldwork typically was conducted. I thought that one should begin a project with clearly defined problems, and even with tentative explanations for these problems. In my own case, I had read widely on theories of development, West African ethnography, and Utopias around the globe; I also had access to three articles that had been published on Olowo. With this background material, I specified three problems as guides to my eventual research: Why was the community founded? How had it managed to develop economically? And what would happen to it after it had been in existence for a generation? For each of these problems, I build models, based on the available literature. At the same time I specified the logical units of comparison in the study, emphasizing especially the advantages of doing comparative work in a village that shared Olowo's religious beliefs, but where private enterprise rather than communalism operated. Much to my surprise, I actually found a village a few miles from Olowo that fitted these requirements, and the comparisons made were important. The same cannot be said about the deductive procedure. The models that I had built prior to beginning fieldwork simply got in the way, distorting what I observed and was told; until I eventually abandoned them and began to work inductively, as most anthropologists do, my research suffered (see Barrett 1976 and 1977).

Because Olowo was a closed community, a Utopia, it was too risky to simply write the *oba* from England, where I was enrolled in a Ph.D. program, and ask if I could conduct research there for a year or so. Instead I travelled to Nigeria and showed up at the community unannounced and without permission. This was not the normal procedure, and throughout the day a few of the guards responsible for the village's security followed me around. Later in the afternoon I saw some boys playing soccer by the seaside, and ran out to join them. That evening I was granted an audience with the *oba*. I explained why I was there, and asked permission to do research in the community for my Ph.D. thesis. I shall never forget the *oba*'s reaction. He said he saw me playing soccer with his boys, and liked it. Without any further hesitation, he said I could stay. Having assumed that there was a good chance that I would be denied permission to do research in Olowo, I had gone to Nigeria with an alternative project in mind. Whether I would have been accepted by the *oba* had I not joined his young subjects at the make-shift soccer field, I shall never know, but somehow I doubt it.

A few weeks later, my wife and I made plans to move to Olowo. We arranged passage on one of the community's small passenger boats that operated in the Niger delta, ran into a violent tropical storm, and almost drowned. That experience, however, created a bond between us and the other passengers, especially the captain and a man who turned out to be one of the *oba*'s favourite subjects. A week after settling into the community, we travelled to Lagos to purchase supplies. When we returned, we were summoned to the palace. The *oba* made no bones about his displeasure. We had left, he said, without his permission, and that was unacceptable. This was an eye-opener. It revealed just how closely regulated the community was, and made it crystal clear that we were expected to conform to the rules. Some allowance, I should add, was made for us. After a discussion with the *oba*, we were allowed to live in the same room in a guest house rather than separately in the female and male sectors. The church was also divided into male and female sections, and there too we sat side by side with the men. Our idea was that we would adapt to the local custom after we had got acclimatized, but we never did.

About two weeks after taking up residence in Olowo, we were awakened in the middle of the night by sounds of shouting and running feet. As we peered out of the window, we could see lanterns bobbing in the darkness. The Biafran War was then in progress, and our first thought was that the fighting had arrived on our doorstep. In the morning we found out that all the excitement had been over an outsider who had slipped into the community during the night, and tried to make off with some goods. This man, we learned, was a deserter, a former member of the community. Just as strict control was exercised over who entered Olowo, the same held for anyone who wanted to leave. In fact, at that time a person fed up with the village actually had to escape. Early in the research, thus, I was made aware of the discrepancy between the community's ideals and actual attitudes and behaviour, and this small incident showed me just how important it was in research simply to be on the spot.

The greatest challenge during the initial weeks was to have the patience to proceed slowly, building rapport and getting to know people, and not to ask sensitive questions. Sometimes people would stop me on the boardwalk and inquire politely about how the research was going. I was amazed, and began to think that perhaps it would be easier to do research in the community than I had anticipated. But the *oba*, of course, had told his subjects that I was there to do research, and only as the months went by and I began asking questions did they begin to appreciate what research involved.

From the very first days in the village I had begun to do unsystematic observation, simply walking around trying to absorb everything around me. In one of the community shops I was surprised to observe people paying money for goods. As I soon discovered, I had entered Olowo just when a small amount of private enterprise had been allowed to emerge. After about a month in the community, I still found it dicey to ask questions openly, except with a few individuals who had become my friends, but I did begin to conduct systematic observation. For example, I began to count all the boats, canoes, motorcycles, and bicycles. It was then, too, with the help of my talented wife, that I began to draw a map of the village, assigning a code number to every street and house.

CHOOSING ROLES

One of the first challenges for the fieldworker concerns impression management. How do you explain your presence? How do you want people to define you? This latter question implies that you have some choice in the matter, but that is only up to a point; your age, sex, ethnicity, and country of origin, and possibly other things such as your religion, all will have an impact. In my case, I presented myself as a graduate student, risking rejection at the outset from the *oba*, but realizing, quite apart from ethical issues, that it would have been impossible to have tried to pass myself off as a potential member of the community. I taught English in the village's secondary school, and gradually became aware that Olowo people saw me primarily as a teacher, not a researcher. Whenever I needed something, such as a canoe, it was the school principal's responsibility to arrange it.

Another question is how far into the community do you want to penetrate? It is conventional, following Gold (1958), to sketch out four distinct research roles, ranging from great empathy to great detachment: the complete participant, the participant who observes, the observer who participates, and the complete observer. It is perhaps understandable that most anthropologists would reject the role of the complete observer, because despite the advantage of apparent objectivity, it nullifies empathy. Yet the complete participant's role has its own limitations, namely that the researcher is constrained from probing analytically and asking questions that would be foreign to a full-fledged member. While my preferred role was that of a participant who observes, in actual fact my role fluctuated over all four positions, depending on whether the community was in a state of harmony or tension. In retrospect, the fact that both my wife and I taught in the local school was exceptionally important, at least in terms of the research project. Teaching legitimated our long stay in the community (fifteen months during the first field trip), and made the community slightly indebted to us, which helped when things got tense.

MANAGING DEVIANTS

As experienced fieldworkers know, the first individuals to cosy up to the anthropologist are usually deviants, people who for some reason or other are marginal in their communities. While their perspectives sometimes are important, which means they should not be ignored, it is necessary to avoid too much interaction with them, otherwise the researcher too risks being labelled an oddball. The first person to seek out our company in Olowo was a pleasant, middle-aged woman. She didn't seem to have any other friends in the community, and I soon learned why. She was a reputed witch, accused of killing new-born babies by eating their souls. Two younger men also began to stick to us like glue. One of them, as it turned out, was thought to be mentally unstable, the other a thief.

The most ridiculous case of all, however, was partly my own creation. When I had been with CUSO, I had met a member of the community while travelling in the neighbouring country of Cameroon. When I took up residence in Olowo, not only did I encourage his visits to my room, but I also called on him nearly every day. These efforts to build rapport came tumbling down a few months later when the *oba* summoned me to the palace and exploded. The man whom I had been so carefully courting, he explained, dabbled in sorcery, and was completely mistrusted by other members. The *oba* made it clear that he despised the man; my only response was a sickly smile, and a promise that I would avoid him in the future.

TECHNIQUES

Participant observation and reliance on informants are usually the fieldworker's basic research techniques, and that was the case in my research in Olowo. On most days I simply wandered around the village, chatting with people on the boardwalks, dropping into their homes, joking around, and joining in community work projects, which occurred on a regular basis. Occasionally my observations would be more systematic, such as comparing what high-status and low-status men, and men and women, did during communal labour.

Participant observation is crucial both for the data it generates and the empathy that it makes possible, but it has its limitations. At some point you need informants to interpret what you have observed, and to provide information to which you have not been privy. Before having fieldwork experience, I greatly underestimated the importance of informants.

Because of the closed nature of Olowo, the people who eventually became my informants initially approached me with caution. Within a few weeks I began to hang around with a half-dozen young men, most of them students or teachers in the secondary school. Each of them, I soon learned, had his own special interests, whether in religion, conflict, or family matters. After approximately three months I analysed the characteristics of these informants, taking into account age, sex, status, and membership criteria (a handful of non-members were teachers in the community). It was immediately clear that I was overloaded in some categories, but thin in others, especially as regards women and high-status elderly men. I immediately attempted to develop informants among these people, but never fully succeeded in doing so.

As the months went by, I realized that I had fallen into a pattern. During the day I mostly did participant observation. When darkness fell, however, I spent a great deal of time with my informants. This may well have been because of the community's closed nature, since in no other project that I have done has a similar distinction between day and night research emerged.

Incidentally, a distinction sometimes is made between moral and transactional informants. The fieldworker's relation to moral informants is based on trust and friendship, not financial remuneration. In contrast, one pays transactional informants. The conventional assumption is that data supplied by the first are more dependable. The main distinction in Olowo was between public and private informants. The *oba* selected individuals to act as my guides, supposedly trustworthy members who would discourage me from trying to get into the back stage, where my private informants took me. When the community was tense, perhaps as a result of a member escaping, I avoided being seen with my private informants, and paraded along the boardwalk with my public ones.

The traditional techniques of participant observation and reliance on informants had certainly proved their worth, but I was determined to try out more systematic techniques and gather quantitative data. About three months after moving to Olowo I decided to do a census of the community, and to include a few questions about status. I purposefully kept out all questions about attitudes, being concerned about validity, and instead asked about objective factors such as whether a person belonged to one of the elite organizations in the community.

Once I had the census/questionnaire form constructed, I took it to the *oba*, who granted me permission to run off as many copies as required on the school's mimeograph machine and to administer it to his subjects. The form couldn't simply be left in each house for people to fill out, since it was foreign to their experiences. Instead, at each house I sat down with the residents, went over each item on the form, filling out their names, village of origin, length of residence, age, occupation, and status memberships.

If there is one truism in fieldwork, it is that nothing ever quite works out as planned. In the case of the census/questionnaire, often nobody would be at home, or there would be a communal work project, or a clash with one of the neighbouring villages. The upshot was that three months later I was still going door to door with the census/questionnaire. I quickly learned that one has to have several projects on the go simultaneously, because it was impossible to keep to a time schedule with any one of them. While still working on the census/questionnaire, I initiated another project based on the card-sorting technique (Silverman 1966). In this project I was attempting to measure correlations among political, religious, and economic authority in the village. Names of several prominent members were written separately on cards, and judges, selected according to age, gender, and status criteria, were asked to sort the deck of cards according to political importance, then religious and economic importance. During this period I also systematically examined particular roles in the village, such as the leaders of each side-street, first constructing a set of questions, and then meeting each leader individually. Sometimes, if rapport was excellent, I would write up the notes as the person was interviewed; otherwise, I would memorize what was said and return immediately to my room to write. Occasionally I was pressured into doing group interviews, such as when I tried to interview a category of women responsible for processing fish. In these situations I merely asked innocuous questions, content to have the opportunity to build rapport. Sometimes as I sat with people, asking questions, they would advise me to save my time and go directly to the *oba* who knew everything, and would write my thesis in a week!

When I began the project I was determined to write up my field notes every day. For a few weeks I jotted down rough notes throughout the day, and turned them into formal, organized field notes during the evening. Soon, however, I found myself in the company of my informants after nightfall, and began to put off the task of writing field notes until the next morning. I made three copies of the field notes, one organized chronologically (that is, as the data came in), the other two organized in terms of themes and categories that I thought were critical to the project. Although some adjustment of these categories was required even after six months in the field, I finished up with reasonably well-organized notes, which made the task of writing a thesis somewhat less painful than it might otherwise have been. I should add that I typed all of the field notes on large index cards, which made it easy to handle masses of data; I also distinguished between the interpretations offered by Olowo people and my own interpretations by placing 'a' or 'b' beside the notes in the margin. From the very beginning of the project separate categories were kept for methods and theory; the first focused on techniques, strategies, characteristics of informants, rapport, etc.; the second consisted of potential explanations, hunches, and the possible relevance of the general theoretical literature.

One of the unusual challenges in this project was how to get rid of scrap paper on which rough notes had been jotted. There was no garbage dump in the community, and indeed not much paper of any kind. So periodically I walked out to the seaside, usually in the early afternoon when people were resting on their porches out of the glare of the sun, started a small fire, and burnt the paper. On one such occasion I had just cut my hair, so I burnt the hair clippings as well. When I walked back into the community, two or three people, having smelled the burning hair, asked me if that was part of my religion. I did not discourage that interpretation, because I knew that it was important not to let body parts fall into unknown hands, otherwise one risked injury from sorcerers.

CRITICAL TURNING POINT

In every research project that I have done there has been a critical turning point – an event or situation that has determined whether the project continued or was abandoned. In Olowo the moment of truth was sparked off by the census/questionnaire. About every two months my wife and I left the community for the Yoruba mainland, a day's trip by boat, and from there to the University of Ibadan where I was affiliated with a research institute. We had lived in Olowo for six months when we decided to take another break. The rapport that we enjoyed by then exceeded anything that we had anticipated. The research was flowing along smoothly, we were healthy, and we enjoyed the company of many friends. Best of all, we had fallen into a routine that reduced our anxiety about living in such an isolated community.

By the time we left for Ibadan I had administered the census/questionnaire to three-quarters of the community. This included everyone in the male sector, and about one half of the female sector. A young man had got into the habit of accompanying me from house to house, and I decided to employ him as an assistant. Before leaving for Ibadan I left him with one hundred copies of the census/questionnaire form, with the idea that I would check a sample of his work on return. About ten days later we were back in the community. Immediately it was clear that something terrible had happened. People refused to greet us at the dock, and ignored us on the boardwalk. Later that evening, one of my closest informants slipped into our room and explained what was going on. Apparently the *oba* and the elders were incensed over the census/questionnaire. The *oba* ordered the young man who had become my assistant to stay away from us, and indeed gave the same command to all of my informants. The next day I tried to arrange an audience with the *oba*, but was refused. Later the following day a formal letter was delivered to my room. In the letter, the *oba* accused me of using the census/questionnaire to collect intelligence information (for whom, I never did find out, but it must be remembered that the Biafran War was then in full swing, and it was common knowledge that I had lived in Biafra for two years).

Needless to say, things were very tense. To make matters worse, I learned that the principal of the school had flogged one of my main informants, simply because he had associated with me. I was incensed, and decided that even if it meant giving up research in the village I was going to make my feelings known. At the school I confronted the principal, accused him of vicious behaviour, and at the same time made some rather nasty comments about the community. While I was at the school, as I later learned, my wife, distraught because of all the tension, had burst into tears. These two incidents – my confrontation with the principal and my wife's anguish – brought everything to a head. We were almost immediately summoned to the palace where the *oba* greeted us with friendliness and compassion. Sitting around him were most of the educated young people in the village. He explained to everyone present that he had granted me permission to use the census/questionnaire, and then indicated what had gone wrong. First of all, the assistant with whom I had left copies of the instrument had entered people's houses and arrogantly ordered them to cooperate with him. This greatly angered the elders, who were puzzled by the instrument in the first place. To make matters worse, when the assistant found nobody at home, he stole valuable items such as radios and sold them at night in a nearby village.

To make a long story short, we were exonerated. The next day the *oba* took me for a ride down the main boardwalk in his car, the only one in the community, and a few days later we were his guests in his speedboat. During the meeting at the palace the *oba* asked me why I was associating mostly with the young men, some of whom he described as rascals. I explained that the high-status elders and women seemed reluctant to talk to me. The next day in the church he ordered these people to give me as much time as I required, and for the next couple of months, thanks ironically to the debacle over the census/questionnaire, I worked with the elders and with women, thus filling a large gap in the data. When we had first returned to the community and I had learned what had happened, I had a sickening feeling that the *oba* would confiscate the nine hundred or so forms of the census/questionnaire that had been completed. The second night back I coded the questions, and transferred all the data to index cards that I fortunately had brought with me. As it turned out, not a word was ever said about the completed forms.

It was clear that I would not be able to operate openly with systematic techniques again. One of my adjustments was to turn to the structured interview. My usual procedure was to select a category of people, such as those who worked in the shoe factory, design a questionnaire, memorize it, and then work with a sample of individuals in the category. I also developed a technique which I now regret having done, because of ethical considerations. From the nine hundred completed forms of the census/questionnaire I would draw a simple random sample, and then arrange for a trusted informant to join me in my room at night to provide information about the people in the sample, such as whether they had more than one wife, or had ever attempted to escape from the village. This technique certainly provided rich, systematic data, but had my informant been discovered, he probably would have been punished, and my wife and I may have found ourselves on a one-way trip to the mainland.

WITHDRAWAL

How do you decide when you've done enough fieldwork? Certainly not on the basis of what you have learned, because you could spend five years or a lifetime on a project and still not know everything. Fieldworkers usually wrap up a project when they have spent a conventional amount of time at the job, formerly a couple of years, now twelve months or so. In my own case, research in Olowo came to an abrupt conclusion when one of my brothers unexpectedly showed up from Canada. By then I had lived in Olowo for fifteen months during 1969–70; had my brother not appeared out of the blue, I don't know when I would have called it quits, and in fact I returned in 1972 and 1974 for two further stints of research.

Case Study Two: The Radical Right in Canada

White people are an endangered species. Inter-racial breeding is more dangerous than the atomic bomb. Race riots are natural manifestations of antipathy between different species, and are occasions to rejoice. Blacks are an inferior species and must be kept in their place. As regards Jews, there is no place in this world for them. There is an international Jewish conspiracy to gain control of the world. Democracy is a Jewish invention to promote the conspiracy. The Holocaust is a hoax. God is the original segregationist. As one fascist put it, 'God is a racist. The seventh commandment means no race mixing. Had God wanted coffee-coloured mongrels, He would have made us this way.'

Such are the pernicious beliefs held by members of the Canadian far right. In the pages that follow, it will be apparent that the methodology in my study of the radical right was quite different than that in the study of the Nigerian Utopia. This was partly because of the different subject matter, partly because the one project was done abroad and the other at home, and partly because in the interim I myself had changed my mind about how to do fieldwork.

CHOOSING THE PROJECT

As I have remarked elsewhere (Barrett 1987), one doesn't just wake up in the morning and decide to study white supremacists and anti-Semites. Several factors took me in this direction. A friend from Nigeria who had moved to Canada was attacked by several youths, and this and other incidents suggested that racism was becoming more pronounced and overt in the country. Then, too, I had stopped believing in a value-neutral, objective social science, and had started to argue that research should contain an explicit moral component. Coupled with all this was the argument that research actually is subversive, undermining those who are investigated, plus the suggestion that white people who want to make a positive contribution to race relations should study white-controlled institutions and the victimizers rather than the victims. Finally, there were my own ascriptive characteristics: small-town background, Protestant upbringing, white skin, and age. As one radical-right member commented, it is perfectly natural to be a socialist when young, but anyone over the age of thirty-five who still is a socialist should be shot.

RESEARCH DESIGN

Because my attempt to proceed deductively in the Nigerian study was a disaster, I made no effort to build pre-existing models in the Canadian study. I did, of course, read widely on racism, anti-Semitism, fascism, political sects and movements, and the existing literature on far-right groups. The purpose, however, was simply to identify analytic problems that were important to investigate. In short, my procedure was conventionally inductive, and my aim was to produce a thorough, rounded ethnography.

GAINING ENTRY

Before fieldwork could begin, two questions had to be answered. First, was the project feasible? Would right-wing members agree to talk to me, and would it be safe to meet them? Second, would the research do more good than harm, or would it simply provide the racists and anti-Semites with free advertising? To answer these questions, I consulted several anti-racist organizations and academics with experience in race and ethnic relations. The consistent answer was that members of the radical right probably would agree to meet me under tolerable conditions, and that a study of the far right would be extremely valuable, especially if it were an in-depth one.

Having been given the green light, I then fell into a trap that often catches fieldworkers: putting off entry into the field as long as possible. The usual pattern is for anthropologists to hide in a hotel room reading Agatha Christie. In this case it amounted to repeated visits to the library, and further consultations with academic specialists. Finally, I took the plunge. I telephoned a man whose fascist roots went back several decades, and arranged to meet him a few days later. His first question when we got together was whether I was a Jew. I said no, and for the next several hours he talked about the far-right movement, and his own deep involvement. This was the beginning of the fieldwork phase of the project, which lasted for almost exactly five years.

CHOOSING ROLES

Compared to the West African project, in the study of the Canadian right wing I had to make a much greater effort to define my role and control the research situation; otherwise my own strong anti-racist views would have made the research impossible. Before attending my first meeting with the member of the radical right, I tried to think of a role that would work. I decided to approach the aging fascist as if he were my grandfather. For an hour or so before meeting him, I concentrated on the grandfather-grandson relationship, and kept it in mind throughout the eventual interview.

This same procedure was followed in other interviews. First, I would try to come up with a plausible, effective role. Then I would spend an hour psyching myself into the role before the actual meeting. For example, early in the project I was virtually forced to meet a huge, middle-aged man whose reputation for violence was intimidating. He had been a noted athlete in his youth, and I decided to approach him as if he was Gordie Howe, a hockey player who continued to dazzle his opponents even at the age of fifty. The first question the man asked me was whether I was gay. I quickly led the conversation in the direction of sports, and the man's own athletic career. Finally, I dropped the topic, and sat back and listened as this reputedly dangerous individual opened up about the right wing, his own organization, and its prospects for the future.

MANAGING DEVIANTS

Early in the project two individuals proved to be particularly chummy. One was a long-time member of the right wing who on occasion had been a police informer. He was a subject of mirth and disrespect in the movement, and not surprisingly saw me as someone who would at least listen to him. The other person actually was a freelance undercover agent – that is, he sold his talents to police forces – but I did not find that out for several months. All that I realized was that for some reason or other he had a great need to associate with me. In fact, by the time I finished the project, this man, a lone wolf if ever there was one, had formed a dependency on me, often telephoning me at home and asking me to meet him for dinner or drinks. As he pointed out, he was in limbo. He had to restrict his interaction with the police in order not to blow his cover; but because he was an agent rather than a genuine member, he could not form any lasting friendships within the far-right movement; nor, due to his personal views about racism, did he wish to do so. Simply put, I became his refuge.

In retrospect, I think that I relied on deviants in the project more than in any other study that I have done, which perhaps was unwise. Given the difficulty of penetrating the far right, however, it was always tempting to spend time with people who knew the inside story and were eager to talk about it.

TECHNIQUES

Two main techniques were used in this project. One was archival. An enormous amount of material on the right wing existed, some of it in newspaper articles, some of it in university libraries and provincial archives. But the most important material consisted of in-house publications produced by organizations such as the Ku Klux Klan, the Western Guard, the Nationalist Party, and the Aryan Nations.

The other technique was the unstructured interview. In order to add depth to the project, I decided to do face-to-face interviews. There is, however, a tremendous difference between interviewing people in a community such as Olowo where one plans to live for a year or so, and the one-shot interviews that characterized the right-wing study. In community research the fieldworker strives, in a sense, to become invisible; when she or he does do interviews, they do not have to be elaborate or exhaustive, mainly because so much complementary information about the interviewees is available from merely living among them. When the interview is the primary source of data, however, the researcher attempts nothing less than to capture the interviewee mentally, to project his or her personality so seductively that people will open up as if they had known the interviewer for all of their lives. That describes the interviews with the members of the far right. Occasionally I did have opportunities to observe these people, usually when I dropped into bars that they frequented, but the main source of data, besides the archives, was the unstructured interview.

My approach can be described as deceptive candour. Racism, I would remark, is widespread in Canada. You bet it is, people would respond, and would add that isn't that wonderful. My reaction was simply to remain silent. Every now and then someone would question me about my personal viewpoint, but for the most part it was assumed that what I thought did not matter, because I had been a victim of a liberal-left education.

Although I usually dressed neatly for the interviews in sports jacket and tie, for some people, especially those with a reputation for violence, I dressed more formally in order to control the degree of social distance. Sometimes I met people in their homes, but most interviews were conducted, by my preference, in public places such as bars, restaurants, and libraries. Although I had anticipated great difficulty in arranging and conducting the interviews, I was unprepared for the depression they created. After each interview, especially with the more fanatical members, I felt soiled. This was to such an extent that I wondered at times if I could continue in the research. In other projects I have conducted two or three interviews day after day. Not so in the study of the white supremacists and anti-Semites. I found that I was only efficient when I did interviews sporadically, two or three at most a week. This is one reason that it took me five years to complete the fieldwork. I should add that in this project there were other benefits to stretching it out. It took a long time to build up contacts, not only in the right wing itself but also in anti-racist organizations and among infiltrators who were goldmines of information. Occasionally I would be taken by an infiltrator (police or otherwise) to a right-wing meeting or house party. Almost always the research would be shallow. The right wingers would be confused, because I had been brought by a person whom they considered to be a genuine racist, as to whether I was a researcher or a potential member. As a result, it was impossible to probe analytically to the depth that was required.

CRITICAL TURNING POINT

The circumstances surrounding the moment of truth in this project were bizarre, to say the least. Almost two years after beginning the interviews, I applied to the Canadian government for a research grant. One day, out of the blue, the head of security at the university where I taught telephoned me and requested an urgent meeting. As I soon learned, a message had been passed on to him by one of the country's police agencies that a far-right organization had managed to get hold of my research proposal. How? A member of the organization worked in the branch of the government that dealt with issues such as multiculturalism and ethnic relations. The leaders of the organization apparently were shocked and angered with what they read in my proposal, and considered ways of dealing with me (none of them, apparently, involving violence). I am not going to spell out in great detail how I handled the situation, except to say that deceptive candour played its part; in short, I met with leaders of the organization, and frankly told them I had received a grant from the government. Not only did they withdraw their threat to cut me off from further contact with the right wing, but curiously the outcome was similar to that which had transpired in Olowo. During the meeting, I had complained about the difficulty of arranging interviews with women and with ordinary (sometimes wealthy) supporters of the organization. Arrangements were made for me to meet these sectors of the membership.

In the Nigerian project I did not use a tape recorder, nor did I in the study of the right wing except when I interviewed James Keegstra, a former mayor and secondary school teacher in Alberta whose peculiar interpretation of Christianity had led him in the direction of racism and anti-Semitism. It no doubt makes sense to use a tape recorder when only a few interviews are planned, and the investigator is dependent on the close analysis of a moderate amount of data, or in projects where exact transcripts of speech patterns are required, such as in discourse analysis. But in a project involving two or three hundred interviews, the tape recorder becomes a cross to bear. The time involved in transcribing such interviews, not to mention the expense if the job is hired out, is enormous. Moreover, taped interviews are often not transcribed until weeks or even months later (sometimes never), by which time the fieldworker may have forgotten the context in which they were conducted.

My dislike of the tape recorder may be purely idiosyncratic, and not something that should be passed on to students. Yet in my judgment the preferred procedure is to write elaborate notes, including interpretations, as one does research. Incidentally, the reason why I taped the interviews with Keegstra was that he was facing a court charge at the time, and I thought I might have to be able to verify what he told me at some future date. Ironically, the batteries went dead halfway through the second interview.

In this project I did not take any notes when conducting interviews. Instead I followed a system of memorization that I had developed in Olowo when it became clear that it was no longer possible to openly employ systematic techniques. As an interview proceeded, I mentally organized the data into categories and themes, and memorized striking quotations. Every few minutes, with part of my attention still on what the person was saying, I rehearsed the growing scheme in my mind. By the end of the interview I had the mental equivalent of a detailed table of contents; transferring it to index cards, which I did in private immediately following an interview, was merely a matter of 'reading' the table and elaborating on the categories. Sometimes this turned out well enough so that no further writing was necessary. Usually, however, I merely took an hour or so to jot down rough notes, and wrote them up more elaborately and thoroughly the next morning.

Although there doesn't seem to be much written about memorizing techniques in anthropology (psychologists have more to say about the subject), my guess is that many fieldworkers have developed aids comparable to my own. And let me make one thing crystal clear: I do not have an unusual capacity to memorize things. In fact, whenever I force my mind to follow the procedure described above, it groans and complains. But what I have found is that once I have made the effort, and got into a routine, the mind eventually cooperates.

As in the Nigerian project, I continued to use index cards for my field notes, but I only made two copies, not three. I also abandoned my earlier practice of placing 'a' and 'b' beside the actor's and the observer's interpretations.

When the fieldworker lives in a community such as Olowo, there is no difficulty in contacting people. In a project like the right-wing research, however, the challenge is much greater. My procedure usually was to ask each person whom I interviewed for names and telephone numbers of other members in the movement. Sometimes I had already been given this information by infiltrators and anti-racist organizations, but could not use it unless the members had a public profile. Whenever I went to conduct an interview, I tried to let someone I trusted know who I was meeting and when I expected to return. Throughout the course of the project I also attempted to keep my family in the background by encouraging right-wing people to contact me, if they wished, at the university where I was employed. Indeed, one of the great differences between this project and the one in Nigeria was the role played by my wife. In Nigeria my wife, although not an anthropologist, collected important data. She also contributed greatly to the rapport we enjoyed, partly because she taught in the school, but mostly because she was so well liked. In the study of the far right, her activity was restricted to keeping tabs on me as I carried out the interviews.

WITHDRAWAL

As I remarked earlier, one usually stops fieldwork when the conventional length of time has been put in. The decision also can be based on one's mental outlook, as occurred in the study of the radical right. After almost five years of fieldwork, I found that I was jaded. I lacked the mental deftness required to conduct interviews, and began to talk back to some individuals. What tipped the scales, however, was a bizarre incident involving one of the several infiltrators whom I had got to know. A right-wing organization, on to his game, put a contract on his head, and the man came running to me for support. That was too much. On the spot, I terminated any further contact with the anti-Semites and white supremacists, content to wrap up some unfinished research with what I termed fringe-right people – those who bridged the gap between the far right and mainstream conservatism.

When one does research at home, however, withdrawal is not simply a matter of jumping on an airplane and flying off to one's country of residence. One continues to live next door to the research subjects, and what one writes is bound to end up in their hands. In the majority of projects this may merely encourage researchers to be more responsible, but in a study like I had done the consequences were potentially volatile. How would the members of the radical right react to my eventual book? What kind of book should I write – an academic tome, or something accessible to lay people? What about tone? Should the book be low-keyed, cool, and objective, or should it drip with outrage that organizations such as the Ku Klux Klan had a foothold in the country? My decision was to write a book with as much clarity as I could muster so that it would be accessible to a wider audience, to subtly underline my own anti-racist stance, but not to sacrifice scholarly soundness.

REFLECTIONS ON THE TWO PROJECTS

When I conducted my first research project, the study of the Nigerian Utopia, I was in what can be described as my scientific phase. Anthropology, I thought, was an objective, value-neutral discipline, or at least should be. At the time I was essentially a structural functionalist, with dabs of conflict theory thrown in. In retrospect, there is little doubt that I overemphasized systematic techniques at the expense of the conventional tools of participant observation and informants. There also were ethical problems which I shoved to one side, under the guise of objectivity. Conventional fieldwork is to a certain degree two-faced, in that even friendships are to be exploited for data. Such was my admiration for a few individuals in Olowo that I decided I would not include them in my research, but these were exceptions. Usually even the most informal encounter, such as exchanging greetings with a man on the boardwalk, was grist for the fieldworker's mill. It is this constant requirement of always being alert, even when sitting around with friends, not to mention the potentially dehumanizing impact, that makes fieldwork stressful.

During my three field trips in Olowo I did not pay informants, preferring to establish a moral relation with them. After the project had been completed, however, I decided I had a duty to do something, and inquired about the possibility of establishing a scholarship with the funds to come out of the royalties from my books. Immediately there was an obstacle. The *oba* demanded the right to select the recipient, and since he apparently had in mind his own offspring, the project fell apart. As an alternative I provided funds to support one of my main informants in school on the mainland, but within a year he had dropped out.

As I think back on the project now, there are many fond memories. It was an experience that enriched our lives. Even a quarter of a century later, we still maintain contact with some of the people in the community, especially those who went on to university. Yet I cannot help but question the right that I had to undertake the study in the first place. This has little to do with whether or not the study was sound. In fact, most members of the community who have read what I have published seem to think that I got at least part of the picture in focus. The issue, instead, as the postmodernists have put it, concerns the presumed authority of the outside scholar to interpret people's lives.

By the time I had begun the study of the right wing, I was no longer wed to the ideology of value-neutral social science. Indeed, I had selected this project with the explicit design of undermining the beliefs and activities of the anti-Semites and racists. My implicit assumption was that a different ethics operates when studying racists compared with studying the victims of racism. No doubt some anthropologists will take exception to this assumption, and will regard what I have labelled 'deceptive candour' as unprofessional. Yet I have written with the victims of racism and anti-Semitism in mind, and I continue to regard my approach not only as justifiable, but also as the most ethically defensible project that I have ever done.

Conclusion

Depending on where one plugged into the anthropological enterprise in the 1960s – the reigning models, the methods literature, or actual field-work – one got a different view of the discipline. The major models such as cultural ecology, social action, and conflict theory all gave the impression of being scientific, or at least of aspiring to science; yet the latter two models unwittingly moved the discipline further away from science. The methods literature, for its part, became even more devoted to the goal of science, while fieldwork itself seemed to be a combination of science and art. To some extent, then, the theoretical literature, the methods literature, and actual fieldwork had begun to head towards different points on the compass, a trend that picked up speed during phase three.

PART THREE: DEMOLITION AND RECONSTRUCTION

6

Theory

By the 1970s and 1980s it was evident that something strikingly different was taking place in anthropology. For the previous one hundred years the discipline had swung back and forth between hard and soft versions of science, emphasizing objective conditions such as technology and environment at one point and subjective conditions at another, portraying people as robots controlled by a rigid social structure, or active, manipulating agents in an ever-changing universe. Yet throughout these various shifts in perspective the goal of a scientific study of society persisted.

With the emergence of three new theoretical orientations – structuralism, postmodernism, and feminist anthropology – the vision of a natural science of society was essentially abandoned. The appropriateness of positivism, with its emphasis on empirical data, evidence, confirmation of hypotheses, and cause and effect relationships, was sharply questioned by the structuralists. The postmodernists and feminists, in turn, aimed their cannons at that shibboleth of anthropology – the fieldwork enterprise. Rather than being objective and value-neutral, ethnographic research was accused of cultural and gender bias, as powerful and privileged academics misrepresented the lives of natives and women for the ultimate benefit of the Western male. Science itself was dismissed as an ideological mechanism which reinforced hierarchy and capitalism. If research is to have a future – and some writers, especially the postmodernists, came close to advocating a post-fieldwork era – explanation can no longer serve as its prime purpose; instead, research must be unapologetically subjective and political, a vehicle to promote the welfare of people who lack power. In other words, the aim was not merely to patch up the scientific foundation of the discipline as had occurred in phase two. It was nothing less than to dismantle the discipline and start all over again.

1. Structuralism

Structuralism in the 1960s and 1970s was a theoretical perspective with a distinctive conceptual and methodological approach that emerged in several disciplines, including anthropology, linguistics, literary criticism, psychoanalysis, and philosophy. Although it offered an alternative to positivism for the human sciences in general, I shall concentrate solely on the version that took shape in anthropology.

BASIC FEATURES

1. *Deep structure versus surface structure.* Rather than focusing on empirical, observable behaviour (surface structure), structuralists examine the underlying principles and variables (deep structure) that presumably generate behaviour. These principles characteristically take the form of oppositions: nature versus culture, male versus female, left hand versus right hand, earth versus sky, hot (thermodynamic) versus cold (static). Or they consist of logical relationships such as the available residential options in a particular descent system (for example, father's or mother's line). Or they allude to deep human contradictions such as incest versus exogamy. In any particular culture these principles are charged with specific symbolic meaning. However, there is no simple and direct connection between them and patterns of social organization. This is because the underlying principles can be expressed in alternative forms at the surface level. This partly explains why structuralists urge us to focus our analysis on deep structure, where the range of key variables is more confined.

2. *Primacy of unconscious over conscious.* Little attempt is made to examine the attitudes and ideas of people, or the norms that supposedly guide them, the assumption being that what motivates people lies beyond their consciousness at the level of deep structure. The Freudian overtones here will be apparent.

3. *Etic versus emic analysis.* Structuralism not only places priority on etic analysis, on the structures that lie beneath the surface of everyday behaviour, but also relegates to the explanatory sidelines the individual human being, whose motives and actions are largely irrelevant and merely distract the investigator. It is understandable, thus, why struc-

turalism has sometimes been described as having an anti-humanistic orientation.

4. *Emphasis on synchrony versus diachrony.* Rather than focusing on change or diachrony, structuralists are concerned with repetitive structures. The assumption is that different forms of social organization are produced over and over again by the underlying principles, which themselves remain relatively constant. In this respect, structuralism seems to be highly conservative, quite out of step with the contemporary emphasis on social change.

5. *Reversibility of time.* A distinction is drawn between chronological (or historical) and mechanical (or anthropological) time. Chronological time is cumulative; events unfold across history. Mechanical time is repetitive; events unfold across space. The underlying assumption, eminently challengeable, is that mechanical time fits the rhythm of the pre-industrial societies on which anthropologists have concentrated, where the social organization supposedly is faithfully reproduced generation after generation.

6. *Transformational analysis.* It is assumed that the different institutions of human existence – economic organization, marriage systems, architecture, play, and ritual – are merely transformations of each other, manifestations of the same finite set of underlying principles.

7. *Linguistic analogy.* Culture is like a language in two respects. First, just as there is no intrinsic relationship between the sound of a word and its meaning – instead meaning rests on the relationship of a word to the words surrounding it – aspects of culture derive their meaning in the context of the overall system of relationships in which they are embedded. For example, to call a man 'a real prince' might be highly complimentary or derogatory depending on the context. Second, culture is like a language in that the various cultural institutions constitute codes or messages. The task of the anthropologist is to decode these institutions, to tell us what they are saying.

8. *Focus on mental life.* While structuralist studies of social organization (including economic life and kinship) exist, the overwhelming emphasis has been on belief systems, cognitive maps, and oral or written thought. Undoubtedly the main focus has been on mythology, understood as a distinctive 'language' or 'code' that reflects the way the human brain operates and articulates fundamental themes, dilemmas, and contradictions in life.

9. *Neurological reductionism.* Behind the level of observable behaviour, or the surface level, lie the principles that generate everyday interaction.

Behind these principles at yet a deeper level is the human brain. The assumption is that culture is modified and restricted in scope by the inherent operations of the brain, which are thought to be universal across humankind. Structuralists strive not only to detect the impact of the brain on cultural organization, but also to explain how the brain works. Given the assumption that the principles of mythology approximate those of the brain, it is understandable why mythology has been the structuralist's workshop.

An everyday example of the impact of the brain on culture concerns the colour spectrum. This spectrum is a continuum, and thus there is no definite point where one colour ends and another begins. Yet we differentiate red, green, blue, etc. The explanation is that the brain naturally discriminates and categorizes phenomena, and that these categories take on symbolic significance in their cultural contexts. A concrete case is the widespread usage of red for stop and green for go, with yellow as the intermediary. In other words, traffic rules are seen as transformations of the fundamental operations of the brain.

10. *Dialectical method.* The brain, like a computer, is assumed to operate in terms of binary oppositions. Conventional anthropological knowledge has long held that binary oppositions are almost universally represented in cultural organization, the result, structuralists would claim, of the impact of the brain. From binary oppositions it was only a short step to the dialectical method: thesis, antithesis, and synthesis, supposedly reflecting the influence of Marx.

11. *Nature-culture bridge.* One of the characteristics of structuralists has been their willingness to tackle deep, philosophical problems. What makes humans human? How did they make the leap from nature to culture? Is there any difference between humans and other animals?

12. *Humans as classifiers.* Central to structuralism is the contention that what makes humans unique is their capacity for classification. This capacity is thought to be intrinsic to the human brain. To think is to classify. The first is impossible without the second. The propensity to classify is said to be universal among humankind, from hunters and gatherers to industrial capitalists, and marks *Homo sapiens* as a special kind of animal: an intellectual one.

13. *Reduced models.* Happily for anthropologists there are analytic shortcuts: reduced models. These are types of culture or categories of culture reduced to their most simple, elementary properties. In these situations, the layers of conscious thought, or ideology, norms, and rationalization, are relatively thin. This means that it is easier to get at the

unconscious or deep structure, and ultimately to expose the operations of the human brain.

One example of a reduced model is supposedly primitive culture. It is said to contain all the basic elements that characterize human existence everywhere, but portrays the essence of the human condition in stark, undisguised reality. The concept of the reduced model, even assuming that it made sense, was a mixed blessing. It justified a continuing focus on primitive society at precisely the point in history where anthropologists had to adapt to the fact that their bread-and-butter territory had virtually disappeared from the face of the earth.

KEY FIGURES

Claude Lévi-Strauss

Structuralism in anthropology was established almost single-handedly by Lévi-Strauss, a cultural hero in his own right in France, who was born in Belgium in 1908. Lévi-Strauss set out to redefine the entire approach to the discipline. He challenged the empirical, positivistic tradition, arguing that culture is more like a language or logical system of signs than a biological organism, which had been the analogy preferred by the structural functionalists. The implication was that the epistemological and methodological approach favoured in natural science was not appropriate for anthropology, or for the social sciences in general.

Lévi-Strauss's massive contribution to structuralism is reflected in the fact that all of the basic features introduced above are developed in his numerous books and articles, including the distinction between surface and deep structure. There are several reasons, according to Lévi-Strauss, for not focusing on surface structure. One is that at the level of observable human interaction there are too many facts, too much going on. Another is that these almost limitless facts are only loosely governed by cause and effect; in other words, at the empirical level there is a degree of randomness that makes systematic analysis exceedingly difficult. Moreover, everyday life, everyday consciousness, is shot through with rationalizations, as people attempt to justify their actions and beliefs to others and to themselves. It makes little sense, therefore, to tap into people's interpretations of their lives, because such interpretations will not likely correspond with behaviour. In redirecting anthropological analysis to deep structure, to the unconscious, structuralism guards the investigator from getting bogged down in the (misleading) data.

To illustrate what Lévi-Strauss is trying to do, let us consider the design on a colourful sweater. Structuralists like Lévi-Strauss would not be interested in the design per se. Instead their aim would be to discover the underlying rules (knit 1, purl 2, etc.) which produce the design. Similarly, when investigating cultural life the focus is on the underlying principles which generate the surface patterns, not the patterns themselves.

Lévi-Strauss refers to the human brain as 'the uninvited guest' in anthropology. His argument is that the cultural realm is significantly shaped by the brain's operations, especially the binary pattern. A fundamental example is the nature-culture opposition. Lévi-Strauss asks why we cook food items such as meat. His explanation is that cooking meat is a means by which nature is transformed into culture, or a means by which human beings distinguish themselves from other animals. Lévi-Strauss defines cooked food as fresh raw food that has been transformed by cultural means. He defines rotten food as fresh raw food which has been transformed by natural means. Lévi-Strauss always tries to reduce data to binary oppositions, and in his analysis of food preparation we have two of them: nature versus culture, and normal (raw) versus transformed (cooked or rotten).

While Lévi-Strauss threw fresh light on a number of classical anthropological topics, from kinship to social structure, totemism, and the logic of pre-industrial thought, he is best known for his imaginative analysis of mythology. He assumes that myths constitute a kind of language, one that stands midway between conventional language and the human mind. Myths, in other words, are vehicles which supposedly take the analyst close to the workings of the brain. Lévi-Strauss is less concerned with what myth tells us about the social world than what it indicates about the brain's operations. His interest, in other words, is not so much in what humans think as in how they think, although one of his major assertions is that myths revolve around fundamental human dilemmas and contradictions, such as that to live means to die.

According to Lévi-Strauss, one version of a myth is not better than another, nor do myths improve or become richer over time with new versions. Furthermore, it is possible to illuminate a version of a myth in 1990 with a version that appeared in 1890, or the reverse. Lévi-Strauss even attempts to explain myths that occur in one part of the world with those that are found in other parts of the world, thus rejecting what has been a basic methodological principle in anthropology: beliefs and behaviour must be explained in their specific cultural context. Lévi-

Strauss's apparently baffling procedure rests on the distinction between chronological (historical) and mechanical (anthropological) time. In mechanical time, cultural materials such as myth do not progress chronologically; they simply are reproduced across space. This explains why Lévi-Strauss jumps from one point in time back to another, or even across continents.

What Lévi-Strauss is advocating is a quite different and radical conception of causality. A cardinal principle in science is that a cause must precede its effect in time; or an independent variable must pre-exist a dependent variable. This type of logic, structuralists assume, is inappropriate in societies geared to mechanical time. Rather than cause and effect, there are transformations, such as the different versions of a myth. Although Lévi-Strauss has drawn a distinction between observation (gathering empirical data) and experimentation (manipulating models consisting of relations abstracted from empirical phenomena), it is important to emphasize that his procedure is not the conventional one of confirming or disconfirming hypotheses empirically. Instead it consists of decoding the messages in a cultural institution, and tracing these codes as they are transformed from one institution to another.

Edmund Leach (1910–89)

Just as Radcliffe-Brown became Durkheim's public relations agent in the English-speaking world, Leach performed a similar service for Lévi-Strauss. Trained by Malinowski at the London School of Economics, Leach established his intellectual credentials with the publication of *Political Systems of Highland Burma* (1965; orig. 1954). Dissatisfied with the equilibrium assumption and organic analogy prevalent in anthropology at the time, Leach drew a distinction between actual behaviour and the anthropological models erected to explain it. Everyday behaviour is dynamic, messy, driven by choice, contradiction, and power; it is never in equilibrium. Anthropological models, in contrast, are always equilibrium models. The best the anthropologist can do is to erect 'as if' fictional models – fictional, because real life is never static. One of the novel features of this study is the assertion that in their everyday lives people do the same thing. They too erect 'as if' equilibrium models, which are ideal representations that provide a sense of orderliness in an otherwise chaotic universe. Leach's achievement was to retain a fundamental feature of structural functionalism, the notion of equilibrium, while simultaneously promoting the social action model contained in

Malinowski's work and later developed by people such as Bailey and Barth.

Leach was not merely a spokesperson for Lévi-Strauss. In several publications (1961a, 1962, 1966) he introduced his own version of structuralism. However, he has probably been best known for his attempts to explain Lévi-Strauss's imaginative capacity to provide new interpretations for old subjects such as myth and totemism. He also applauded Lévi-Strauss's success in making broad cross-cultural comparisons respectable once again. In another of his influential books, Leach (1961b:2) expressed a strong preference for Lévi-Strauss's grand comparative generalizations over the more controlled comparative method pursued by Radcliffe-Brown, dismissing the latter style as mere 'butterfly catching – of classification, of the arrangement of things according to their types and subtypes.'

Despite being Lévi-Strauss's English prophet, Leach, always a pugnacious maverick, did not hesitate to take the occasional swing at his hero. Whereas Lévi-Strauss saw structuralism as a special method, Leach stated that 'structuralism is neither a theory nor a method but "a way of looking at things"' (1973:37). Leach also pointed out that although Lévi-Strauss recommended that anthropologists spend a great deal of time in the field, his own fieldwork experience was brief and scanty. Leach also commented caustically on Lévi-Strauss's tendency to ignore the facts if they did not fit his preconceived assumptions, and to argue that if any facts corresponded with his theory that was enough to prove it valid (1974:20). Overall, however, Leach's appraisal of structuralism was enthusiastic. Indeed, at one point he remarked: 'Lévi-Strauss often manages to give me ideas even when I don't really know what he is saying' (1968:xvii).

EVALUATION

Lévi-Strauss placed the big questions about humankind back on the anthropological agenda. What does it mean to be human? How does the human mind work? On what basis can it be argued that all humans are the same given the immense range of cultural variation? In some respects his approach to anthropology was decidedly progressive. He contended that the West is not privileged compared to the rest of the world; indeed, there are no superior societies. And he rejected the old anthropological distinction between pre-logical and logical thought, or between the pre-industrial and the industrial world.

Lévi-Strauss threw out conventional, positivistic science, but not science per se. His argument was that structuralism constituted the appropriate scientific procedure for the investigation of culture. He conceptualized culture as a language system to be decoded, rather than a mechanism with synchronized parts or an organism with functions. In terms of epistemology, he offered us transformations rather than cause and effect, and defined social structure not as a general representation of the empirical world, as Radcliffe-Brown and others had done, but rather as an abstraction or model in which the variables consist of logical relationships between things instead of the things in themselves.

In the 1960s and 1970s Lévi-Strauss was probably regarded as the most eminent anthropologist alive, and indeed he was widely read by people in other disciplines. Even in those days, however, sceptics abounded. Both Maybury-Lewis (1970:161) and Burridge (1968:114) complained that it was impossible to subject structuralist claims and hypotheses to empirical confirmation.[1] More recently, Hill and his associates (1988) have demolished the distinction Lévi-Strauss drew between mechanical and chronological time, corresponding to what he labelled cold and hot societies, especially in connection to myths. Their counter-argument is that myths do contain an historical, chronological dimension, and that the societies in which they proliferate are diachronic rather than synchronic.[2]

What is mildly astonishing, given the stature of Lévi-Strauss in the 1960s and 1970s, is just how quickly he has fallen from grace. Today the number of prominent anthropologists who continue to follow structuralism probably could be counted on the fingers of one hand. This may have been partly due to a growing impression that structuralism was more clever than valid. Yet the main reason that it lacked staying power, in my judgment, was that it dealt almost exclusively with mentalist data, failed to relate such data to the material world, and sidestepped the major social and political issues of the day. What it did instead was to rivet anthropology once again to a romanticized and distorted image of unchanging primitive society.

1 But see Mepham (1973:105–6) for an argument that rules for the empirical confirmation or testability of theories are ambiguous in science in general, and simply inappropriate for perspectives like structuralism where the focus is on transformations rather than correlations and empirical generalizations, and on language rather than mechanical and functional systems.
2 For a good discussion of Hill, as well as an argument that contemporary society continues to be impregnated with myth, see Zimmerman (1993).

2. Postmodernism

The 1960s and the years surrounding them, which correspond to phase two in my overview of theory, were marked by a deep crisis in anthropology. The old colonial empires had disintegrated, and the leaders of newly independent nations were not enthusiastic about the prospect of another wave of Western ethnographers, given their historical connection to colonialism and the emphasis on the traditional and the exotic. It was at this time that the expression 'data imperialism' made its appearance, with the charge that Western scholars were 'robbing' Third World nations of one of their valuable commodities. In face of a growing demand that research be useful and relevant, that knowledge for its own sake was insufficient, a new focus on 'development' and 'modernization' emerged (more often than not equated with Westernization), and a shift towards research in the rural sectors of Western Europe occurred, and even tentative steps towards fieldwork at home.[3] It was during this period that the first signs of a gap between theory and method became noticeable, with the methods literature continuing to pursue science, and writers such as Bailey and Gluckman introducing more complex models that pushed that goal further from reach.

In phase three things really began to change. Although Lévi-Strauss thought that he was still engaged in scientific work, it was a radically different version of science: non-positivistic and non-verifiable. With the recent prominence of postmodernism, the screw has turned full circle, for science has been pronounced dead. As Tyler stated, 'scientific thought is now an archaic mode of consciousness' (1986:123). Prior to postmodernism, some anthropologists may have doubted the possibility of ever achieving the rigour of the hard scientist, partly because they could not experiment with human beings in anything comparable to the controlled laboratory, and partly because of the immense complexity of human interaction; nevertheless, science was the ideal to which they usually aspired. Not so the postmodernists. For this new breed of scholar it was no longer the case of science being unobtainable due to technical obstacles. Instead, the very idea of a science of culture was

---

3 There was nothing very novel about the notion that research should be useful to society. Long ago Marx, Weber, and Durkheim had said much the same thing. It is a lot easier to talk about social engineering, however, than to meaningfully put it into practice. Not surprisingly, thus, it is dubious that the massive social scientific research on 'development' in new nations has had much practical benefit.

challenged on epistemological and ethical grounds. With regard to epistemology, the assumption that had guided anthropology since the turn of the century – that not only was it possible to describe and interpret other cultures, but that it was an advantage to do research abroad in order to achieve objectivity – was held up to question. As for ethics, postmodernists regard fieldwork as a political activity whereby powerful Westerners have traditionally represented (read 'misrepresented') the lives of non-Westerners, depersonalized and objectified them as scientific specimens, and indirectly propped up the West's hegemony over the rest of the world.

Postmodernism has penetrated several disciplines, such as literary criticism, philosophy, geography, and architecture. Although my focus will be on the version that has taken root in anthropology, it will not be possible to avoid some discussion of literary criticism, for to a very great degree it has driven the anthropological experiment.

BASIC FEATURES

1. *Challenge to anthropological authority.* The idea here is that it is incredibly arrogant for anthropologists to assume that they have both the capacity and the mandate to describe, interpret, and represent the lives of people in other cultures. The underlying assumption, reflecting the power imbalance in the colonial past between the West and the rest of the world, and the privileged status assigned to science, has been that people in other cultures lacked the capacity to speak for themselves.

2. *Dialogical and polyvocal approaches.* Postmodernism has more than its share of technical language, or jargon, such as dialogical and polyvocal.[4] These terms suggest a very different approach than the monological one which had previously dominated ethnography, with the only voice heard being the anthropologist's. Postmodernists argue that an ethnography always consists of multiple authors: the anthropologist, whose voice we hear as describer, analyst, and interpreter; and the voices of the research subjects and informants which are suppressed in

---

4 Commenting on the manner in which postmodernists pepper their publications with jargon, Abu-Lughod remarks: 'Despite a sensitivity to questions of otherness and power, and the relevance of textuality to these issues, they use a discourse even more exclusive, and thus more reinforcing of hierarchical distinctions between themselves and anthropological others, than that of the ordinary anthropology they criticize' (1991:152).

the ethnographer's text.[5] Postmodernists portray fieldwork as a deep and complex dialogue between the ethnographer and 'the natives,' a joint venture out of which meaning and interpretation emerge, and elevate the role of the subjects in a research project to a level equal to the fieldworker's.

A dialogical approach, it must be stressed, does not merely amount to tapping the actor's point of view. Most anthropologists (the cultural ecologists and evolutionists excepted) have always tried to do that. Instead, the anthropologist in her or his monograph relinquishes the mantle of authority and (somehow) provides equal room for the voices of the research subjects.[6]

3. *Ethnography as a literary text*. One of the novel features of postmodernism is the focus on ethnography as a type of writing, a type of literature, a text to be analysed by the tools of literary criticism. All ethnographies are said to be fictional, not in the sense of being make-believe or unreal, but in the sense of being made, fabricated, created. Just as a poem or novel can be analysed in terms of tone, style, and literary devices, the same holds for the anthropologist's monograph. This perspective highlights a critical dimension previously ignored – that a great deal of what anthropologists do is to write: inscribing myths and rituals, composing field notes, and producing articles and books for publication. One upshot has been to place ethnography within the fold of the humanities rather than the sciences. Another has been to make anthropologists more conscious about literary genres, and even to experiment with them. A case in point is Stephenson's highly readable 1986 account of the Hutterites, where straightforward ethnographic fact, theoretical and methodological commentary, dialogue, and snippets of the author's personal life are combined in a style that is deliberately discursive.

4. *A focus on interpretation and meaning rather than causality and behav-*

---

5 There is yet another voice – the reader's. Rather than portraying readers as passive passengers carried along in a single direction by the 'objective reality' of a text, postmodernists argue that each reader creates her or his unique interpretation of a text. Once again, then, the author's authority is undermined, because the author's control over a text's message is far from absolute.

6 One of the ways to do this is to follow the procedure of Boas and Malinowski of collecting and publishing vernacular texts. As Clifford (1980:525) points out, this serves two purposes. It permits the research subjects themselves to reappropriate their own texts, and it enhances the reader's capacity to evaluate and reinterpret the author's representation.

iour. Culture is regarded as a system of signs and symbols, a complex of meanings, a language – indeed, a text in its own right.[7] The task of the anthropologist is to join forces with 'the natives' and interpret it. The buzzwords in this procedure are hermeneutics and deconstruction. Hermeneutics is a literary device that supposedly enables the investigator to comprehend the manner in which natives decipher and decode their own texts or culture. Deconstruction involves breaking down 'essences' such as the family, female, and male into their individual components in order to illuminate the embedded dimensions of ideology and power.

5. *A trend away from grand theory and generalization*. All-embracing models, explanation, and prediction – the building blocks of positivism – are out. Positivism is regarded as both inadequate and immoral. It can't cope with the vision of culture as an endless complex of changing and contested individual interpretations and meanings; and by erecting abstract models of human interaction it promotes order and consistency at the expense of individual autonomy and variation, ultimately providing support for the dominant ideology.

Postmodernists, in contrast, emphasize the particular and the unique, valorize 'the other' (the subjects of research), and are comfortable with an image of social life that is inherently fragmented, disjointed, and incomplete.

6. *A renewed emphasis on relativism*. Relativism, a doctrine pioneered by Boas, emphasized the uniqueness of each and every culture, and milder versions of it were generally accepted throughout the discipline. This should have meant, one would have thought, the undermining of anthropology's comparative, cross-cultural method. Yet what relativism eventually boiled down to was the rather simple view that customs had to be understood initially in their specific cultural context, and that it was unacceptable to comment on the moral worth of customs, especially by comparing them negatively to those in one's own culture.

What is curious about postmodernism, especially at the current period in history where globalization and immigration have thrown cultures together at an unprecedented pace, is that relativism has been rediscovered with a vengeance. Yet the emphasis on relativism is perfectly consistent with the postmodernist mission to valorize the lives of

---

7 A text in the postmodernist sense need not be a written document. Oral tradition, folk tales, culture – indeed, anything infused with meaning and requiring interpretation – qualify as a text.

'the other,' and to promote (and even glorify) difference rather than sameness.

7. *Author-saturated rather than data-saturated ethnography*. Before postmodernism made its appearance, one's ethnography was judged by the quality of the data and the elegance and incisiveness of the analysis. Unlike sociologists, who were more prone to mimicking the style of the scientific paper, anthropologists often wrote in the first person. Yet even in anthropology the author's presence could not be prominent, because that might cast doubt on the soundness of the data and the objectivity of the investigator.

With postmodernism, it has been the author (or the multiple authors, if the dialogical aim has been realized) who has taken the centre of the stage. Reflections now abound on epistemological and subjective issues – how the author 'knows' a culture and interprets the data, how meaning is negotiated between the researcher and the researched, as well as self-conscious musings on the subjective experience of fieldwork. As Nader has observed, 'Anthropologists have moved from insisting that the anthropologist stay out of the ethnography to having the anthropologist's presence dominate the ethnography' (1988:153). Not surprisingly, then, in the postmodernist monograph we often learn almost as much about the author as about the people on which the research is focused.

8. *Postmodernism as an empirical entity*. A great deal of the debate between those attracted to and repelled by the postmodernist perspective gives the impression that what is involved is no more than an academic exercise. In fact, as Singer has put it: 'Postmodern anthropology is academic sport' (1993:23). The implication is that postmodernism is merely another theoretical perspective dreamed up by jaded (or perhaps mischievous) academics, with little connection to people's lives. This is decidedly not the case. Paralleling the academic postmodernist perspective are massive, ongoing, revolutionary changes in the empirical world.

The advent of modernism is conventionally traced back to the seventeenth century, the Enlightenment era of Voltaire, when science, rationality, and orderly progress began to be championed. The postmodern world, in contrast, is marked by cultural fragmentation on a global scale. Transnational corporations and mass communications have undermined cultural and national integrity. Wars, famine, and economic hardship have shifted Third World populations to First World nations, a phenomenon that Appadurai labels 'deterritorialization'

(1991:192). It is the West, however, where the postmodern academic movement has had the greatest impact, that has been most affected by these changes. As Trouillot has put it, 'the metanarratives of the West are crumbling' (1991:20). Included among these metanarratives are included the institution of science. Science now is regarded as just another type of story, no better than, and indeed possibly inferior to, the indigenous explanatory systems in other cultures. There has been a loss of faith in the West's economic and political superiority and a tendency for the fragments within nation and culture – ethnic groups and other kinds of interest groups – to displace well-defined social institutions, and for particularism and sentiment to overshadow the general and the rational.

Harvey (1989) regards postmodernism as a shield that protects scholars from the hard reality of global power and inequality. Perhaps he is correct, but the important thing is that behind the academic deception (or game) lie massive changes on the world scene – expressions, Jameson (1984) argues, of the late stages of capitalism.

KEY FIGURES

James Clifford and George Marcus

The turn towards, if not the origin of, postmodernism in anthropology can be traced to a single publication: *Writing Culture* (1986). Consisting of contributions from nine scholars, and edited by Clifford and Marcus, this highly influential volume sketches out the basic premises of the postmodernist perspective. Clifford begins his introductory essay with a focus on writing. Writing is what ethnographers do. But writing does not consist of the objective representation of other cultures, as we have usually assumed (or hoped), but rather of the invention or fashioning of ethnographic fictions. Ethnographies are fictional, Clifford explains, in the sense that they are partial constructs, incomplete images of the world as interpreted by the ethnographer, rather than in the sense of being false or fanciful.

If ethnographies are fictional, then they can be analysed as literary texts, plumbed for stylistic conventions, rhetorical devices, and allegory. In his later chapter, 'On Ethnographic Allegory,' Clifford asserts: 'Ethnographic texts are inescapably allegorical' (p. 99). What this means is that any cultural account tells a story about something else, something beyond the immediate data. To illustrate his point, Clifford turns to the

Mead-Freeman controversy which I discussed in chapter one. Mead, as we saw, portrayed the Samoans as a happy, stress-free, sexually-liberated people, a marvellous example of the malleability of human culture. These same Samoans, according to Freeman, were violent and anxiety-ridden, captives of biological conditions that control all humans. The Mead-Freeman controversy, Clifford observes, is not really a question about which account is accurate. Instead, it is an allegory depicting a Western mythic opposition: Mead's Apollonians and Freeman's Dionysians.[8]

In a literate world which includes indigenous anthropologists in other cultures, and a trend among Western ethnographers to do research at home, the anthropologist has ceased to be an heroic, authoritative figure. As Clifford points out, 'Anthropology no longer speaks with automatic authority for others defined as unable to speak for themselves' (1968:10). Although Clifford would probably not put it so crassly, one possible way of preventing the discipline from slipping even further is to adapt a strategy which gives voice to the subjects of research, to be dialogical rather than monological.

The other contributors to *Writing Culture* cover similar issues, from the failure of positivism to the author's pretence of authority, the power embedded in language, and the promises of a new perspective that treats ethnography as a literary text. Rabinow's chapter, 'Representations Are Social Facts: Modernity and Post-Modernity in Anthropology,' merits special attention because of his willingness to evaluate postmodernism critically, rather than promoting it as a religious-like revelation. Rabinow points out the parasitical nature of Clifford's approach: he feeds off the texts created by the ethnographer, rather than creating his own ethnography. While recognizing the benefits that accrue in treating ethnographies as literary texts, Rabinow remarks: 'The insight that anthropologists write employing literary conventions, although interesting, is not inherently crisis-provoking' (p. 243).

Clifford, according to Rabinow, argues that from Malinowski onwards anthropologists have employed two devices to establish their authority. First, there is a personal, subjective account which establishes to the reader that they actually were there, in the field, face to face with the natives. Second, the personal element in the body of an ethnography

---

8 These terms were employed long before by Ruth Benedict in *Patterns of Culture* (1934) in order to contrast people living in cooperation and harmony with others bent towards competition and destructive urges.

gives way to the supposedly objective presentation of the data, which stamps the work as scientific. Along the way, Clifford contends, the dialogical dimension of fieldwork is suppressed. Yet as Rabinow points out, Clifford's own publications (or texts) are not dialogical. In fact, by insisting on dialogue, Clifford has merely established his own criterion of authority (p. 244). Furthermore, states Rabinow, dialogical texts can be just as staged or contrived by an author as the old style monological ones.

George Marcus and Michael Fischer

Marcus was not only co-editor of *Writing Culture*, but also joint author of another influential study, *Anthropology as Cultural Critique*. Also published in 1986, the Marcus and Fischer volume attempts to evaluate what the reorientation of anthropology towards literary criticism has meant to the discipline. It should be noted that while they employ the expression 'interpretive anthropology' rather than postmodernism, the two terms mean much the same thing to them. Thus, early in *Anthropology as Cultural Critique* we are informed that behind the efforts to experiment with new, non-monological forms of doing ethnography lies 'a crisis of representation' (p. 8). That is, in a transformed world, where the ethnographer's mantle of authority has worn thin, what does an acceptable ethnography look like?

Marcus and Fischer state that ethnography has undergone a 'shift in stress from behaviour and social structure, undergirded by the goal of "a natural science of society," to meaning, symbols, and language, and to a renewed recognition, central to the human sciences, that social life must fundamentally be conceived as the negotiation of meanings,' (p. 26). Moreover, the ethnographic monograph, hitherto regarded as a straightforward presentation (not representation), has been rendered complex. On what basis can it be considered 'accurate' or 'truthful'? How is knowledge (or assertion) manufactured? What literary devices are used by the author to control the representation? What factors beyond the author's control – cultural and historical ones – shape a study's representation of cultural life, in a manner comparable to Said's Orientalism?

At the very heart of interpretive anthropology, according to Marcus and Fischer is relativism: 'interpretive anthropology might best be understood as the reinvigorated and sophisticated heir of relativism, the perspective which cultural anthropology pioneered and on which it was founded in the 1920s and 1930s' (p. 32). Previous anthropologists, they charge, had greatly minimized the degree of cross-cultural diversity in order to legitimate universal generalizations. Relativism not only corrects this error, but also enhances dialogue across unique cultural realms.

Two of the most important aims of Marcus and Fischer are to sketch out a meaningful procedure of cultural critique, and to demonstrate how to integrate the soft issues (meaning, symbols, voice, etc.) of interpretive anthropology and the hard issues of politics, economics, and historical change. The usual style of cultural critique, they contend, leaves much to be desired. Anthropologists have typically presented a romanticized version of other cultures in order to devalue materialistic Western society. Moreover, the comparison usually has rested on nothing more solid than the ethnographer's own experience as a member of Western society. Marcus and Fischer reasonably argue for a new style of anthropological critique in which the fieldwork at home is as extensive and thorough as that abroad.

Their attempt to integrate interpretive anthropology and a political economy perspective is considerably less impressive, and the stumbling block is culture, or at least its presumed causal impact. They complain that the political economists, especially Marxian-oriented ones such as Eric Wolf, downplay the significance of culture, assigning it mere ideological status. Yet Marcus and Fischer themselves recognize that, as a consequence of worldwide changes, the very notion of authentic, distinctive, self-contained cultures is an anachronism. It is somewhat curious, then, that they continue to envisage the anthropologist's role as documenting the 'distinctiveness among cultures' (p. 43).

Clifford Geertz

Geertz, an American cultural anthropologist, enjoyed an international reputation as far back as the 1960s, but it was in the 1970s and 1980s that his influence peaked, especially as a result of his efforts to establish a new perspective: interpretive anthropology. In recent years he has nudged Lévi-Strauss aside as the discipline's reigning genius. In his widely read 1973 essay, 'Thick Description,' Geertz wrote: 'Believing, with Max Weber, that man is an animal suspended in webs of significance he himself has spun, I take culture to be those webs, and the analysis of it to be therefore not an experimental science in search of a law but an interpretive one in search of meaning' (p. 5). Rather than generalizing across cases, which is the normal scientific procedure, interpretive anthropology aims for 'thick description' by generalizing deeply *within* cases (p. 26).

Geertz's name is closely associated with the turn to postmodernism, especially the emphasis on texts and writing and the switch from structure and causality to meaning and interpretation. In a footnote in 'Thick Description' (1973:19), the opening and key essay in *The Interpretation of Cultures*, he remarked: 'Self-consciousness about modes of representation (not to speak of experiments with them) has been very lacking in anthropology' (p. 19). In another influential article, 'Deep Play,' (1973:448), he portrayed culture as 'an assembly of texts,' and compared ethnographic analysis to the penetration of a literary document. Elsewhere he stated (1973:15) that 'anthropological writings are themselves interpretations, and second and third order ones to boot. (By definition, only a "native" makes first order ones: it's *his* culture.) They are, thus, fictions; fictions, in the sense that they are "something made," "something fashioned" ... not that they are false.'

All this sounds remarkably similar to the version of postmodernism later developed by James Clifford and his colleagues, and indeed several commentators (Harris 1993, Shankman 1984, and Marcus and Fischer 1986) have pointed to Geertz as the scholar who laid the perspective's foundation. In my judgment, however, there is a sizable gap between Geertz's brand of anthropology and postmodernism. For one thing, Geertz continues to regard his interpretive perspective as a science. Then, too, not everyone agrees that Geertz's interpretive anthropology and postmodernism are identical. Rabinow (1986) separates and contrasts the two perspectives. Clifford (1983:132:3) observes that in 'Deep Play' Geertz suppresses the dialogical element, allowing only his own voice to be heard. Spencer (1989:147-9), who refers to Geertz as 'one of the discipline's foremost literary dandies,' claims that since the 1960s Geertz's writings allow less and less space for readers to agree or disagree with him. As Spencer wrote, 'In Geertz's world ethnographic accounts are assessed on a take-it-or-leave-it basis' (p. 148). Crapanzano (1986:74) refers to Geertz's 'phenomenological-hermeneutical pretensions,' and says that Geertz only gives us *his* interpretations, not those of the natives. The usual criticism of the previous generation's ethnography was that it was underanalysed. Ironically, Crapanzano's charge is that Geertz's ethnography is overanalysed.

Sangren (1988:422) alludes to 'the patricidal' treatment of Geertz in *Writing Culture*, many of the contributors having previously been heavily influenced by Geertz. Geertz, on his part, refers to *Writing Culture* as 'an interesting collection of the very good and the very bad, the knowledgeable and the pretentious, the truly original and the merely dazed' (1988:121). Geertz also talks about the tremendous loss of nerve on the part of anthropologists today, reflected in and possibly caused by postmodernism. In his words, 'Indeed, the very right to write – to write ethnography – seems at risk' (1988:133). All this suggests that while postmodernism was partly inspired by Geertz, he is less than thrilled by the direction in which this new perspective has moved. Karl Marx, reflecting on the manner in which his own arguments were distorted, apparently quipped, 'I am not a Marxist.' One of these days we may hear Geertz state, 'I am not a Geertzian.'

EVALUATION

Although postmodernism has undeniably had an immense impact on anthropology, the critical reaction against it has been vigorous. My impression, indeed, based on the corridor talk that takes place informally in academia, is that many anthropologists who possess only the most rudimentary knowledge of postmodernism have been quite prepared to dismiss it as nonsensical. Let me enumerate some of the criticisms.

First, postmodernists demand that the author as the sole authority step down, that books be dialogical, recognizing all the voices that are involved. Critics retort that this goal is not feasible. Ultimately, it is the author who selects the evidence and themes, and organizes the study. Recall Rabinow's comment that even Clifford's writings are not dialogical. Yet Clifford would not disagree. He fully recognized that the author remains in the 'executive, editorial position,' and he alludes to plural authorship as a utopia (1983:140). His point merely is that dialogue is the goal to which ethnographies should strive.

Second, postmodernism may amount to a post-fieldwork model. If research, especially in other cultures, is unsound both on epistemological grounds (how can we 'know' the other) and on ethical grounds (what right do we have to represent the other), why not give up the exercise completely? Jonathan Spencer suggests that postmodernism provides an excuse for not doing primary research at all,[9] and adds

9 Jarvie makes much the same criticism, and dismisses postmodernism as navel gazing (1988:428).

about *Writing Culture*: 'it seems more than likely that the book will pro-
voke a trend away from anthropology, and towards ever more barren
criticism and meta-criticism' (1989:161). A related comment is that postmodernism, by encouraging self-conscious reflections on what it was
like to be in the field, and on how the fieldworker makes sense of the
data, is incredibly self-indulgent. Yet Marcus and Fischer condemn
exactly this tendency, labelling it a form of exhibitionism, and implying
that it is not a necessary feature of postmodernism (1986:42).

Third, postmodernism, with its heightened sensitivity to 'the other,'
and its critique of positivistic, colonial anthropology, appears to be radical, even revolutionary. Yet Spencer has commented: 'If *Writing Culture*
is to be taken as evidence for a more wholehearted subjection of anthropology to literary theory the possible gains look meagre indeed. I would
go so far as to suggest that, despite its trappings of political and intellectual radicalism, it is in some of its preoccupations a depressingly reactionary document' (p. 145).

It would appear that by placing so much emphasis on ethnographies
as texts, and analysing them independent of political and economic
institutions, some of the most significant dimensions of social life such
as who eats and who starves are ignored. Recall, however, the attempt
of Marcus and Fischer to integrate the postmodernist and political economy perspectives. It also is relevant to point out that in his preface to
Writing Culture, Clifford candidly observed that a textual analysis can
only partly cope with the larger issues of institutionalized inequality
and global political and economic constraints. What he requests is that
the limited explanation that postmodernism does provide be evaluated
with fairness rather than bias.

Fourth, it sometimes is contended (Bailey 1991, Harris 1993) that
there are no standards in postmodernism, that one cultural account is as
good as any other, that anything goes. Clifford heatedly rejects this criticism, and implies that 'good' ethnographies can be regarded as 'true fictions' (1986:6 and 24). While the criteria in literary criticism employed to
measure the quality of a text may be ambiguous and debatable, the
same can be said about so-called scientific criteria, at least when applied
to cultural materials.

Fifth, Sangren (1988:408–9) sees postmodernism primarily as a power
play, with academics jockeying for influence, mobility, tenure, and promotion. While postmodernists never really deny this aspect – indeed,
Rabinow (1986 and 1991) has gone on at length about the micro-politics
of academia and the hiring game – Friedman (1988:427) charges that

Sangren fails to understand that postmodernism is articulated with changes in society that have undermined science and Western academic authority.

Sixth, some anthropologists such as Bailey and Harris take postmodernism to mean that the very foundation of the discipline as the study of other cultures has been a false program, and that cross-cultural comparisons are impossible. I suppose that is one possible interpretation of the swing towards a revitalized relativism. Yet cross-cultural analysis, as we have seen, is at the very heart of the study by Marcus and Fischer. Moreover, what postmodernists seem to be advocating is a means of communicating cross-culturally that will actually work in a world where the authoritative voice of the ethnographer has lost its clout. Dialogue, in fact, can be taken to mean not just a variety of voices assembled together in a text, but rather a profound exchange between individuals located in different cultural settings.

There does seem to be, nevertheless, a lingering contradiction within postmodernism. If the ethnographer cannot know a culture other than her or his own, if the dialogical aim is utopian, and if anthropological texts are distorted representations which enhance domination of 'the other' – all of which undermine the epistemological and ethical basis of ethnography – the obvious solution would seem to be to switch the focus of research to one's own society. Certainly writers such as Clifford and Marcus and Fischer occasionally recognize that there now is a bona fide anthropology at home. Yet the works that they hold up as models for the postmodernist perspective have almost entirely been based on fieldwork in other cultures. Indeed, it is quite remarkable just how many of these have been set in Morocco (Crapanzano 1980, Dwyer 1982, Rabinow 1977), a country with a heavy-handed political apparatus and a wide gulf between the haves and the have-nots – much like the colonies which attracted anthropologists in the past. Some critics, as it was shown, regard postmodernism as a post-fieldwork orientation. It could be argued that by placing so much emphasis on reworking old ethnographies, postmodernism, like structuralism, has salvaged anthropology's focus on other cultures (especially in the pre-industrial world) at the very moment when it has been threatening to disappear.

The last comment notwithstanding, it would be unjustified to dismiss postmodernism out of hand. If the massive changes in the empirical world that have been lumped under the postmodernist rubric are in fact real – and there is little reason to doubt it – our theoretical and methodological stances must fall into step. It may well be that some of the claims made by postmodernists, such as the death of science, will not stand the test of time. Yet it is difficult to imagine a future anthropology insensitive to textual dimensions, unaware of representation and all that it entails. In the final reckoning, the fate of postmodernism will be played out in the fieldwork setting, because a theoretical perspective which is debated almost entirely in the abstract cannot long endure. Lévi-Straussian structuralism is a case in point. Assuming that there is much to praise about postmodernism (as well as much to criticize), I suppose that its future will depend on the flexibility and inventiveness of ethnographers themselves.[10] This is because it is quite possible to imagine an anthropology without postmodernism. But an anthropology devoid of fieldwork is a contradiction of terms.

3. Feminist Anthropology

Two intellectual revolutions have swept through academia in recent years: postmodernism and feminism. Perhaps even more obviously than in the case of postmodernism, academic feminism has been paralleled and fuelled by ongoing actions and changes in the empirical world, notably in connection to the women's movement. Although feminism, like structuralism and postmodernism, cuts across several disciplines, prominent among them being sociology, philosophy, and literature, my main focus once again will be on anthropology, and for good reason. Anthropology has provided the basis for exploring numerous issues significant to feminism, such as whether gender roles and female oppression have been universally the same or culturally diverse.

BASIC FEATURES

1. *All social relations are gendered.* Not only all social relations but also all knowledge of them is gendered (Warren 1988:10). This means that gender must be included alongside class, status, role, power, and age as one of our basic or primitive terms – primitive in the philosopher's sense of being elementary.

This would seem to be an important breakthrough in social science

---

10 Two of my students have sketched out research programs guided by postmodernism. Shawn Chirrey (1994) has mounted a postmodernist study of medical practice. Jean Becker (1993) has examined what she claims to be a remarkable degree of overlap between the tenets of postmodernism and Aboriginal thought.

investigation, but it is not without controversy. Some writers such as Acker et al. (1989:77) applaud the focus on gender, rather than the more narrow focus on women, which they argue marginalizes and ghettoizes feminist studies. But in the words of Stanley and Wise, 'we see the study of gender as a de-politicized version of feminism akin to studying "race relations" rather than racism and colonialism' (1990:45).

2. *A distinctive epistemology*. The separation of subject and object, or researcher and researched, is rejected. Research should be a collaborative, dialogical affair. Subjectivity is associated with females, and is superior to 'male' objectivity (Whittaker 1994). Meis (1983) urges female scholars to incorporate their own subjective experiences of oppression into their research projects. MacKinnon (1983: 543) argues that the analytic basis of feminism is sexuality, and that its method is consciousness-raising.

3. *A distinctive ethics*. Knowledge for its own sake is insufficient. The primary purpose of research is to empower women and eliminate oppression.

4. *Anti-positivism*. The language of science is regarded as the language of oppression. Procedures involving hypotheses, operational definition, scales, evidence, and rules of disconfirmation are rejected. Positivistic research is said to serve the interest of elites. Value-neutrality, even if it were possible to achieve, would be ruled out, because feminist research unapologetically promotes the interests of women. The image of the orderly universe, another cardinal feature of positivism, and the tidy, logically tight models favoured in the past, are displaced by incomplete and fragmented ethnographies that arguably more accurately reflect people's lives.

5. *Preference for qualitative methods*. A distinction is drawn between 'male' quantitative methods and 'female' qualitative methods (Stanley and Wise 1990: 21). Mainstream, quantitative methods become 'male-stream' methods. Qualitative research has been given a shot in the arm by feminist scholars. Empathy, subjectivity, and dialogue supposedly allow the investigator to understand the inner worlds of women, helping them to articulate and combat their oppression.

Even interviewing, a central technique in contemporary anthropology, sometimes is accused of being too positivistic. In fact, Oakley (1981) bluntly asserts that interviewing women is a contradiction in terms. The explanation is that interviews have conventionally implied a distinction between expert and layperson, the purpose being to generate a body of objective knowledge. Genuine 'female' methods, in contrast, bring researcher and subject together as equals driven as much by politics as by knowledge.

6. *The life history*. A specific qualitative technique, the life history, quite prominent in the social sciences before the Second World War (see Dollard 1935), but pushed aside since then by the trend towards quantification, has been rediscovered by feminist writers. The life history is seen as a means to give voice to people, vividly to capture institutional and historical forces as they impinge on and are experienced by individuals; and to guard the wholeness and integrity of individuals rather than slicing them into analytic pieces which are packaged into generalizations, reflecting abstract features of the social structure.

7. *A female essence*. As it will be pointed out below, there is considerable controversy about whether it is justifiable to speak of a female essence (and thus of a male essence too). Such an assumption, one would think, would allow too much room for biological reductionism, and would fly in the face of diversity among women. Nevertheless, the notion of a distinctive female essence, of Woman writ large, has proved attractive as a counterbalance to misogynist representations.

8. *Universal sexual asymmetry*. Anthropology has proved to be fertile ground for examining two key questions. First, has gender inequality existed in all cultures at all times? The debate around this question has focused on gatherers and hunters. Some writers, especially Marxists (Leacock 1977 and Sacks 1979) have argued against the 'universal sexual asymmetry' thesis, contending that gender relations in gathering and hunting societies were egalitarian. Even the tendency in the literature to extol 'man the hunter' and ignore 'woman the gatherer' can be written off as another example of male bias. While there is general agreement that in comparison to other types of society, hunters and gatherers were remarkably unstratified, the jury is still out according to Lamphere (1977:624) as to whether they were completely egalitarian.

The other question is a great deal less ambiguous: as human society has moved through history from hunting and gathering to agriculture and industrialism, has gender equality increased or decreased? Although structural functionalists, as Tiffany points out, may have been inclined to argue that with modernization, and development gender equality has progressively increased, the overwhelming judgment of both Marxists and non-Marxists is exactly the opposite. Boserup (1970), Atkinson (1982), and Cebotarev (1986) all argue that with the emergence of agriculture and the state, with colonialism, modernization, and international aid programs, women's economic and political autonomy has declined. That may be the case in developing nations, but what about Western democracies? The general impression is that significant advances towards gender equality have been made, but like race relations, the gap between female and male worlds may be widening, and violence may be on the upswing.

9. *Anthropology of women versus feminist anthropology*. The anthropology of women was the forerunner to feminist anthropology. It began to take shape in the 1960s and 1970s in reaction to the implicit assumption in ethnography up to that point that the male world represented the entire world. To correct the gender bias there emerged a focus on women's roles and worldviews, such as Weiner's 1976 restudy of Malinowski's Trobrianders.

The anthropology of women perspective has sometimes been referred to critically as merely the 'add women and mix' stage. It certainly made the focus on women and gender inequality legitimate in the discipline, but it did not constitute a new perspective, one capable of transforming the existing male-oriented paradigm. Feminist anthropology, the second stage, marked a qualitatively different approach. The aim no longer was simply to expand the discipline's scope to include women's roles alongside men's; instead, it became nothing less than to erect a new paradigm that would serve as an alternative to conventional anthropology, thereby possibly revamping the entire discipline.

Feminist anthropology itself has gone through several mini-stages. First, there was the hope of an androgynous anthropology, in which the distinction between male and female would become meaningless; but given anthropology's androcentric history, this was an unrealistic aspiration, at least in the short run. Second, there was a shift in emphasis to female essence. Instead of minimizing gender differences, attention switched to the special, positive attributes of the generic female, offsetting old stereotypes that had undervalued women. Third, there emerged an emphasis on female diversity. This change in perspective largely came about because of criticisms that feminist scholarship was controlled by middle-class, Western, heterosexual, white women, who implicitly represented the so-called female essence. By stressing diversity, feminist scholars attempted to be more sensitive to the class, racial, and sexual orientation divisions among women, plus the different positions occupied by women in industrial and pre-industrial societies and in immigrant and non-immigrant populations.

Finally, there were signs of the emergence of a feminist paradigm. As Atkinson remarked, 'The ultimate goal of feminist anthropology should be not simply to supplement our knowledge but indeed to realign our disciplinary approaches' (1982:255). Feminist anthropology, in other words, should not amount to merely one more theoretical orientation alongside existing ones. Instead, it should constitute an alternative to conventional anthropology, one that both female and male scholars can embrace. This new paradigm often has been designated by the more narrow label of feminist methodology, reflecting the centrality of features such as dialogue and empowerment.

KEY FIGURES[11]

Marjorie Shostak

In 1969 Shostak took up residence among the !Kung, a gathering and hunting people also known by the pejorative term Bushmen who lived in Botswana on the edge of the Kalahari desert in Africa. Shostak was following in the footsteps of a Harvard team of anthropologists (see Lee 1979 and Lee and Devore 1976) who six years earlier had initiated an ambitious study among the !Kung ranging from nutrition, genetics, and child-rearing practices to ritual and folklore. From the outset Shostak was not satisfied with the generalities about social organization and belief systems that have been characteristic of ethnographic investigation. She wanted to probe deeper, to discover what it was like to be a !Kung, how they saw their own lives, what made them happy and sad, how they felt about their spouses and children. As a young woman caught up in the women's movement in the United States, she especially wanted to find out what it meant to be female among the !Kung.

Over a period of twenty months Shostak concentrated on learning the language and gaining a general understanding of !Kung life. During this period she interviewed eight women, finding it easier to work with women than men. It was only two weeks before her departure that her research came sharply into focus, resulting eventually in the publication of *Nisa: The Life and Words of a !Kung Woman* (1981). Based on fifteen taped interviews with one woman, this life history of Nisa (a pseudonym) presents in her own words the sweep of her existence from her

---

11 There is an enormous feminist literature, and I cannot pretend to have a reasonably firm grasp on more than a portion of it. I should add that the choice of authors who are described here as key contributors has been quite arbitrary, reflecting those works which have particularly influenced me.

earliest memories as a child through marriage and the birth of her children to the edge of old age.

Atkinson (1982:251) has remarked that *Nisa* might well become a classic, and with good reason. The book is well-organized and clearly written. The author provides an excellent introduction to the !Kung as gatherers and hunters, plus short and relevant prefaces to each chapter. As an example of the dialogical approach and the aim of providing a rounded portrait of the individual rather than gross generalizations, and of conveying the meaning of life through a woman's lens, *Nisa* triumphs.

The story of this one woman, told vividly in her own words, unfolds smoothly – perhaps too smoothly, reflecting the guiding hand of the author. Shostak's achievement, I might note, has not gone unnoticed by the postmodernists. In *Writing Culture*, both Pratt (1986:42–9) and Clifford (1986:98–110) selected *Nisa* for special attention as an experiment in ethnography that is both polyvocal and humanistic.

As impressive as *Nisa* is, it is not unblemished. Some eyebrows may be raised by the fact that only in the two-week period before Shostak's departure did the focus on the woman called Nisa crystallize. Yet that is exactly what often happens in fieldwork; the well-organized designs in research proposals go out the window as soon as one steps beyond the cocoon of the university setting. Shostak, indeed, deserves to be congratulated for adjusting to what she was observing and experiencing in the field. Much more bothersome is her lukewarm rapport with Nisa and other women. In her words, 'I did not become Nisa's "best friend," nor did she become mine. She rarely asked much about me, nor did she seem particularly interested in my life, and there was no doubt that the financial arrangements were important to her' (p. 42).

This apparent lack of deep rapport, and the businesslike arrangement that Shostak was forced into with Nisa in order to obtain her cooperation, raise considerable doubt about the validity of the central theme of the book: Nisa's obsession with sex. Indeed, it might not be too strong to describe *Nisa* as a mild form of pornography. Did Nisa's life actually revolve around sexual matters, or was she simply making it all up? Shostak herself candidly expressed scepticism about the trustworthiness of Nisa's information, and wondered out loud whether her own concerns with sexuality had led Nisa on. In the end, with the benefit of another fieldwork stint among the !Kung four years later, Shostak stuck to her guns: a pervasive interest in sexual matters did run through !Kung society. Nevertheless, Shostak revealed that another anthropologist had learned 'that the !Kung depicted me in one of their amusing (and often scathing) character portrayals as someone who ran up to women, looked them straight in the eye, and said, "Did you screw your husband last night"' (p. 350). Such was the reputation of Shostak's line of inquiry that apparently a woman only had to talk to her in order for her husband to suspect that she was having an affair.

Can Nisa be dismissed, then, as another example in which 'the natives' have spun a fanciful story to please the anthropologist and amuse themselves? Possibly. Yet *Nisa*, flaws and all, remains a successful experiment in feminist methodology. This is not only because it gives voice to and humanizes a !Kung woman, but also because of its honesty. Previous generations of ethnographers rarely exposed themselves to criticism by revealing their inadequacies as fieldworkers, or weaknesses in their data. Shostak's self-conscious, candid reflections elevate the ethnographic enterprise to a higher level.[12]

Marilyn Strathern

Is feminist anthropology merely a branch of mainstream anthropology, or do the two constitute separate approaches or paradigms? This question is provocatively examined in Strathern's 'An Awkward Relationship: the Case of Feminism and Anthropology' (1987a). Strathern, a British social anthropologist, begins by commenting on the failure of feminist studies to transform the disciplines that form the basis of academic study. Such a failure, in her judgment, is unsurprising, because feminist studies cut across disciplines rather than being isomorphic with them, thereby challenging vested interests. But anthropology, she suggests, is a different kettle of fish. Often singled out for its receptiveness to feminist thought, anthropology has in fact been *too* tolerant; it has absorbed feminist studies as just another approach among many. In other words, room is made for feminist anthropology without posing any challenge to the discipline as a whole, which thus thwarts the ultimate aim of feminist studies.

12 Much less known but possibly superior to *Nisa* in terms of textual analysis and dialogical approach is Julie Cruikshank's *Life Lived Like a Story* (1990). This book is much more complex than *Nisa*, mainly because the author allowed its organization and themes to be determined by the three Yukon women whose stories are related, reflecting their ways of looking at the world rather than the literary conventions of the academic writer. While Cruikshank's study is admirably collaborative, it is interesting to note that she did not intentionally set out to produce a postmodernist work (personal communication).

The 'awkward relationship' refers to the clash between interdisciplinary feminism and autonomous disciplines, and to the dissonance between the feminist goal of transforming anthropology and the mainstream response of packaging feminism as just another specialty within the discipline. It also turns significantly on a major difference between the discipline in general and feminist anthropology. This concerns the relationship to the other. In mainstream anthropology, and especially in the recent variety known as postmodernism, there is always a dichotomy between the researcher and the other; yet the central conceit of anthropology is that it is able to bridge the gap by promoting the actor's point of view, and perhaps even becoming multivocal. In feminist anthropology there is also a gap between the researcher and the other, the other denoting patriarchy or the male. However, rather than trying to bridge the gap, feminist anthropologists try to sustain it. In fact, as Strathern states (1987a:288), the other is a necessary condition for the existence of the feminist self. Collaboration with the other, so central to postmodernism, is by definition out of the question in feminist anthropology.

Strathern's work too found its way into *Writing Culture*. As Rabinow (1986:255) observes, Strathern is not trying to demonstrate feminism's compatibility with or contribution to mainstream anthropology; rather, she wants to reinforce the wall that separates them. The ironies, as Rabinow points out, are delicious. On the one hand we have postmodernists (most of them male) adapting a posture towards the other that is nurturing, sharing, and inclusive. On the other hand we have Strathern's anthropological feminists dwelling on difference, power, and hierarchy.[13]

Elvi Whittaker

In 'Decolonizing Knowledge: Towards a Feminist Ethic and Methodology' (1994), Whittaker, a Canadian anthropologist, provides an admirably clear picture of the problems and aims of feminist scholarship. She begins by observing that while feminism and postmodernism are often viewed as women's and men's struggles respectively, both are fundamentally concerned with representation – the representation of women by men, and of the cultural other by Western social scientists. Whittaker

---

13 For a more explicit treatment of postmodernism by Strathern, see her paper 'Out of Context: the Persuasive Fictions of Anthropology' (1987b).

argues that the relationship between women and men is comparable to that between the colonized and the colonizer. In both cases, Western, white, heterosexual males have imposed their worldview on the other (women and colonial peoples), subjugating the other and consolidating their stranglehold on the levers of privilege. Science, according to Whittaker, has played its part in the hegemonic control enjoyed by men, pushing the dubious assumption of objectivity, demanding a separation between subject and object, and claiming a 'truth,' an explanatory status superior to any other body of knowledge. In reality, Whittaker counters, science is a culturally fashioned, gendered enterprise which helps to reproduce the conditions that sustain patriarchy.

Feminist scholarship instructs women how to talk back, to articulate their own voices. Central to the feminist endeavour are epistemological and ethical issues, both of which are addressed vigorously by Whittaker. Feminist research, she argues, is 'an intellectual system that knows its politics' (p. 357). Knowledge for its own sake is secondary to the undermining of oppression and the active support of women's goals. Political activism and responsible scholarship are one and the same thing. The separation of the researcher and the researched has no place in feminist methodology. Subjectivity rather than an artificial objectivity prevails. Grand theory and all-encompassing models merely depersonalize and distort; feminism promotes multiple, contested truths (science being merely one of them), and ethnographic texts that are fragmented and incomplete rather than neat and polished finished products – the artifacts of science. Not only does the ethical mandate inform the choice of research topics and the use to which research is applied, but in addition feminism rejects the competitive 'buy and sell mentality' characteristic of male research, replacing it by collaborative, nurturing principles more akin to the mother-child relationship.

In case any ambiguity remains about Whittaker's forceful and polemical vision of feminist methodology, consider the following: 'The "research" scene in itself disappears. There are no questions, no questioned, and no curiosities to be satisfied. Instead there are agendas of mutual concern and knowledge constructed in consort with others. Ideally, the results do not have authors and authorities ... Interviewing and other positivistic techniques disappear. The authority of the researcher dissipates' (p. 358).

Whittaker offers us an elegant statement of the ideals of feminist anthropology, but just how feasible are these ideals in actual fieldwork? It is interesting to note that in her earlier study of the white experience in Hawaii (1986), an innovative experiment in ethnographic reporting in its own right, she found that the strong anti-positivistic stance that had accompanied her to the field could not be sustained. Like it or not, positivism intruded. While this does not necessarily mean that fieldwork will require a similar adjustment to feminist methodology, a question that she was moved to raise at the end of her 1994 paper is at least suggestive: 'What would a text resulting from feminist research look like?' (p. 359).

CULTURAL FEMINISM VERSUS DECONSTRUCTIONISM

What is a woman? That question goes to the heart of a debate between cultural feminists who assume a female essence and deconstructionists who claim that there are no essences at all, merely ideological constructs (such as 'woman') that reflect cultural bias and power. 'Cultural feminism,' explains Alcoff, 'is the ideology of a female nature or female essence reappropriated by feminists themselves in an effort to revalidate undervalued female attributes' (1988:408). The assumption of a knowable female essence has been intrinsic to the male representation of women. Cultural feminists reverse the negative image so that passivity becomes peacefulness and sentimentality connotes nurturing. From the perspective of the deconstructionists, the notion of a female essence, defined by either women or men, is nonsensical. Once constructs such as woman and man are stripped free of their ideological baggage, there is virtually nothing left, merely individual actors reduced to units in the social structure, devoid of will, meaning, and autonomy.

The cultural feminists and the deconstructionists both pose almost insurmountable obstacles for feminist anthropology. As pointed out by Abu-Lughod (1991), cultural feminism amounts to reverse Orientalism. In Said's critique, this meant accepting the rigid cultural representation imposed on the East by the West, but attempting to turn it into an advantage, such as Gandhi's emphasis on the greater spirituality of Hindu India. In similar fashion, cultural feminists portray the female essence in a positive light. The problem is that the representation of the East by the West and of women by men is not dislodged, exposing and destroying the underlying mechanisms of power and ideology. Indeed, in a way these representations are reproduced, because the positive twist introduced by Gandhi and the cultural feminists depends on their prior and continuing existence.

The implications of deconstructionism are, if anything, even more devastating. If the construct woman is merely a fiction, if woman does not exist except in an ideological sense, how can there be a feminist perspective and movement? As Alcoff observes, deconstructionism 'has the deleterious effect of de-gendering our analysis, of in effect making gender invisible once again' (p. 420).

Does the perspective emphasizing female diversity offer a reasonable middle ground between cultural feminism and deconstructionism? In such a perspective women constitute a socially significant category, but there is no typical female and thus no single feminism but rather several feminisms, reflecting differences in class, sexual orientation and race and ethnicity. As Harding observes, 'in many cases women's lives are not just different from each other's, but structurally opposed' (1992:181). Yet this immediately plunges us into another quagmire. In the face of female diversity, how can one say anything about gender in general? Is every segment of the female population unique? Does experience count for all, meaning that a person of colour cannot understand a person of European origin, and vice versa? Harding recognizes that women of colour, for example, through their lived experiences, do have a head start in terms of understanding themselves. And she argues forcibly that white women cannot speak *as* or *for* women of colour. Yet Harding also contends that categories such as gender, race, and sexual orientation constitute social relationships. That is, women define themselves in relation to men, and the converse, and also in relation to other women. For example, a middle-class, white, heterosexual woman is one who is not lower or upper class, not a person of colour, and not a lesbian. Harding's achievement, in other words, is to elevate female diversity into a holistic feminist perspective in which all the parts are interconnected.

Harding also offers some penetrating comments about female experience. Such experience is the bedrock on which feminist consciousness rests, but, she argues, it is not incorrigible. In her words, 'it cannot be that women's experiences or "what women say" in themselves provide reliable grounds for knowledge claims about nature and social relations. Women say all kinds of things – misogynist statements, illogical arguments, misleading statements about an only partially understood situation, racist, class-biased and heterosexist claims' (p. 185). If experience is not a sufficient basis or prerequisite for generating feminist knowledge,[14] does this open the door a crack for men's contributions? As Har-

14 Harding, not surprisingly, is critical of feminist standpoint theory (see Smith 1986 and 1987), which begins with the everyday world of women rather than with issues and

ding put it, 'it cannot be that women are the unique generators of feminist knowledge. Women cannot claim this ability to be uniquely theirs, and men must not be permitted to claim that because they are not women, they are not obligated to produce fully feminist analyses' (p. 183).

FEMINISM AND MARXISM

There would appear to be an almost natural affinity between feminism and Marxism. Both centre on issues of inequality and oppression, with women compared to natives, and both sometimes are presented as alternatives rather than supplements to conventional social science. In the anthropology of women stage in the 1960s and 1970s, Marxists such as Leacock and Sacks were prominent, and more recently Acker et al. (1989) had argued for a feminism based on Marxian principles. Yet there has been considerable disagreement, and even acrimony, between Marxists and feminists. Marxists charge feminism with promoting gender at the expense of class, resulting in an analysis that props up the ruling class. Feminists, in turn, accuse Marxism of being a male-oriented approach that serves the interests of men by promoting class at the expense of gender, thus obscuring women's issues (see MacKinnon 1982:517–18). The obvious solution is to bring gender and class together under one umbrella, but as Meis has observed, despite all the gains of the women's movement, there still is no clear understanding of the relationship between the exploitation of women and class exploitation (p. 117).

FEMINISM AND POSTMODERNISM

Feminism and postmodernism also appear to have a great deal in common. Recall the attention paid to Shostak's *Nisa* in *Writing Culture*, and Whittaker's observation that both feminism and postmodernism are fundamentally concerned with the issue of representation. Several other feminist writers have pointed out the parallels between the two approaches. Stacey (1988:25) argues for a greater degree of cross-

---

problems dictated by the literature. Stacked against feminist standpoint theory, according to Harding, is not just that women's experiences can be corrigible, but also the fact 'that there is no typical "woman's life" from which feminists should start thought' (1992:181).

fertilization between them. Opie has written: 'Following postmodernist theory I have argued for the production of texts which incorporate multiple voices' (1992:59). Stanley and Wise have actually used the expression 'feminist postmodernism' (1990:27).

When we consider the central importance of representation, the dialogical goal, and the preference for the life history technique shared by feminism and postmodernism, only one conclusion seems to be obvious: they are, if not intellectual siblings, then at least first cousins. Yet not everyone would agree. *Writing Culture* did not include any contributions expressing a feminist perspective, although it did include one female author.[15] Perhaps anticipating the flak that would follow, Clifford explained that 'we were confronted by what seemed to us an obvious – important and regrettable – fact. Feminism had not contributed much to the theoretical analysis of ethnographies as texts' (1986:19). Feminism, in other words, has not been sufficiently experimental. Yet it would be difficult to describe some books such as Bowen's *Return to Laughter* (1954), a sensitive and novel account of the human dimension of fieldwork, as anything but experimental.

Feminists began to question the value of an academic approach hinging on Western literary theory for the analysis of power relations that lay at the heart of women's struggles. It also was pointed out that there are significant differences in the relationship between the researcher and the researched in the two approaches. Postmodernists begin with a gap between the investigator and the other, which they attempt to bridge; but feminist scholars are part of what they study: women. Perhaps the sharpest criticism of all was launched by Mascia-Lees et al. (1989). They pointed out that postmodernism emerged at that juncture in history when Western white males no longer controlled the production of knowledge, when the anthropological other began to talk back, a consequence of the West's (supposed) reduced influence in the world. The response of Western males, no longer able to define the truth, was to claim that there is no truth, only literary conventions and multiple stories.

Mascia-Lees and her collaborators concluded not only that feminist theory and practice has much more to offer than postmodernism with regard to the task of understanding and confronting the political mechanisms that sustain patriarchy, but also that 'postmodernism may be

15 Abu-Lughod points out that not only feminists but also 'halfies' – people with mixed ethnic backgrounds – were left out of *Writing Culture*.

another masculine invention engineered to exclude women' (p. 427).[16] If that is so, postmodernism lines up next to traditional liberal anthropology and Marxism. All three supposedly have had one thing in common: they have subverted women's interests.

EVALUATION

Feminist anthropology, especially when fused with overlapping concerns in postmodernism, amounts to a powerful critique of positivistic anthropology, but a few doubts must be voiced. It is one thing to argue that knowledge for its own sake is not enough, that research must be driven by a strong ethical mission which translates into the improvement of people's lives. It is quite a different thing to reduce research primarily to a political agenda, with advocacy as its raison d'être. One reason is that this merely encourages the pendulum to swing in the opposite direction, back towards the arid production of knowledge for its own sake, an outcome which always seems to be encouraged by the culture of academia. What we end up with, then, is a split between activists in the street and analysts in the university.

In this context the history of Marxism is instructive. Marxists too advocated a fusion of theory and action (or praxis). But it has been mostly those committed individuals in Marxist organizations such as the International Socialists who have carried the ball. The more Marxism became accepted as a legitimate scholarly perspective in the university setting, the more it became tamed, with explanation overshadowing politics and its proponents mounting critiques of society while simultaneously digging themselves deeper into conventional middle-class existence (Pincus 1982). There are already signs, according to Meis , that feminism has experienced a similar fate: 'The present world-wide interest in Women's Studies may also be attributed to certain efforts to neutralize the protest potential of the movement. In many countries there is already a gap between Women's Studies and the Women's Movement' (1983:138).

Although there are several varieties of feminism, they all start off from the assumption that conventional social science has been male-biased. Eichler (1986) indicates four reactions to this charge. The first: don't do anything, it's business as usual; this, she argues, has been the

16 Their pungent attack on postmodernism did not go down well with everyone. See the exchange between Kirby and Mascia-Lees et al. in Kirby (1991).

manner in which most social scientists have responded (or failed to respond). The second: add women when convenient to one's analysis; Eichler labels this the liberal response, and it pretty well sums up the limited reaction of the majority of male scholars, including my own efforts in a recent study of rural Ontario (Barrett 1994). The third: woman-centred research. The fourth: nonsexist research.

While Eichler thinks that this last option is our ultimate goal, in her judgment it is necessary first to concentrate on the third option. Yet even woman-centred research is not necessarily free of male bias. In her words, 'a study may be totally on women, but if these women are seen only in relation to a social universe constructed around males it remains as sexist as if the work was totally on males' (p. 51). This observation underlines just how important it is to carve out a genuine feminist perspective, one that rivals conventional anthropology rather than is absorbed by it. It is an open question, however, whether feminist anthropology has achieved that stature, or can do so in the future, and even whether the gains that have been made will not eventually be whittled away by the conservative forces of old-time anthropology. Perhaps the realistic contribution of feminist anthropology will consist of the *process* involved in striving towards a non-sexist, liberating discipline, rather than in realizing the goal per se.[17]

Conclusion

In phase one the strong version of science was represented by British social anthropology (notably in connection to structural functionalism), the weak version by American cultural anthropology (principally in relation to historical particularism). In phase two the situation was reversed; it was the American school of cultural ecology that approximated nomothetic inquiry, with conflict theory and social action constituting pale versions of the scientific enterprise. In phase three it no longer made sense to talk in terms of strong and weak versions of science. Social anthropology, once the dominant school in the discipline, was deflated, reduced to scrambling in the direction of postmodernism in order to catch up to the action. Cultural anthropology, for its part, did not merely opt for a weak version of science: it rejected science itself.

There was, as always, more going on in the discipline than postmodernism and feminist methodology, even during phase three. A sort

---

17 For a useful source book on women in anthropology, see Gacs et al. (1988).

of underground anthropology, consisting of the conventional approaches in the past, continued to thrive, even if lip service was paid to postmodernism. I have assigned to this type of anthropology the somewhat unflattering label of no-name anthropology, a theme that will be explored in the next chapter.

Finally, what causes old theoretical orientations to die out and new ones to emerge in their place? In the hard sciences, the answer often has to do with the discovery of a superior model or technique, ones that can cope with unresolved puzzles. Rarely has that been the case in the social sciences. Instead, the main source of theoretical shift has been the special properties of their data base. The social world, to a degree unmatched in the world of nature, constantly (at times dramatically) changes. New theoretical perspectives must emerge to keep pace with social transformation. In addition, theoretical orientations in disciplines such as anthropology tend to rebound from existing orientations. For example, a new orientation such as postmodernism often consists of the polar opposite properties that were prominent in the orientations that they usurped, such as cultural ecology and political economy. Then, too, there has been a certain degree of circularity and repetition in anthropological theory. A case in point is the common ground between postmodernism and historical particularism, especially as regards the emphasis on subjectivity, relativism, and the presumed fragmented nature of culture. If all this seems to suggest that our bodies of theory do not always reflect the social world that prevails at any particular point in time, that is my intention. To expect more from theory is to misunderstand the sources that create them.[18]

---

18 For a fuller discussion of the sources of theoretical shifts in anthropology, see Barrett (1984b: chapter four).

7

Method

With the emergence of postmodernism and feminist methodology, science took a pounding. It was either pronounced dead or dismissed as an incomplete, biased story that propped up privilege. Yet in the methods literature the hope remained that qualitative research could be rendered as rigorous and explicit as quantitative research. In phase three it was not simply the theoretical and methods literature that were out of tune. The same held true for the fieldwork situation. In fact, a great deal of current ethnography simply ignores both the theoretical and methodological literature. The explanation, I assume, is that many ethnographers cannot stomach the scientism of the methods literature or 'the end of fieldwork' thrust in structuralism and postmodernism, and what might be called the sophisticated irrationality that characterizes much of postmodernism and some of feminist anthropology.

The type of ethnographic work that sidesteps both the methods literature and the two dominant theoretical orientations of the 1980s and 1990s is what I have labelled no-name anthropology. No-name anthropologists (if I can get away with the oxymoron) continue to do long-term fieldwork, to treat the data as if there was something more solid about them than the investigator's arbitrary interpretations, to employ techniques such as the interview, and to offer generalizations and identify causes and correlations. In other words, no-name anthropologists continue to do conventional ethnography. Some of them may well operate within an identifiable perspective from the past such as cultural ecology or social action, but by doing so they fight an uphill battle against a powerful opponent: the combined forces of feminism and postmodernism.

No-name anthropology may be both a good and a bad thing. It may be good in the sense of keeping the fieldwork enterprise alive during a period when so much of the literature is choked with agonizing discussions of meta-theory and meta-method. It may be bad if postmodernism and feminist anthropology, rather than being curious fads on the intellectual landscape, prove to have staying power. In that eventuality, no-name anthropologists will have scripted their own death sentences.[1]

The Methods Literature

In terms of the goal of science, it was business as usual in the 1980s and 1990s for the methods literature, which continued to be dominated by American anthropologists, although British anthropologists and sociologists had begun to contribute as well. General introductory texts, '10 easy steps to successful qualitative research,' still flooded the market (Agar 1980, Babbie 1983, Berg 1989, Burgess 1982, Ellen 1984, Hammersley 1992, Hammersley and Atkinson 1983), including a hefty volume edited by Denzin and Lincoln (1994). The same was true for retrospective texts in which fieldworkers reconstructed the methods employed in their projects (Dietz et al. 1994, Shaffir et al. 1980, Van Maanen 1983), and for the confessional genre in which the reader was invited to empathize with the fieldworker's experience (Anderson 1990, Ward 1989, Werner 1984). The list of publications on specific techniques and issues continued to expand: participant observation (Spradley 1980), sampling (Honigmann 1982), interviewing (Brenner et al. 1985, De Santis 1980, Douglas 1985), analysis (Gubrian 1988, Strauss 1987, Strauss and Corbin 1990), statistics (Gephart 1988), reliability and validity (Kirk and Miller 1986), semiotics (Manning 1987), educational ethnography (Burgess 1985, Dobbert 1982), and gender (Warren 1988).

During this period a new series appeared on qualitative methods, the Sage Series, but the books published in it, some of them seemingly aimed at the lowest common denominator in undergraduate courses, were uneven in quality, much below the standard of the Holt, Rinehart

---

1 In a sense there have always been no-name anthropologists. Many scholars have refused to identify themselves with any particular theoretical orientation, preferring instead an eclectic approach that draws from numerous orientations. I should add that the very notion of a theoretical orientation is somewhat ambiguous. A theoretical orientation essentially is what people in a discipline agree is an orientation. Usually it becomes identified as such when it is realized that a great number of researchers have used roughly the same approach in their studies. Occasionally, as in the case of Lévi-Strauss, the approach taken by a single, dominant figure can achieve the stature of a novel perspective.

and Winston series (see Kent 1989). Some methodological issues received more emphasis than was the case in the 1960s and 1970s, such as the politics of fieldwork (Adler et al. 1986, Brajuha and Hallowell 1986, Punch 1986), anthropology at home (Greenhouse 1985, Messerschmidt 1981, Narayan 1993), and critical evaluations of fieldwork (Borman and Taylor 1986, Bryman 1984, Geertz 1988, Richer 1988, Stocking 1983). Undoubtedly, however, the major change was the emergence of a literature on the use of computers in qualitative research.

Back in the 1960s Gilbert and Hammel (1966) and Hymes (1965) had written about computer applications in anthropology, but it was not until the 1980s and 1990s that the message began to get through (Bernard and Evans 1983, Conrad and Reinharz 1984, Fielding and Lee 1991, Gerson 1984, Podolefsky and McCarty 1983). By this time, of course, the typewriter belonged to the horse and buggy age, and writers who still put a pen to paper were virtual dinosaurs. As Tesch put it, 'Today, any qualitative researcher not using a computer at least for word processing is considered an oddity' (1991:225). The development and increasing sophistication of software programs such as the ETHNOGRAPH (see Seidel and Clark 1984; Seidel, Kjolseth and Clark 1985; and Seidel, Kjolseth, and Seymour 1988) and NUDIST (see Richards and Richards 1987, 1989, 1991), with their promise of a solution to the task of coping with the masses of chaotic qualitative data, made anthropologists stand up and take notice.

Richards and Richards (1987), the creators of NUDIST, condemned the degree of mystification that still existed in qualitative research, and contended that the program is much more than 'a super filing cabinet.' NUDIST is an acronym for Non-numerical Unstructured Data Indexing, Searching, and Theorizing. It is divided into a document system, an indexing system, and an analysis system. In the judgment of the Richards, it is the capacity of NUDIST to generate and test theory that is its most significant feature. The analysis system, they wrote, 'is a set of facilities for manipulating the indexing database in various ways in processes of category creation designed to help the researcher define and explore research ideas, find text relevant to complex ideas, pursue wild hunches in all directions, keep the fruitful ones, and formulate and test hypotheses' (1991:308).[2]

---

2 In this article, Richards and Richards join force with Anselm Strauss, emphasizing the compatibility of NUDIST with grounded theory, an analytic approach that I shall discuss in some detail in the next chapter.

While there can be little doubt about the value of computer programs for specialized fields of research such as discourse analysis, it is the claim that the computer can do the job of theorizing and interpreting in conventional ethnographic projects that raises the eyebrows of field-workers. Most of them, unless they are masochists, would probably agree that some sort of systematic organization of qualitative data is necessary. It is therefore easy to agree with Tallerico that programs like the ETHNOGRAPH do fill the bill as a super filing cabinet. The big question is whether they can do more than this. Tallerico, for one, is doubtful. She argues that 'the most important conceptual tasks can not be delegated to the microcomputer.' Software programs are no substitutes for the researcher's insights and interpretations. She also warns that there is a danger that the researcher will be seduced by the computer, giving it more attention than the data (1991:281–3). In her experience, students who use programs such as the ETHNOGRAPH have a tendency to exaggerate the scientific quality of their reports and dissertations, assuming that because they have used a computer their work must be valid.

Similar doubts have been voiced by Pfaffenberger (1988). He points out that the procedure of using key words to retrieve data glosses over their various connotations, from the literal to the ironic. Whereas most academics, even if they are sceptical about the capacity of the computer to take over the task of theorizing, would acknowledge the tremendous advantage of using the computer as a word processor, Pfaffenberger is even sceptical in this respect. He challenges the conventional view that the word processor is an asset in writing. A limitation of the word processor, he states, is that in writing it is important to see the overall structure of one's work, not just what is on screen. The solution would seem simple: print out a hard copy. But, as Pfaffenberger observes, this gives the impression of a beautiful, finished product, and puts us under the spell of 'the authority of the printed text' (p. 19). Because it all looks so good – so professional – there is a tendency to accept it prematurely as the final word.

It is, I suppose, an open question whether computer-assisted ethnography is the wave of the future, and whether the next generation of field-workers will find the awesome task of ordering, retrieving, and analysing their data to be no more complicated than playing around with a keyboard. I would, however, like to sound a mild warning. My impression is that those scholars who have been most enthusiastic about computer-assisted ethnography have themselves rarely done long-term field research. For these individuals (many of them sociologists), programs such as NUDIST almost seem to be a substitute for in-depth research, since on the basis of little data one can run dozens of cross-tabulations and correlations. This was not, of course, the scenario envisaged by the creators of these programs. What will be interesting is to see whether it becomes the model for ethnography in the twenty-first century.

The Fieldwork Situation

By phase three there was, obviously, an enormous gap between the theoretical and the methods literature, with the former veering sharply away from conventional science and the latter still hot on its tail. Both bodies of literature have been concerned with demystification, but in quite different senses. The methods literature engaged demystification at the level of technique, and attempted to show us how to do better science. The theoretical literature, especially postmodernism and feminist anthropology, approached demystification at the level of epistemology, and argued that it was science itself that was mystifying. The remedy was not more or better science; instead, it was less science and more humane, non-authoritarian, empowering, responsible scholarship.

A great deal of the energies of ethnographers during phase three was directed not to fieldwork as such, but to abstract debates of methodological, epistemological, and ethical issues, although feminist anthropology inspired more original research than did structuralism and postmodernism. Dorothy Smith (1986), for example, has examined the everyday life of women in the context of broader social and economic processes, taking care not to transform women into objects of research. Her starting point is women's experiences, and her aim is to provide women with the analytic tools needed to understand, and thus confront, the manner in which their experiences are shaped by the institutions in which they live. I think it is accurate to observe, however, that even today only a minority of ethnographers have done research guided by feminist methods.

By the 1990s a few changes in the fieldwork situation had become apparent. The life history had been revived as perhaps the principal technique. The comparative method was not quite dead – after all, even prominent postmodernists such as Marcus and Fischer continued to push it – but it was breathing hard, and for understandable reasons. The comparative method belongs to nomothetic inquiry. It has been the anthropologist's alternative to the controlled laboratory experiment. Indeed, it used to be thought that unless one could specify a number of logical comparisons in a project, one's 'problem' was neither sharp nor fruitful. With the attack against science in postmodernism and feminist anthropology, the comparative method has been pushed to the sidelines.

The ethnographer's conception of community has also changed once again. By phase two it had been recognized that no community was isolated, and that the external forces that impinged on it had to be taken into consideration. By phase three there was a subtle modification; outside forces didn't just intrude into the small community; they were an intrinsic part of the community, as central as the local council. In a sense, then, the macro-micro divide, often thought to parallel the urban and rural realms, no longer existed. It must be added that the conception of community also has been affected by theoretical concerns. By the 1990s community had become just another essence to deconstruct, like woman, man, or science. Little wonder, then, that contemporary ethnographers have moved away from rounded community studies, erecting instead life histories and favouring talk over observation.[3]

The tendency in phase two towards a shorter period of fieldwork has continued in phase three, possibly even more so. There was a time when an ethnographer's Ph.D. project constituted possibly the major piece of research that he or she would ever do. In fact, if one did not publish the thesis, one's reputation suffered. That no longer seems to be the case. Nowadays the attitude sometimes conveyed is that the thesis is an obstacle that has to be got out of the way so that one can finally turn to meaningful research.

While the major theoretical debates in the 1980s and 1990s centred around postmodernism and feminist anthropology, the bulk of ethnography continued to follow the techniques that had been forged in phase one, the rules of thumb that emerged in phase two, and various theoretical orientations that predated the two recent intellectual revolutions. This is what I have called no-name anthropology. It has not, however, escaped the influence of postmodernism. Postmodernism has to a considerable extent become the new orthodoxy against which ethnography

---

3 As Arensberg (1954) argued long ago, community study is not the study of community as such, as a territorial reality or subject matter. Instead it is a distinctive methodological approach. The small community, for Arensberg, constituted a naturalistic setting where social relationships could be investigated in the raw. In Arensberg's own words, 'Community study is not the study of whole cultures, or of communities ... It is the study of human behaviour *in* communities,' (p. 120).

is measured (Sangren 1988:409; Nader 1988:153). A case in point is *The Queen's People* by Carstens (1991), a study of the Okanagan people in British Columbia by a highly experienced ethnographer, based on extensive archival research and long-term fieldwork. The academic reviews of this study have varied from applause to cat-calling, sometimes a sign that an innovative work is involved. Lanoue (1991) patted Carstens on the back for allowing the voices of the Okanagan to be heard, and commented that it was 'as if the Okanagan and not Carstens' had written the book. In sharp contrast both Barker (1992) and Trigger (1993) criticized *The Queen's People* for failing to present the natives' point of view. According to Barker, only the author's voice is heard in the study. Barker ends his review by wondering whether the Okanagan regard themselves as the Queen's People, or whether that is only Carstens's imposed interpretation. From the book itself, Barker observes, the reader can't tell.

The Queen's People offers a sympathetic ear to the sufferings of the Okanagan at the hand of white people over the decades, and stresses the hegemonic throttlehold held by mainstream Canadian institutions. Yet Trigger argues that a major weakness in the book is its failure to recognize and analyse the degree to which Aboriginal people like the Okanagan have engaged in effective resistance since the white person's arrival.

Even more damning is a review by Wickwire and McGonigle (1991). Evoking the postmodernist critique of conventional, scientific anthropology, they dismiss *The Queen's People* as cultural appropriation, in which the author has robbed the Okanagan of their story and imposed his own interpretation. As Wickwire and McGonigle remark, 'it is Carstens' voice, not the voices of the Okanagan people, that is being heard' (p. 113). Even Carstens's explicit condemnation of white racism and hegemonic control is attacked by Wickwire and McGonigle. They too, like Trigger, censor Carstens for overlooking the capacity of subordinated peoples to resist, to fight back and survive. A generation or so ago it is probable that *The Queen's People* would have been universally praised both for its data and for its humanistic stance. In today's intellectual and political climate, however, the book has been easy prey to the guardians of the new orthodoxy.

Case Study Three: Social Change in Rural Ontario

Although I can think of several recent books that could be taken as examples of no-name anthropology, I doubt whether many of my colleagues would be pleased to have this label pinned on them, and in order to keep the peace I have selected my own 1994 study of social change in rural Ontario. As in case studies one and two, my aim is to convey in more detail what is involved in fieldwork methodology. For purposes of comparison, I shall later provide a brief description of my methods of research employed in a fourth project organized in terms of feminist anthropology and postmodernism: the study of gender and violence in Corsica.

Paradise, as I call the town in rural Ontario on which I focused, was founded in the late 1800s by British immigrants, the majority of them Protestants from northern Ireland. Set in the midst of farming country, it has been for most of its history a sleepy little community – until, that is, the 1970s. It was then that an invasion took place, as people from the city in search of affordable housing and a better quality of life moved en masse to Paradise and surrounding communities. Within the space of a handful of years, its population, previously about twelve hundred, almost tripled. The impact sent a shock wave through the village, splintering the values and identity that had once been so prominent.

It was not size alone that did the damage. Equally important was the diversity of the newcomers. Most people in Paradise had belonged to the United and Anglican churches. Among the newcomers were members of numerous Protestant denominations, plus Catholics, Hindus, Sikhs, Muslims, and Buddhists. The newcomers also transformed the ethnic landscape, their countries of origin spread over the globe; and for the first time in the history of the Paradise region there was a significant number of visible minorities, especially people who traced their ancestry back to Africa, India, and Pakistan.

CHOOSING THE PROJECT

The study of Paradise, unguided by postmodernism and feminist methodology, is not only an example of no-name anthropology, but also of anthropology at home – in this case, really at home, because it was where I lived for the first dozen years of my life. My interest in doing research in Paradise actually dated back to the project in West Africa. The two communities were roughly the same size, and I often compared them in my mind in order to understand more deeply the special characteristics of the Nigerian Utopia. Growing up in Paradise in the 1940s had been pleasurable in many respects, with baseball in the summer, hockey in the winter, trout fishing, and just enough hell-raising to make life interesting. Yet what stuck most in my memory were the different levels of the class system, with a few powerful families out of reach at the top, a bottom layer of penniless families, and hardly any movement upwards or downwards from one generation to the next. When I began research in Paradise in 1988, it was with the intention of studying the stratification system.

RESEARCH DESIGN

My plan was to undertake a systematic comparison of social class in the 1950s and 1980s. When I learned about the massive number of newcomers in the community, I expanded the focus in two directions. One was to study the migration process. This meant examining the reasons why people had moved to Paradise, and how they had adjusted to small-town life. It also involved an analysis of the commuting phenomenon, because for most of the newcomers Paradise was only their bedroom; their jobs remained in placed like Mississauga and Toronto, a distance of fifty to sixty miles. A portion of the newcomers, as I indicated, were visible minorities. Ever since I had completed the study of the radical right, I had been curious about the nature of racism and anti-Semitism among ordinary Canadians. When I discovered the tremendous ethnic diversity in Paradise and the area around it, I decided on a third focus: race and ethnic relations in rural Ontario.

The Paradise project was similar to the radical right project in that the procedure was inductive, with questions and problems to guide the fieldwork rather than preconceived models. It was similar to the Nigerian project in that some comparative work took place, but in a much less systematic manner. In Nigeria I had conducted a rigorous comparison between Olowo and another village that I called Talika. In the Paradise study I did research in surrounding villages and among farmers mainly to gauge whether there was anything atypical about Paradise.

GAINING ENTRY AND CHOOSING ROLES

In stark contrast to the radical right and Nigerian projects, gaining entry into Paradise was effortless. The community was located about an hour's drive from the city in which I lived, and I simply got in my car and showed up at the town hall. Because I had grown up in Paradise, and some of my relatives continued to live there, in my mind I still belonged to the community (at least to some degree), and I suppose my assumption, justified or not, was that I had a right to study it. Nevertheless, the reason I went to the town hall was to establish semi-formal contact with officials.

From the moment I entered the town hall, it was clear that research in Paradise would be a different experience from anything I had previously encountered. The town clerk, after hearing my name, came over to shake my hand, explaining that he had known my parents well and remembered my brothers. After chatting for a while, he personally escorted me to the building in which the local archives were kept, unlocked the door, and told me I could close up whenever I felt like it. When I returned to the town hall later that first day, one of the secretaries introduced herself, and quipped that she did not belong to the well-known family in town with the same surname. The reason for the qualification was immediately obvious to me; I remembered the other family as one of the poorest in the village when I had been a boy, with a reputation of being at the bottom of the ladder. Had I not lived previously in the town, I would never have grasped the significance of this woman's comment.

The role I adopted for interaction with the newcomers and minorities was uncomplicated. I merely presented myself as an anthropologist interested in social change in rural Ontario. Almost always I would explain that I had been brought up in Paradise, hence my interest in the community, but I never dwelt on the issue. This was because relationships between the newcomers, including the minorities among them, and the natives of the town were strained. From the perspective of many of the natives, the newcomers had destroyed the old way of life. From the perspective of the newcomers, the natives were stuck mentally in the nineteenth century, unwilling to put out the welcome mat.

My role for interacting with the natives was a great deal more complex and partly beyond my control. The natives saw me as both an outsider and an insider, a researcher and a bona fide Paradise resident. Most of the time this was an asset. It enhanced rapport, and took me quickly into the back stage. There were, however, problems. One was the ambiguity in some people's minds about my identify. A few of the older people who had known my parents and grandparents found it difficult to relate to me as a researcher. From their point of view, I was the son of old friends and acquaintances. As a consequence, interviews with these people were never satisfactory. It was simply impossible to probe analytically, at least to the degree that I wished. Nor was it a one-way street. I too was reluctant to transform human relationships into research.

Colleagues had forewarned me that there would be lots of obstacles to studying my own community, and they were right. Occasionally I experimented with interviews with childhood friends, but soon gave it up. Only if I had been willing to promote my research role at the expense of friendship – which I was not prepared to do – could I have continued with the interviews. Fortunately, however, in a town of over three thousand residents there are almost always an adequate number of candidates in any particular sector or category to make it unnecessary to select old friends. Overall, in fact, my past experience in Paradise was entirely beneficial. Not only did it help greatly with rapport, but it meant that I was in possession of information that would have taken an outsider years to accumulate. In a sense, in the study of Paradise I was my own informant.

MANAGING DEVIANTS

Given my past fieldwork experience, I would have been surprised if I had not encountered deviants early in the Paradise project. In one case it was not merely a question of an individual who did not quite fit into the community, but an entire family. Branded with a reputation for hard-drinking and indolence, and located at the bottom of the social scale, the members of this family were exceptionally bitter about their lives in Paradise. They believed that 'the hierarchy,' as they referred to those who controlled the town, had thwarted every attempt they had made to raise themselves out of poverty. Their complaints, apparently, were old hat in Paradise and generally ignored, which probably explains why they were so eager to talk to me.

Early on in the project I began to run into a middle-aged man almost everytime I stepped into town, and finally realized that he was attempting to make contact. He was an unusual individual, reputed to be extremely clever with machinery, and he was the one citizen of Paradise who drove the local politicians mad. Whenever there was an election, he loudly accused council members of corruption and ineptitude. This idiosyncratic man, a loner for the most part, had a most interesting and penetrating perspective about Paradise. His case illustrates a point made in an earlier chapter: while too much exposure to deviants can harm the fieldworker, they should not be ignored, because sometimes they have important things to say. I should add that in my experience not all, or even most, of the people who might be labelled deviants seek out the anthropologist. In Paradise, for example, there were individuals who kept everyone at arm's length, including me.

Incidentally, there is another kind of person the fieldworker is almost certain to encounter. This is the staunch defender of the public image. Such individuals are difficult to recognize early in a research project, because at that stage almost everyone offers a fictionalized version of the community. Because public defenders want more than anything else to keep the fieldworker away from the back stage, there is a tendency to avoid them, or to dismiss their perspectives as misleading nonsense. Yet to do so is a mistake. The ideal structure of a community, or the front stage, is as much a part of a community as the actual structure, or back stage. I have learned to welcome contact with the public defender in order to gain a clear picture of what a community is supposed to be like.

TECHNIQUES

My research in Paradise went through three stages. First, there was the pilot study, lasting about six months. My principal techniques then were archival, participant observation, and unstructured interviews. The local archives were rich in data, quite valuable for gaining a picture of the early years in Paradise, and for comparing the 1950s to the 1980s. During this period I intentionally tried not to focus on any specific problem, in order to be receptive to significant but unanticipated issues.

After about six months I turned to the technique that dominated the project – the structured interview. The version used with the natives consisted of thirty-three questions, and at the beginning I actually read each question from the form, and wrote down what people said. The result was disastrous. People were put off by the formality, too nervous to open up. Of course, I should have known better than to proceed in this stilted manner, and I soon changed my approach, memorizing all the questions, asking them informally and not necessarily in their order on the interview form. The cost of this more casual procedure is that not every question is always raised or answered fully. The benefits are much greater depth and more spontaneous, candid reactions from the interviewees.

In this project I took notes openly during each interview, which usually lasted two or three hours. Normally I did two interviews per day, occasionally three, but that was pushing it. It required just as long a period to write up an interview as to conduct it, and usually I did this late at night, or the next morning if I had arranged to meet someone or attend an event during the evening. As in my previous projects, I put all my field notes on large index cards and made two copies. The cards were arranged into categories important to the project, the largest ones consisting of natives, newcomers, and minorities. Like many other field-workers, I also kept a diary on methodological issues.

By the time the project was finished I had done more than three hundred interviews. In retrospect, I quite frankly am surprised that I put so much emphasis on the interviews. In my only other experience with a community study, Olowo in Nigeria, I also conducted interviews, but they were much less important than participant observation and informants. The reason that I think I turned to the structured interview as the principal technique in Paradise was that the community was so much less cohesive than Olowo. In Olowo there was a single church, and everyone knew each other. That was almost the way Paradise was back in the 1940s and 1950s, but not in the 1980s. By then the Ontario town was divided into natives and newcomers, with minimal interaction between them. It also was divided in terms of social class, and indeed it would have been difficult to locate any social event or situation which brought all the residents together. The structured interview was a way of coping with the limitations of participant observation, given the heterogeneity and fragmentation of the community.

I hasten to add that I did do a fair amount of participant observation. It became the dominant technique during the third stage of the project. My concern was that the structured interviews were too artificial, not sufficiently embedded in social life as it unfolded. More particularly, I was worried about a methodology that placed so much emphasis on what people said, on their reported attitudes. During the last six months of fieldwork I still conducted interviews, but concentrated mostly on participant observation, hoping to fill in the cracks between the interviews, and measure what people said against what they did. At the same time I spent a great deal of time with the several informants who had emerged over the previous three years, relying on them to interpret issues that puzzled me, and inviting their critical comments on my version of the community.

CRITICAL TURNING POINT

The critical turning point in this project was entirely personal in nature. About eight months after fieldwork had begun, one of my closest relatives died and was buried in the Paradise cemetery. For several months I found it mentally impossible to do concentrated research, and began to doubt my wisdom in deciding to study my home town. Eventually my spirits revived and I got back into the swing of research. Quite frankly, however, had I been able to foresee the family tragedy I might never have launched the project, because there is something unseemly about pushing the memory of a loved one aside merely to keep alive an academic exercise.

Something else was going on which slowed the project down, although it would be an exaggeration to describe it as a critical turning point. Like many academics, I had dismissed postmodernism and feminist methodology on the basis of nothing more than my own prejudices. I had not read these literatures, and the little that I knew about them was snatched from conference presentations and corridor talk. Halfway through the Paradise project I began to read widely on postmodernism and feminist anthropology. So many of the arguments touched a nerve. The prospect of an anthropology that reduced the authority of the writer, encouraged collaboration between interviewer and interviewee, and even empowered the subjects of research was seductive. Postmodernism and feminist methodology seemed to offer answers to ethical dilemmas that had agitated me ever since I had begun to study anthropology. I started to regard my approach to the Paradise study as out of date, a throwback to the days when the fieldworker made his or her way into the backstage by hook or crook, and when there was a predisposition to dismiss anything people said as fanciful.

Despite misgivings, I did carry on with the Paradise project. The book I eventually produced is solid enough, I hope, at least in terms of the type of (no-name) anthropology that it represents. Yet that is not the point. I suspect that when people express their displeasure about a book that has been written about them, it is not so much that they find the contents inaccurate and invalid – in fact, they may not even have read the book thoroughly; what upsets people is that they have been put under a microscope, treated like scientific specimens, and in that way dehumanized. As I continued to absorb the literature on postmodernism and feminist anthropology, I became acutely conscious of the moral limitations of my approach to Paradise.

WITHDRAWAL

As fieldwork comes to an end and the writing stage commences, a decision has to be made about whether to use fictitious names for the communities that have been studied. I used pseudonyms in the West African project, mainly because I had uncovered so much conflict that I thought it would be impossible to write about it without taking steps to protect the identity of the village. Yet Olowo was so well known in Nigerian academic circles that the pseudonym served little purpose. The same question arose with the study of the community in rural Ontario. After considerable reflection, I again decided to give the town a fictitious name, mostly because I had promised to protect the identities of the individuals who had been interviewed.

It might take people unfamiliar with Paradise a while to work out the identity of the town, but it is a different story for Paradise residents themselves. On a recent visit to the community I was surprised to learn about the impact of my book on the local council. If a meeting went well, councillors apparently exclaimed: 'Paradise found!' If a meeting was rancorous, they quipped: 'Paradise lost!'

Case Study Four: Gender and Violence in Corsica

If I had to sum up the essence of Corsica in a couple of words, it would be beauty and violence. This French island in the Mediterranean has it all: towering granite mountains which glow pink in the sunshine, chestnut trees and olive groves on the plateaus, deep green valleys through which flow trout-filled (and eel-filled) rivers, and stretches of clean, sandy beaches around almost every bend in the road. Then, too, there is the violence. From the sixteenth century to the beginning of the twentieth century, the dominating factor in Corsican life was the vendetta or family feud. In a population of just over one hundred thousand, the vendetta at its height claimed about one thousand lives per year. While both the victims and the killers were mostly men, women too were victims, and sometimes they avenged the deaths of family members. In one critical dimension, women were the principal players: it was their responsibility to sustain a state of vengeance, to instil hatred and revenge in the minds of their children.

Today the vendetta is a thing of the past, but violence in Corsica remains widespread. Bombings occur frequently, some of them connected to the island's independence movement, others motivated simply by personal enmity. There has, however, been one significant change. Whereas during the vendetta era both men and women were active participants, either as victims or perpetrators, in the contemporary era violence has become mainly 'men's work.' If women are involved at all, it is almost entirely as victims. In the past it was accepted that a man had a right to kill his wife even if he merely suspected that she was having an affair, and archival records show that in such cases the fine for murder was as little as ten francs. While it would be an exaggeration to state that nothing has changed since then, it is a fact that today when marital relations sour, Corsican women are often at the risk of severe physical violence.

Although I have not yet completed this project, I have included a brief description of it here as an example of research influenced by feminist anthropology and postmodernism, and to show just what can go wrong when one embarks on fieldwork.

The focus of gender and violence has a complicated and bizarre past. To begin with, I chose Corsica as the research site for all the wrong reasons. At the University of Sussex in England, where I was enrolled in a Ph.D. program, the majority of students were doing fieldwork in mountain villages in Spain, France, and Italy. Realizing that I might not be given permission to study Olowo, I had to have a viable alternative, and somebody suggested Corsica. I knew nothing about the place, but the very mention of the name of the island raised images of romance and intrigue in my mind. In 1974, en route to Nigeria, I spent a few weeks in Corsica, and was captivated. Somehow I had to do research there. As I talked to Corsicans and read about their history, the one thing that stood out in terms of anthropological significance was the vendetta. Consultations with Corsican scholars revealed that the only major study of the vendetta had been published in 1920 by a lawyer.

In 1978 I returned with my family to Corsica in order to begin a study of the vendetta. The first thing that went wrong had to do with my methodology. As I pointed out in an earlier chapter, while the problem under investigation is supposed to dictate our methods, we more often than not let our methods determine the project and the problem. That is precisely what I did at the beginning of the Corsican study. I was a fieldworker, and fieldwork I was hoping to do. After several weeks in a mountain village, however, I finally realized that if I was serious about studying the vendetta, rather than contemporary village politics or some other such problem, I had to give up fieldwork and concentrate on archival research.[4]

---

4 It should be noted that in recent years there has been an upsurge of research employing historical and archival sources and methods. See Wolf (1982), Goody (1976 and 1983), MacFarlane (1979), and Sahlins (1981). At the same time there has been an increased interest in the history of anthropology. See Trautman (1987), Ackerman (1987), Stocking (1987), Darnell and Irvine (1994), and Thornton and Skalnik (1993). For an interesting commentary on these trends, see Jarvie (1989).

I reluctantly made the adjustment, moved to the Corsican city where the main archives were located, and began to work with dusty papers rather than living people. About four months later the critical turning point of the project crystallized, and once again it was a personal matter. My daughter, less than a year old, became seriously ill. When her health failed to improve, we packed up and returned to Canada.

For the next few years I busied myself with other projects, and when I began to think about reviving the Corsican one in the late 1980s, I discovered that someone else had produced the book on the vendetta that I had had in mind (S. Wilson 1988). It was around this time that I was reading as widely as possible on postmodernism and feminist anthropology. Eager to begin a research project guided by these orientations, I began to think of Corsica as a possibility, especially the comparison of gender and violence in the vendetta era with Corsica today.

As stated earlier, I am still in the midst of fieldwork in this project, but what I am aiming for is a book in which the anthropologist's voice is muted, in which there is collaboration between the researcher and the researched, and in which Corsican people feel empowered rather than exposed by the study. Towards this end, my plan is to produce a few carefully constructed life histories of women and men, and even to explore the possibility of joint authorship with these people.

Quite frankly, I do not know if these goals are feasible. It is easy to enumerate the merits of a theoretical perspective and to sketch out an attractive methodological approach while sitting in the library. It is quite another matter to carry the plan off in the field. This project will be complicated from the outset by virtue of the two different sources of data: the archives for vendetta material, and fieldwork for contemporary material. Then, too, there will be self-imposed pressures to put the Corsican case into a broader comparative context, which will push the project towards conventional, scientific anthropology. Finally, even if these hurdles can be overcome, a question will remain about just how much a male anthropologist can contribute to gender studies. To reiterate what has been said before, men cannot write for or as women, but only about women.

Backlash against Feminist Methodology

A number of writers, most of them women, have launched a vigorous counterattack on feminist methodology. Michele Barrett (1986), for example, accused the advocates of a distinctive feminist methodology of having hijacked feminism, and blamed them for the unwillingness of the majority of sociologists to take gender seriously. Clegg (1985) contended that there is no such thing as feminist methodology. Coser, who uses the language of positivism such as 'testing our theories' and 'propositions,' stated: 'There is no male science, or female science' (1989:201). McCormack (1989) and Acker (1989) pointed out that there has been little that is new in the feminist critique of positivism, most of it having already been said by critically-oriented male social scientists. McCormack predicted that women who argue for a radical feminist methodology, who oppose science and reject objectivity and rationality, will never be taken seriously in academia. In a forceful reaction to feminist methodology, Lynn McDonald (1993) emphasized the manner in which positivistic, empirical research has benefited her own life-long work as a feminist. She traced the social sciences back to the philosophical era that predated the works of Marx, Weber, and Durkheim, and demonstrated the degree to which the contributions of female social scientists such as Florence Nightingale have been ignored. Rather than being conservative and reactionary, positivistic social science from its early days, according to McDonald, has often been radical, highly critical of the status quo. The various writers to whom I have just referred have made no bones about their opposition to feminist methodology and their attraction to old-fashioned positivism and empiricism. It must be pointed out, however, that some of the criticisms have come from scholars who have been much more sympathetic towards the goals of feminist methodology. Acker et al. (1983), for example, found that it was impossible to eliminate completely the treatment of the women in their study as objects. They had decided to share their data and analysis with these women but ended up only doing so with those who agreed with their feminist perspective. They even wondered if it had been ethical to impose their perspective on women in the project who were not feminists.

Then there was the goal of treating those who were researched as equal partners. As Acker et al. revealed, in their own project they could not avoid assuming the privileged position of experts (p. 429). In fact, the women in the project who did read the research report demanded deeper analysis and interpretation, not simply accurate description. In other words, they encouraged the experts actually to act as experts, thus widening the gap between academic and lay persons.

Opie (1992) concluded that no matter how hard one tries to let the voices of those who are studied be heard, it is impossible to eliminate appropriation entirely, because the researcher always decides in the end on what quotes to include and how to interpret the data. Both Harding (1992) and Shields and Dervin (1993) rejected the assumption of an automatic rapport between female researchers and subjects. The reason is that women's lives, rather than being uniform, are often structurally opposed, divided by class, gender orientation, and race and ethnicity. Shields and Dervin also pointed out that collaborative research employing qualitative, participatory methods is not always appropriate, such as when studying up. On what ethical principle is it justifiable to empower elite women?

Finally, some advocates of feminist methodology have found that qualitative research is not necessarily liberating. Stacey, for example, came to the conclusion that qualitative methods are just as ethically problematic as quantitative ones, and possibly more so. Not only does the qualitative-oriented investigator still compose the book or article, thus giving the lie to the appearance of equal collaboration, but she also uncovers a great deal of highly sensitive data. As Stacey stated, 'Indeed, the irony I now perceive is that ethnographic method exposes subjects to far greater danger and exploitation than do more positivist, abstract, and "masculinist" research methods. The greater the intimacy ... the greater is the danger' (1988:24).

Experienced ethnographers, both female and male, will find this unsurprising. What might make them raise their eyebrows is the assumption in feminist methodology that qualitative research is intrinsically more on the side of the angels than quantitative research, and especially more 'feminine' than 'masculine.' After all, it was in androcentric anthropology that qualitative methodology was fashioned. Yet as I pointed out earlier, qualitative research does not necessarily imply non-positivistic research. In fact, for most of the history of anthropology the opposite has been closer to the truth. Perhaps Eichler (1986:43) got it right when she suggested that any method, qualitative or quantitative, can be used in a sexually biased manner, and possibly in a non-sexist manner as well.

Are Women Better Fieldworkers than Men?

As fieldworkers, women arguably have several advantages over men; they are said to be better communicators, more sensitive and empathetic, more perceptive of subjective material, less visible in the field, less threatening, and enjoy greater role flexibility. At least, this is what is suggested in the literature, most of it written by women at a time when fieldwork was still done in other cultures.[5]

Harris, for example, argued that female researchers create less suspicion than their male counterparts, unless, she added, tongue in cheek, they are stunningly beautiful, in which case they might be taken for spies.[6] Along the same lines, Fischer (1970:275) asked who would think a women could trick them? Several writers, Harris included, have pointed out that because of their outsider status and educational qualifications, women in the field are not bounded by the rules that restrict local women. In fact, the claim is made that female researchers actually are granted more role flexibility than male researchers. Male ethnographers are usually restricted to the male world. Female ethnographers not only have access to the female world, and thus to the special knowledge possessed by women about genealogies, scandal, and household budgets, but also considerable access to the male world too. As Nader commented about her research in Mexico, 'I capitalized on their indecision as to how to categorize me and gained the greatest freedom of movement among both men and women' (1970:104–5).

Mead too (1970:322) believed that a woman has access to a wider range of a culture than does a man, and Powdermaker (1966) and Du Bois (1970) have both suggested that research is easier for a young unmarried women than for a young unmarried man. As Du Bois wrote, The young unmarried woman can rely on her status as an educated person, her privileged role as a foreigner, her helplessness, and her access to women' (p. 235).

There is, however, another side of the story. Fischer (1970) thought that women were more vulnerable than men to threats and attacks. Powdermaker revealed that Radcliffe-Brown insisted that she took a gun with her to Melanesia, which might be a telling comment on his own inadequacies as a fieldworker. According to Golde ,women who do fieldwork often have to deal with sex-linked problems, including offers of marriage (1970:90).[7] One's unmarried status apparently creates spe-

---

5 My main source here is Peggy Golde's *Women in the Field* (1970), a collection of articles written by twelve prominent female anthropologists. This book falls clearly into the positivistic tradition, reflected in Golde's own words: 'The anthropologist is first and foremost a scientist – using the particular to illustrate the general' (p. 13).

6 Her article on female fieldworkers was part of a mimeographed volume on fieldwork available to students at the University of Sussex in 1970.

7 On the subject of sex in the field, see Cohen and Eames (1982:35–7) and Warren (1988).

cial dilemmas for women in the field. Male anthropologists, Warren says, are much less likely to be hassled if they are single. 'But an unmarried, childless adult woman,' she continues 'has no fully legitimate social place in most cultures unless, perhaps, she is elderly and thus androgynized' (1988:13). In this regard, Mead suggests that the older a woman looks, the easier fieldwork becomes.

More so than men, women in the field have to pay great attention to their reputations. Ann Fischer pointed out that a man can get away with 'going native,' but not a woman (p. 274). Female researchers also have to be very careful with regard to their interactions with other Europeans. As Mead has explained, 'Fieldwork is in most cases lonelier for women than men. Women's activities are more restricted; contacts with other Europeans have to be managed with more skill and tact. Where a male fieldworker can afford a night on the town in an outstation, a woman ... cannot' (1970:322). Mead also had some caustic comments about husband and wife anthropological teams. In such cases, she argued, the woman on the team usually ends up in a subservient role, promoting her husband's research at the expense of her own – the price of continued marriage (p. 326).

Are women, then, better at fieldwork than men? Warren referred to this as 'the focal gender myth of field research' (pp. 39 and 64). She even has suggested that the myth may be based on the tendency of women, more than men, to conceal the flaws and weaknesses in their fieldwork, such as poor rapport, so that their credibility will not be questioned. In my own judgment, it is far from conclusive that women are indeed more sensitive and empathetic than men. In this regard, I cannot agree with Meis (1983:121) who argued that because women have been oppressed, they are more capable of studying exploited people; shared experiences of oppression do not necessarily put people on the same side; oppressed individuals sometimes avoid other oppressed people in order to enhance identification with the dominant group.

There also, of course, is the question about the source of supposed gender differences – whether in nature or in culture. Regardless of which side of this debate one comes down on – and not surprisingly, being a social anthropologist, my bias is for culture – it does seem that in at least one dimension women in the field do have an advantage over men: role flexibility. The various possible threats to women notwithstanding, the fact that they have access to both the female and male worlds is not insignificant.

Anthropology at Home

The subject of anthropology at home has come up several times already in this book, and here I shall take a closer look at what it entails. In the 1960s it was almost unheard of to do fieldwork in one's own country. The only exceptions that I recall concerned married women and Third World students studying in Western universities. Sometimes a married woman with children and a husband was allowed to do a project on her doorstep, but only if it contained an anthropological flavour, such as a religious sect or ethnic group; the assumption of the day was that married women did not have the liberty to hive off to a South Sea island. As for students from the Third World, what was curious, given the supposed advantages of stranger value and objectivity in anthropology away from home, was the expectation that they would return to their natal countries for their dissertation research.

One of the earliest pleas for an anthropology at home was made in 1972 by Laura Nader, the same scholar who advocated studying up. Other prominent anthropologists such as Fried tried to forestall this new development, arguing that without cross-cultural research the discipline will die. Nader, however, had pointed out that in view of the wide ethnic diversity in North America, one can actually do cross-cultural research at home. So great was the growth of anthropology at home that by the 1980s Messerschmidt was able to write: 'Anthropology at home is not a fad; neither is it a stopgap for unemployed Ph.Ds. It is, instead, a well-established branch of anthropology that has deep roots and a strong heritage ... it is here to stay' (1981:1).

Messerschmidt is probably right, but not everyone has been pleased with the type of work done at home. Ortner, for example, points out that most studies have focused on marginal sectors of society, such as street gangs (1991:166). Even more damning is Ortner's criticism that anthropologists who have turned their attention to home have largely ignored social class (presumably the key to Western society), and have tended to 'ethnicize' the groups investigated, as if they were exotic, isolated tribes. When I myself decided to switch my research focus from West Africa to Canada, most social scientists to whom I went for advice simply assumed that I would want to select an ethnic ghetto or an Aboriginal community. No wonder I sometimes have been asked if my studies of the radical right and class and racism in rural Ontario represent real anthropology.

Aguilar (1981) points out that there are both advantages and disadvantages to doing research at home. On the positive side, because ethnographers in this situation are insiders, they can blend more easily into the culture. They have better rapport, greater linguistic competence, and a greater capacity to appreciate the nuances of non-verbal, subjective data. They also are less likely to construct misleading stereotypes of people. On the negative side, sensitive data sometimes are withheld from them, in case they use the information against the research subjects. Another problem is that inside researchers, because of their familiarity with everyday life, may accept it unquestioningly rather than analysing it. Then, too, insiders may lack sufficient social distance to ask questions – a problem that arose in my study of Paradise – and, unlike the foreign researcher, no allowance is made for inadequate cultural performance; they are expected to know the rules and conform. Finally, inside researchers, because of their professional status, often are marginal among the people they study, especially in projects that study down.

Anthropology at home is a rather vague concept, and in order to clarify what it entails Messerschmidt (1981:13) breaks it down into three categories: insider anthropology, the term applied to anthropologists from dominant ethnic groups who do research at home; native anthropology, the term applied to anthropologists from ethnic minority groups who study their own people; and indigenous anthropology, the term for Third World anthropologists who do fieldwork in their own societies.

Native anthropology is often thought to be politically oriented, a reaction against conventional, Western social science. Thus Gwaltney, an African American anthropologist, defines native anthropology as a perspective opposed to 'the settler social scientist establishment' (1981:48). Another African American anthropologist, Delmos Jones, wrote: 'By a "native anthropology," I mean a set of theories based on non-Western precepts and assumptions in the same sense that modern anthropology is based on and has supported Western beliefs and values.' The problem, Jones pointed out, is that while there are native anthropologists, there is not yet a native anthropology, or a body of theory built around the perspectives of 'tribal, peasant, or minority peoples.' Nor, Jones continued, are the data and insights produced by native anthropologists necessarily superior to those generated by mainstream anthropologists (1982:472, 478).

Then there is the issue of rapport, and the apparent advantage enjoyed by the native anthropologist. Jones indicated that when he did research in Thailand he was suspected of being a missionary. But when he did research in a black community in Denver he was suspected of being a Black Panther. The reaction of people in the latter project ranged from those who didn't really care about the research, others who thought it was marvellous that a black person was studying a black community, and a third group who opposed such research, no matter who did it, arguing that enough studies already had been done, and what was needed was action.

While it is probably correct to describe native anthropology as ideological, the same holds true for insider and indigenous anthropology. Insider anthropology tends to be highly critical of the status quo. Indigenous anthropology may be more complex, but equally ideological. From my experience in West Africa, it seemed that Nigerian anthropologists doing fieldwork at home were committed to studies that would contribute to nation-building. However, most of these scholars had been trained in North America or Britain and had often bought into the ideology of objective social science. In some cases Nigerian anthropologists operated much like insider anthropologists: nation-building, they assumed, was promoted by studies that exposed and criticized the state and its institutions.

The difference between doing fieldwork at home and abroad is nicely described by Wolcott (1981). In his research in urban Africa, in a Malay village, and among the Kwakiutl, he avoided confronting sensitive issues, and was highly detached. In his research on education in the United States he was deeply involved and critical, more than willing to expose flaws in the system. Wolcott quite candidly admits that compared to the fieldwork that he has done at home, his work abroad has been superficial, but still important because of the cross-cultural perspective that it encouraged.

A particularly interesting research role is the combination of insider/ outsider. In the 1960s Gloria Marshall, an African American, conducted fieldwork among the Yoruba in Nigeria. Her African heritage seemed to provide her with remarkable rapport. She dressed in Yoruba clothing, plaited her hair, and tried to adopt Yoruba mannerisms. The people in the town, in turn, apparently went out of the way to make her welcome. Yet she did not go native, nor was she treated as a native. In fact, she pointed out, the townspeople never forgot that she was a foreigner, and ironically her African heritage generated its own special problems. Usually anthropologists are accused of being spies, missionaries, or, during the colonial era, tax collectors. Marshall was accused of being a Yoruba. People in the markets that she studied did not always believe that she was from America. Some of them thought she was a Yoruba who pretended not to speak the language in order to collect information for the Nigerian government.

Overlap between Anthropology at Home and Feminist Methodology

There is considerable similarity between feminist methodology and one category of anthropology at home: native anthropology. In both cases there is homogeneity between researcher and research subject: African Americans studying African Americans, women studying women. There also are common aims, namely empowering the people who are studied, elevating their pride and capacity to resist oppression. Then, too, there are the theoretical goals. Both native anthropologists and feminist anthropologists have striven to erect new paradigms, ones that are liberated from the dominant white male Western culture.

Native and feminist anthropology might also be said to share some of the same pitfalls. Just as ethnic research programs have been criticized as inherently biased, the same charge has been levelled at studies influenced by feminist methodology. It also has been pointed out that the supposed homogeneity between researcher and research subject is more apparent than real. Ethnic minority scholars often occupy a different class position from the people they investigate, and are integrated into the wider society in a way that is impossible for less-privileged people. As for women, it has long been charged that the women's movement has been controlled by people from the middle class, and in recent years the efforts of minority women to exert their influence has deepened the divide. Finally, both native and female anthropologists are torn between a split audience: their academic colleagues and the people in their research projects. For whom are they to write? To please one of the audiences may not be difficult. To please both may be almost impossible.

Conclusion

Let us return to the current chasm between the theoretical and methods literature. How can it be explained that in the one case science has been virtually dismissed, and in the other case almost frantically pursued? Part of the explanation is that feminist methodology and postmodernism have concentrated on the big issues: what is the nature of fieldwork, what are its underlying assumptions? To do this, they have dealt with epistemological and ethical issues. The specialized literature on qualitative methods, in contrast, has been much narrower in focus: how does one conduct systematic research? This literature has dealt mainly with technique.

I might add that it is almost impossible to render field methods systematic without standing inside the shadow of quantitative methods, with their positivistic assumptions. As I pointed out earlier, fieldwork is essentially a non-linear activity. Any attempt to reduce it to a set of public, replicable rules and procedures converts it into a linear approach, with quantitative analysis as its model. It should also be pointed out that a considerable amount of the recent literature on qualitative methods has been produced by non-anthropologists, especially sociologists. The discipline of sociology has always been more jargonistic than anthropology (except for kinship studies), and more self-conscious about its status as a science. The tendency of sociologists to ignore feminist methodology and postmodernism seems to be even more pronounced than in anthropology.

Finally, what is the status of qualitative research in academia today? Historically, qualitative research was the reserve of anthropologists. In the 1920s and 1930s it also was the preferred procedure of the famous Chicago school of urban sociology, its leading figures being Park, Thomas, Znaniecki, Burgess, and Hughes. More recently, ethnographic or qualitative methods have not only become more widely utilized in sociology (especially the sociology of education) and in feminist research, but they have also been closely examined by literary scholars and philosophers. As Hammersley (1992:123) has stated, qualitative methods are no longer regarded merely as tools suitable for preliminary, pre-hypothetical investigation. In fact, such is their growing popularity, he argues, that in some fields of investigation there is a danger that quantitative research will become a thing of the past.

PART FOUR: ANALYSIS AND INTERPRETATION

8

The Last Frontier: How to Analyse Qualitative Data

Given the massive literature on qualitative methods that now exists, plus the literature on feminist methodology and postmodernism, it is fair to say that the techniques of fieldwork and related issues such as stress, ethics, literary devices, appropriation, and epistemology have been thoroughly examined. Yet there remains a missing link: the *analysis* of qualitative data. This is what I call the last frontier, the one part of ethnography still cloaked in mystery – a state of affairs, let it be clear, that very much applies to the type of conventional, positivistic anthropology that preceded postmodernism and feminist anthropology. In this chapter I shall deliberately ignore these last perspectives, assumming that our first job is to attempt to clarify what analysis means in relation to the style of anthropology that has dominated the discipline for most of its history, and continues today in the form of no-name anthropology. À propos these observations, I want to ring three little warning bells, especially for students.

The first is that you won't get much help on how to proceed analytically in the field by turning to general theory, or by expecting a particular theoretical orientation such as cultural ecology or postmodernism to serve as a meaningful framework for your study. This is not because such orientations will fail to fit your data. The problem, rather, is that they will fit the data in almost any project conceivable. In other words, the relationship between theory at this level and the empirical case under investigation is vague, imprecise, and superficial. In fact, to invoke one of the well-known theoretical perspectives as a guide to research amounts to little more than a labelling exercise at best, and distortion at worst.

There is, let me hasten to add, a definite place for general theory in ethnographic research. Such theory enhances one's anthropological imagination. When one enters the field and begins to collect data, one is almost dazzled by their potential theoretical significance. Indeed, the fieldwork experience prompts one to think about almost everything that one has read in the discipline. However, the creative juices released by the confrontation with data are a mixture of theoretical orientations, rather than a pure sample of one specific orientation; in other words, the fieldworker draws bits and pieces from any body of theory that seems relevant. Moreover, the illumination provided by one's knowledge of a wide spectrum of theoretical perspectives is only a single aspect of the explanatory procedure. As I shall argue below, several additional steps are involved, some of them more appropriate and powerful.

My second point is that you won't find much direction about how to proceed analytically in existing ethnographies and monographs. The reason is that hardly anyone (including myself) is explicit about the analytic exercise. Authors may say something in an appendix about why they chose a project and about their techniques, but rarely do they attempt to explain their analytic procedure. Ethnographers are equally reticent about the reasons they organized their books as they did, even though such organization is a statement about analysis. Most ethnographies fall into two types. One is the sandwich; here the book opens with an overview of theory (often in the guise of a literature review), followed by the presentation of the data, and finally a brief reconsideration of the theory. The other type is more deliberately inductive, supposedly truer to the ethnographic tradition. From the very first chapter, and continuing throughout until the concluding chapter, the reader is presented with the 'raw' data, often divided into subsystems such as family, economy, polity, and belief system. Only in the concluding chapter (if at all) is a stab made at theorizing, usually in the form of offering empirical generalizations. Yet these generalizations, which supposedly emerge from the data that have been presented, and thus are marvellously (almost inevitably) valid, are often only the disguised assumptions with which the authors began their books, and which gave their monographs a semblance of coherence.

My third warning is that unfortunately you won't get much assistance from the textbooks on qualitative methods. Most of the literature simply sidesteps the troublesome issue of how to analyse qualitative data. In recent years a few brave souls such as Agar, McCracken, and Strauss have ventured into the last frontier. Their contributions, I shall argue, still leave a lot to be desired, but in my judgment they are among the most impressive that have been made to date.

The Literature on Qualitative Analysis

Agar's *The Professional Stranger* (1980) is a widely used introductory text-book with a difference: the author does attempt to say something mean-ingful about the analysis of qualitative data. He announces at the beginning (p. 3) that his goal is to demystify fieldwork, and he proceeds to deal with a wide range of issues such as obtaining funds for research, gaining entry into the field, choosing techniques, and analysing the data. He criticizes anthropologists for failing to spell out exactly what is involved in qualitative analysis. Yet when he addresses this issue him-self, he abandons qualitative analysis and turns to quantitative analysis: scales, surveys, samples, and statistics.

This is all part of what he calls the funnel approach. The fieldworker begins a project at the wide end of the funnel, building rapport, doing participant observation and informal interviews, and covering a wide range of ground in an unsystematic manner. At a later stage the field-worker shifts to the narrow end of the funnel, where quantitative analy-sis and hypothesis-testing take over. As Agar stated, 'I advocate hypothesis-testing in the classic sense as a potentially strong way to check out informal ethnographic conclusions' (p. 172). It is probable that many anthropologists have followed the funnel approach, even if they didn't have a label for their efforts, and I did much the same thing in my research in West Africa. However, we would all be fooling ourselves if we thought we were pushing back the frontiers of *qualitative* analysis; we were merely ducking that challenge by opting for the more straight-forward procedure of quantitative analysis. The funnel approach, unfor-tunately, resuscitates the old assumption that qualitative research is merely a preliminary stage for the ultimately more important task of quantitative research.

One section of *The Professional Stranger* is labelled 'Analysis of Infor-mal Interviews' (pp. 103–5). Here we are advised to go over our taped interviews and try to sort out what people have said into categories, and arrange the categories according to themes. We can then wade back through the interview material and, using a pair of scissors, cut it up and reorganize it in terms of the categories. Later in the book (pp. 163–70) the author makes another stab at advising us how to analyse qualita-tive data, but essentially repeats what was said earlier. The procedure advocated by Agar is neither sophisticated nor novel – what ethnogra-pher doesn't search for themes and categories? And in one respect it is quite misleading. In ethnographic research, analysis should never be put off until all the data are collected. Analysis begins with the first notes that the fieldworker jots down, and continues on a day-to-day basis throughout the fieldwork phase. This is one of the major differences between qualitative and quantitative research, because in quantitative research, data analysis usually occurs after a survey has been completed.

There are several inconsistencies in this book, the major one being a plea for a more sophisticated qualitative approach but a solution that revolves around quantitative analysis. Agar also criticizes the sink or swim school, in which one starts off with minimal preparation, but he informs us that that is precisely how he wrote *The Professional Stranger*; he only consulted the literature on qualitative methods later, and said he is glad he did it that way. Agar is quite impatient with the manner in which ethnographic research proposals are written, arguing that it is simply not good enough to say one is going to do participant observation or interviews. But his alternative, once again, is to sidestep qualitative methods and concentrate on quantitative techniques and measurements. This advice is offered despite the author's recognition that most of the quantitative stuff has to be abandoned when we actually get to the field, because it will simply get in the way.

There is, of course, an element of truth in what Agar says about successful proposal writing, and perhaps he should be applauded for his honesty. The reaction of my students, however, is to question the ethics of a procedure that is tantamount to ripping off funding agencies.

As I have said before, ethnographic research is a highly personal experience, and possibly this is why even a general introductory text such as *The Professional Stranger* seems so obviously autobiographical. It appears that Agar has never done a traditional piece of research, living in a community for a year or more. He only spent six months doing research in India, and even less – two months – on a project in Austria. The vast bulk of his fieldwork appears to have focused on junkies in North American cities. This may explain his preference for 'talk' over observation, and his opinion that field notes are not very important. It may also account for his bent towards quantitative methods. Apparently drug-related research is dominated by quantitative-oriented scholars, and if one hopes to compete for scarce funds, one has to play the quantitative game.

As an introductory text, there is much to praise about *The Professional Stranger*, not least of all the engaging style in which it is written and the portrayal of contemporary ethnography as much more than the study of

Third World cultures. Yet in terms of the analysis of qualitative data, this book, regrettably, has little to offer.

Let us turn to another study, McCracken's *The Long Interview* (1988). This book, written in a less engaging but more succinct style than *The Professional Stranger*, does have a great deal to say about qualitative analysis. McCracken reasonably observes that such analysis 'is perhaps the most demanding and least examined aspect of the qualitative research process' (p. 41). Yet he is confident that 'someday we shall see these qualitative methods pass routinely between even the most disenchanted teacher and unenchanting student' (p. 19). His solution to analysis is the long interview, which consists of a four-step procedure: a review of analytic categories (translation: a literature review); a review of cultural categories (translation: basically thinking about the topic under investigation in local cultural terms, leading up to the appropriate research design); the discovery of cultural categories (translation: constructing an open-ended questionnaire and using it to interview people); and finally, the discovery of analytic categories (translation: the analysis of qualitative data).

The fourth stage in turn is broken down into five more stages. The first concerns an observation made about a statement in the transcribed interviews; the second is an expanded observation; the third is an observation linked to even more observations; the fourth is the isolation of a theme from the foregoing stages; and the fifth is the creation of an interview thesis, or a central argument derived from the data. The author points out that each stage shifts to a higher level of generality, interconnecting observations about the data with the literature and cultural reviews, producing at the end the patterns that express the central thesis or argument of a study.

To McCracken's credit, his procedure is a great deal more explicit and systematic than anything offered by Agar. The big question is whether it amounts to a sophisticated breakthrough in the analysis of qualitative data, or mere empty formalism. My guess is that most experienced researchers would dismiss the four-stage procedure, and especially the five analytic steps in the fourth stage, as superficial, bearing little resemblance or relevance to their own experiences in the field.

How, then, did McCracken, a specialist in historical anthropology, come up with his scheme? Once again, part of the answer may be autobiographical. Although widely published, McCracken's fieldwork experience appears to have been quite limited. It seems that he has never done a community study, nor worked in other cultures. On the face of it, these facets of his scholarly experience should have little impact on his methodological stance. Yet early in *The Long Interview* (pp. 10–11) we find the curious argument that conventional fieldwork is no longer possible because neither the research subjects nor the researcher have sufficient time, and because North Americans place too much value on privacy to let anthropologists into their homes and lives. Nothing about my knowledge of ethnographic work in North America suggests that these assumptions are anything more than personal projection (and confession). McCracken also states (p. 37) that in many projects eight respondents are sufficient. How this figure was arrived at is an intriguing question on its own, but the point of course is not the number of respondents, but rather the depth of inquiry. There might, indeed, only be one respondent, interviewed repeatedly, as in Shostak's *Nisa*, and that might be adequate. Yet McCracken implies that the actual interviews with people in his procedure only take two to three hours to complete. This is the standard length of the unstructured interview in most ethnographic projects, where the average number of respondents might be two or three hundred people. Eight interviewees might make sense to a scholar in a hurry, but I imagine that the majority of anthropologists would be bemused rather than impressed.

There are further curious assertions in *The Long Interview*, such as the implicit assumption that qualitative research is non-positivistic, but I think that enough has been said. Like Agar's book, McCracken's serves a useful purpose in that it speaks to a new and significant direction of anthropology – anthropology at home. The efforts of the author to tackle the last frontier also deserve our praise. Even if my critical comments about McCracken's proposed analytic procedure are sound, he at least has had the courage to gaze at a phantom from which most of his colleagues have shrunk.

Agar and McCracken are both anthropologists, but the most ambitious attempt to demystify qualitative analysis has been made by a sociologist, Anselm Strauss. More than a quarter of a century ago Strauss joined forces with Glaser to produce *The Discovery of Grounded Theory* (1967), a book which Strauss has rewritten several times since then (Schatzman and Strauss 1973, Strauss 1987, Strauss and Corbin 1990). Here I shall focus on the 1987 version entitled *Qualitative Analysis for Social Scientists*. Like Agar and McCracken, both of whom referred to grounded theory, Strauss is confident that the process of analysing qualitative data can be demystified. In his words, 'The analytic mode introduced here is perfectly learnable by any competent social researcher' (p. xiii). Elsewhere he states: 'Good research analysis can be taught and learned: It is not at all merely an innate skill' (p. 13) Grounded theory, according to Strauss, is not restricted to any particular discipline; it is a style of analysis that can be used in a variety of fields, including anthropology. Unlike postmodernism and feminist methodology, grounded theory does not challenge the scientific tradition; to the contrary, its raison d'être is to render qualitative research more scientific.

Grounded theory, according to Strauss, systematically generates and tests theory. It is virtually synonymous with interpretation, and is a procedure that milks the theoretical significance out of data. All this sounds laudable, and indeed there is much about the approach that is impressive. Strauss opposes grand theory, or speculative theory, as represented in the works of Marx, Weber, Durkheim, and Parsons, arguing that it is too abstract to be of any value for specific research projects; and he complains, with justification, that what often passes for theory is lip service to the great figures of the past.[1] He wisely argues that analysis isn't something that is tackled when fieldwork is completed, but occurs throughout the data-collection phase. Nor, he states, is fieldwork a linear activity. Instead one constantly shifts back and forth between gathering data and analysing materials, and the very focus of research often moves in unanticipated directions, changing according to what one learns in the field. Although anthropologists used to insist that the fieldworker's personal biography be kept separate from the research process, otherwise the data would be tainted, grounded theorists reasonably argue that experiential data can often be highly relevant and useful. For example, if one has worked in a hospital, and later ends up studying nurses or doctors, one becomes one's own informant. Finally, perhaps most impressive of all is Strauss's recognition that qualitative research consists of rules of thumb or guidelines, rather than rigid prescriptions like a manufacturer's directions for assembling a toy. Given the fluid and often unpredictable nature of fieldwork, the flexibility implied in rules of thumb is perfectly appropriate.

That is the good news. Now let me tell you what is wrong with grounded theory. For one thing, there is the enormous amount of jargon associated with it. Grounded theory consists of a number of technical

---

1 Ironically, it is not uncommon nowadays for social scientists to pay lip service to grounded theory, with little evidence that they have actually used the approach.

operations including what is labelled coding, dimensionalizing, memoing, theoretical sampling (comparing), diagramming, and integrating. By following these operations, the researcher supposedly will produce a level of sophisticated explanation and interpretation unrivalled in qualitative investigation. To prove his point, Strauss provides several lengthy excerpts from his own work (pp. 217, 241–8). Yet what is striking about them is their superficiality and triteness. If these under-analysed, casual reflections represent grounded theory at its best, fieldworkers can look for the promised land elsewhere.

At several points in the book (pp. 161, 165, 294), Strauss remarks that the researcher can have too much data, a statement which should immediately make any anthropologist agitated. One might come out of a research project with such a pile of data that managing it is difficult, especially if it was not recorded and organized systematically while in the field. But in terms of explanation, one simply cannot have too much data, because the more one gathers, the deeper one penetrates. Having too much data only makes sense if one is wed to a set of technical operations such as those associated with componential analysis or grounded theory, because technical tinkering becomes unwieldly when working with more than a few cases. The good thing about such formal approaches is that the data are closely examined, stripped down, and recombined in a manner that exploits their potential theoretical significance. The bad thing is that the technical operations may be regarded as more important than the quality of the data.

The question of quality can be traced back to the first version of grounded theory presented by Glaser and Strauss. In the course of mounting their opposition to deductive research, where one enters the field armed with models and hypotheses, they stated: 'Indeed it is presumptuous to assume that one begins to know the relevant categories and hypotheses until "the first days in the field" at least, are over' (1967:34). The first days! Most experienced fieldworkers, I imagine, would be thrilled if they knew these things after six months of research. Glaser and Strauss also remarked that at an advanced stage in a project the researcher 'may observe in a few minutes all that he needs to know about a group with reference to a given theoretical point' (p. 72). In the later stages of a project, they add, 'establishing rapport is often not necessary' when the investigator is verifying hypotheses, and indeed the investigator 'may obtain his data in a few minutes or half a day without the people he talks with, overhears or observes recognizing his purpose' (p. 75). This is fairyland. If only social life were so simple and predictable.

The terminology associated with grounded theory certainly provides qualitative research with an aura of scientific respectability which distances the enterprise from the lay person. Yet stripped of its high-tech jargon, there is little to grounded theory that is new. From the time of Malinowski onwards, anthropologists have proceeded in the same rough fashion: gathering data, getting hunches, checking them out, generating tentative hypotheses, rejecting them as contradictory data emerge, arranging their data into categories, searching for themes and patterns, and conducting comparative research. The difference is the absence of a specialized vocabulary in anthropology, and the much greater emphasis on long-term fieldwork. It might be said that, like the individual who was surprised to discover that he had always been writing 'prose,' anthropologists have always been doing grounded theory (or at least a sensible version of it); they just didn't have a label for it.

Flawed they may be, but the works of Agar, McCracken, and Strauss are still more impressive than almost anything else available regarding the analysis of qualitative data. Other studies such as *Analysing Field Reality* (Gubrian 1988) and *Analysing Social Settings* (Lofland 1971) seem to be vague and abstract in comparison, although the second half of Lofland's book, where it deals with the collection, organization, and writing of qualitative materials, is sound. Hammersley and Atkinson (1983:175–205), who also refer approvingly to grounded theory, include a chapter entitled 'The Process of Analysis' in their text. Analysis, they suggest, consists of reading over and thinking about the collected data, searching for patterns and inconsistencies, and creating concepts, categories, and typologies. The chapter trails off into a general discussion of triangulation (using a mixture of methods), the comparative method, and different types of theory – from the macro to the micro. Once again, the degree to which the analysis of qualitative data has been demystified is minimal. At this juncture it may be hard to repress the thought that perhaps this is the one part of qualitative research that simply can't be demystified. Let me turn, nevertheless, to my own attempts to do so.

A Modest Alternative

Although I am less confident than Agar, McCracken, and Strauss about the prospects of demystifying qualitative analysis, I think some of the fog can be pushed aside. In sociology it is conventional to distinguish between large M and small m methodology. The first concerns the logic of research, and includes design, focus, concepts, operational definitions, and decisions about whether to precede deductively or inductively. The second deals mainly with the techniques used and steps taken to collect data. My starting point is draw a similar distinction between large A and small a analysis. Large A represents the most general level of analysis and interpretation that is uniquely addressed to a specific research project. Small a represents the minimal level of analysis and interpretation in a project, a level that hovers close to the data. The pure case, or exemplar, of large A is the model; it is a product of imagination and logic. The pure case, or exemplar, of small a is the burst of insight; it is a product of imagination and perceptiveness.

The Model

The model is the most elegant, condensed, abstract statement in one's study. It provides the reader with a snapshot of the major themes, variables, and arguments. In a sense it is like poetry: a densely packed message expressed in minimal words, a metaphor for the empirical universe that has been investigated. The model is not a theoretical orientation, although it might very well have implications for general theory. The model's scope is purposefully limited to the project at hand; to the extent that it has wider applicability, that is merely a pleasant bonus, and not the fieldworker's primary concern. The model could be verbal, but I prefer to represent it in a diagram. The model is neither valid nor invalid; it is useful or not, in the sense of providing an overall picture of the central features of a research project.

The model could be erected prior to research, based on general theory and the relevant literature, and then refined in light of the research findings, but I am quite opposed to this deductive procedure; the risk is too great that the fieldworker's perceptions and interpretations will be distorted. The model then, should not be a guide to research, but a product of it. It should grow directly out of the data that one has collected. As one does fieldwork, one might erect several partial models, usually addressed to specific analytic problems. The task of building an overall model, however, should be put off until fieldwork is completed, partly because one must continue to have a capacity to be surprised by the data, leading one to unanticipated interpretations; another reason is that it is only after one has left the field, and has had an opportunity to read and re-read one's field notes, and to reflect deeply on them, that one is likely to have a sophisticated appreciation of the entire research project.

Most fieldworkers do not include models in their ethnographies, being satisfied to relate their data to themes and issues in the relevant literature. However, as students we could pick up any ethnography and carve a model out of the data; whether it would be as useful as what the author could have produced is another matter. In my West African study I presented two models, one addressed to the community's early economic success, the other to its transformation and decline. These models grew out of the data, but they certainly were not what I originally had in mind. I had begun research in the Nigerian community with models of development and decline; only after I finally discarded them and adopted an inductive style did I begin to understand the community.

In my study of organized racism and anti-Semitism in Canada, I began with specific problems (or questions), but I did not make the mistake of taking preconceived models into the field; nor, in this project, did I present a model in my eventual book. The main reason was the anticipated audience. I had hoped that the book would be read by lay people, not just academics, and eschewed model-building so that it would be easier reading. In retrospect, I wonder if it would not have actually helped lay readers to have had a concise and clear model in front of them.

It is not an easy thing to build a model (at least I don't find it so), and in order to give some idea of the process involved let me turn to my community study in rural Ontario. After a few weeks of exploratory fieldwork, I had decided to focus on stratification, migration, and race and ethnic relations. A short time later I wrote a research proposal in which these topics were placed in the context of the relevant literature. At that juncture I raised a number of questions and theoretical issues that seemed pertinent to the topics under investigation, but what I did not possess then was an overall theoretical grasp of the project.

With the fieldwork phase completed, it was time to put it all together and produce a book. For the first month or so, all that I did was to read the field notes – over and over again, to the point that they were almost memorized. What I was searching for was a unified picture, a framework based on the data in front of me that would pull everything together. I can actually recall the very afternoon when it happened. I had been jotting down themes and ideas, speculating about the manner in which different themes were interdependent, doodling on scrap paper, when out of nowhere came the model presented below.[2]

2 Of course, it is somewhat disingenuous to say 'out of nowhere,' because in actual fact the model was a straightforward product of the weeks spent in familiarizing myself with and reflecting on the data.

Model of Social Change in Paradise

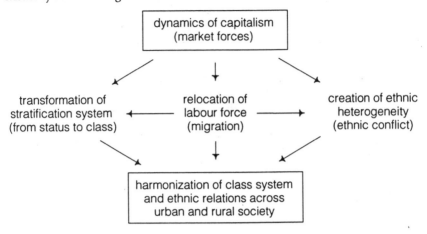

I shall not attempt to spell out in detail the various arguments contained in this model (for a fuller explanation see Barrett 1994:31–3). Whether this model is the most useful one that could have been lifted from the same data set is quite a different question, and no doubt other fieldworkers may have carved out quite different (and possibly superior) models, especially, as is likely, had they focused on different topics. From my point of view, the strength of the model was to bring together the three topics of the study, to suggest how they were interconnected, and to provide a dynamic overview of the entire project – a guide to the chapters that followed.

SECONDARY LARGE A TASKS

While the model is the core of large A analysis, a number of additional exercises are involved:

1. *Focus, Issues, and Themes*

If fieldwork is done well, the anthropologist will depart with data on a wide range of issues and topics. However, one cannot look closely at everything, which means that it is necessary to concentrate on a limited range of topics. The decision will be partly personal, reflecting one's own interests. For example, it is quite possible, given the relative paucity of anthropological studies of racism, that few fieldworkers would have selected it as a focus in Paradise. The decision will also be partly analytic, reflecting the issues and themes that are currently in vogue in a discipline.

2. Topic versus Problem

There is an important difference between a topic and a problem. A topic is simply a subject matter on which to focus. A problem implies a puzzle to be solved. In the Paradise study, racism in rural Ontario was a topic. To have analytic bite, such topics must be converted into problems. For example, is racism in rural society greater or lesser than in urban society? Or does increased contact between races mean greater or lesser tolerance? Should one wish to do so, such problems can readily be stated in hypothetical form.

3. Concepts and Conceptual Issues

One of the first steps in research is to identify and define the basic concepts. This is not as easy as it might seem. One reason is that it assumes that the researcher already has a clear picture of the topics and themes of the study. Another reason is that one's concepts probably will be a combination of those derived from theory and those that are embraced by the research subjects (or observer and actor concepts). For example, in the Paradise study I focused on residents native to the community, white newcomers, and visible minority newcomers. But how does one define a native? How long does a person have to live in a community before qualifying? And does the fieldworker take his or her criteria from existing studies in the literature, or listen to what residents themselves have to say about the issue? The task of defining racial categories is even more complex inasmuch as most anthropologists, including myself, would argue that racial classifications obfuscate rather than clarify; in this situation, does the fieldworker reproduce the definitions offered by the research subjects, knowing full well that they consist mostly of stereotypes?

Equally challenging are the concepts tied to complicated theoretical issues, such as class and community. How many classes are there in a community? Does the number perceived vary with the actor's own class position? What is the difference between class and status? Is class an objectively identifiable entity, or a subjective one? Should the fieldworker follow Marx's conception of class, or Weber's or Warner's? A similar set of questions surrounds the concept of community. Does community constitute a specific sociological type, bounded concretely by territorial limits and characterized by a distinctive value system and culture? Or, as some critics would contend, is community a fiction, and thus theories of community meaningless?

One of the peculiarities of ethnographic research is that the task of defining key concepts often continues throughout the fieldwork phase. It is possible to begin research with a tentative idea of what to focus on and how to define concepts. However, the researcher must remain sufficiently flexible in order to be instructed by the people in a study about what these concepts mean to them. For example, I entered Paradise with the contrasting theories of stratification embraced by Marx, Weber, Warner and others in my mind. Yet it was not until near the end of the project that I decided on my own approach, taking a lead from Krauss (1976). The same was true for the concept of community. There are literally dozens of definitions in the literature of community. Which to pick? My procedure was to listen to what Paradise people had to say: community in the 1950s may have meant something, but not in the 1980s.

What I am pointing out is that even when it comes to the most rudimentary exercises such as selecting topics and themes and identifying and defining concepts, ethnographic research is maddeningly inductive. No doubt it would be more elegant and simple to settle all these issues arbitrarily before entering the field, allowing them to be dictated by one's favourite theoretical perspective; but that would undermine the peculiar strengths of ethnography which justify its unsystematic procedure.

The Burst of Insight

The burst of insight does not resemble the logical manipulations involved in building models or comparing one theoretical orientation to another, although even these exercises, if they are original, will be stamped by imaginative insight. Nor is the burst of insight a mechanical activity, patiently teasing out trends and correlations from one's data, although once again flashes of insight may be produced by such activities. Instead, the burst of insight involves deep penetrations into the minute details of people's everyday life, quick perceptions that allow the fieldworker to understand their innermost motives. The burst of insight is comparable to shouting eureka when suddenly what was previously puzzling or only superficially understood makes sense.

When I talk about the burst of insight I do not mean to imply that the fieldworker uncovers or sees into 'the key' to a community or group. In my judgment, no such key or fundamental factor exists in social life; instead, in successful research projects bursts of insight occur time after time. The burst of insight is even more important than the model. Indeed, without repeated bursts of insight during fieldwork, it is improbable that a meaningful model can be built. Therefore, I would regard as superior those ethnographies that are rich in bursts of insights but lacking models rather than ethnographies that provide elegant models based on drab, superficial data.

Although long periods of fieldwork and hard work are prerequisites to sound ethnography, these alone will not generate bursts of insight. What is required is a well-developed sociological imagination and a flair for perceptiveness. At this point it may be thought that I am getting pretty close to what I referred to in an earlier chapter as 'the genius syndrome,' the assumption that anthropologists possess an extraordinary capacity to comprehend social life. That is not my intention. To the contrary, what I am advocating is that students, rather than merely being provided with a range of fieldwork techniques, should also be alerted to the fundamental importance of deep and repeated insights. If this is done, students will be more aware of the degree to which good research depends on imagination and perceptiveness, rather than mere technical virtuosity.

To illustrate what is meant by bursts of insight, let me turn again to the Paradise study. My first example concerns a sixty-year-old man who was employed as a clerk in a small store, a job that he had held for more than twenty years. He told me that he had only accepted the job as a stop-gap measure, something that would put food on the table until he managed to land a good position in a nearby city. As I listened to this man, I suddenly realized that in his mind life had not really begun yet. Although he stood on the edge of old age, he still was waiting for things to fall into place so that he could relocate in the city and enter the ranks of the middle class. This man's story touched a common chord, especially (but not solely) among people struggling to make ends meet. For many of these individuals, life had a temporary quality. They may have worked for thirty or forty years as clerks or domestics, but in their minds that was simply because they had not yet got untracked. Then, tragically, they found themselves in their sixties or seventies, and what had been meant as a temporary situation turned out to be the defining feature of their lives.

My next example concerns commuters. A large number of those people who had moved from the city to Paradise continued to work in the city. For most of them, commuting was a necessary evil, something that had to be done to make their mortgage payments. They complained about the wear and tear the commuting exacted on their bodies, the strain that it placed on their marriages, and the obstacle that it created in their efforts to get to know their neighbours and enjoy small-town life. One day I interviewed a man with quite a different perspective. He insisted that he enjoyed commuting. As he talked, he gave the impression of being a loner. The last thing he wanted was to interact with his neighbours. It was then that I realized that for this man, and a handful of others like him, commuting was the equivalent of the high-rise apartment building in the city: a mechanism that created the anonymity that they desired. I should add that not all people who found commuting to be attractive, or at least tolerable, were anti-social. Some of them simply appreciated the opportunity to collect their thoughts, and put their lives in order.

A third example deals with social class. My interviews had revealed a contradiction between two norms. The one was that allowance was always made for one bad apple in a family. The other was that it only took a single alcoholic or shifty character to ruin a family's reputation. As research progressed, it became apparent that the first norm applied mainly to the higher classes, the second to the lower classes. It was then that I realized that each individual in Paradise began life with a measurable degree of social credit – the higher the class, the greater the amount.

A fourth example concerns racism. The influx of the newcomers had a dramatic impact on social interaction. People, the locals included, no longer automatically greeted each other on the street as they did in the past. They were inclined to stick to themselves, to guard their privacy jealously. As one man observed, people didn't 'neighbour' any more. When individuals belonging to visible minorities moved to the Paradise area and attempted to become friends with their neighbours, they were generally rebuffed. Paradise natives defended themselves against charges of racism by pointing out that the time was gone when people leaned over their fences and chatted with the individual next door. However, it struck me that the current quality of fragmented interaction served as a convenient cloak to cover up the racism that indeed was widespread in the region.

My final example also concerns racism. One of the peculiar things about Paradise, a town which until recently had been inhabited primarily by British-origin people, and which had no direct experience of racial conflict, was that people readily thought in terms of racial stereo-types and did not hesitate to offer racial classifications, ranking visible minorities at the bottom. How to explain? My sense was that in small communities like Paradise there existed what could be labelled a racial capacity. That is, generated by media accounts and perhaps by the very nature of capitalist society, in which racial conflict divides the working class for the benefit of the elite, racism as an ideology existed long before visible minorities began to make the town their home, but laid dormant, ready to be activated by their arrival. Critics might object that it is pre-tentious to label the notion of a racial capacity as an insight, or all the other examples for that matter. Such criticism does not disturb me in the least, as long as it is accepted that what is objectionable is the quality of my examples, not the importance of the burst of insight per se.

SECONDARY SMALL A TASKS

The burst of insight is the pure case of small a analysis, but several addi-tional steps are involved.

1. *Empirical Generalizations*

Some examples from the Paradise study: male newcomers tended to adjust better to small-town life than their spouses; the amount of social interaction varied with the class level, with the least at the top and the bottom; the higher the class position of a person, the more probable rac-ism was expressed in biological rather than economic terms, and the converse.

I do not include these examples as bursts of insight because that is not their character. Instead, these generalizations were based on observa-tions over time of repeated patterns in the data, rather than on quick flashes of perception.

Merton (1949) distinguishes empirical observations from correlations and trends. I suppose it would be possible to generalize about a single variable, whereas a correlation always contains a minimum of two vari-ables. For example, one might generalize that most churchgoers are eld-erly women; but even in this case there is an explicit second variable: elderly men (or age and gender). In Paradise I found that there was a relationship between social-class level and church affiliation, with the Anglican church attracting people from both the highest and lowest classes. Is this an empirical generalization or a correlation? My reaction, unscholarly as it might be, is not to waste any time worrying whether one is producing empirical generalizations, correlations or trends, and simply get on with the job.

2. *Ex Post Facto Explanations*

Merton warns us that such explanations are the weakest type of theorizing. The reason is that the investigator can lift contradictory explanations from the data, but have no criteria to indicate which of them is valid. For example, if it is found that unemployed people read a great deal, the explanation might be that they have the leisure time to do so. But if it is discovered that they read almost nothing, the ready explanation is that they are too anxiety-ridden for such pleasures. From a logical point of view, Merton's position would seem to be unassailable. Nevertheless, I do not think that it is possible to avoid ex post facto explanations in qualitative research. The very inductive procedure of ethnography dictates their necessity. All that one can hope for, I suppose, is that the research has been sufficiently thorough to enable one to exercise sound judgment.

3. *Comparisons with Existing Studies*

If an ethnography is rich with data, there is no need to fill it with reviews of the literature. There will be times, however, when a theme in one's data has such a close fit with existing studies, or is so strikingly unique, that comparisons become obligatory and relevant. In the Paradise study, for example, there was an ideology of egalitarianism, the character of which I compared to similar ideologies in other community studies. I also drew on these community studies in order to judge whether the degree of racism in Paradise was relatively high, average, or low. Then there was the working-class level of the majority of the newcomers. Inasmuch as the literature on migrants from the urban to the rural regions in the United States stressed their middle- and lower-upper class positions, it was important to introduce this literature in order to highlight the special character of the Paradise case.

4. *Implications for and Guidance from General Theory*

As I argued at the outset of this chapter, it is fallacious to think that general theory can serve as a meaningful framework for a fieldwork study.

However, during research one will uncover data that have obvious implications for specific aspects of theoretical orientations. In my West African project, for example, the fact that the village was a theocracy and had enjoyed tremendous economic success made it pertinent to evaluate the applicability of Weber's Protestant ethic thesis, in which he argued that there was a rich congruence between the values of Protestantism and the values of capitalism, leading to the West's economic development. Sometimes an aspect of a general theory will be relevant because it is so completely at odds with what one finds in the field. Durkheim had argued that society evolves from repressive to restitutive law. In Olowo, however, I found the reverse trend. As the community moved into its second generation of existence, repressive law sharply increased, largely to enable the elite to cope with an uncooperative population as private enterprise slowly replaced communalism, and the elite attempted to claim more than its share of the village assets.

In Paradise I discovered that as the community was transformed by the influx of newcomers, ranking by status, based on family reputation and honour, began to disintegrate, leaving in its place a stratification system dominated by class, measured in terms of a person's economic success. This was exactly what Weber had predicted would happen under conditions of rampant social change, and it was entirely relevant to tie the Paradise case to this aspect of his theoretical framework.

5. Quantitative Analysis

While qualitative data and analysis rightfully dominate ethnographic research, it is silly to argue that there is no place for quantitative data and analysis. In fact, anthropological fieldwork has always made room for quantitative materials. The fieldworker need not get carried away with sophisticated statistical measurements. All that is required is to count things that are readily accessible and significant for one's research aims. Earlier, for example, I indicated how I counted canoes, bicycles, motorcycles, and radios in Olowo. Often, as in Paradise, the local archives will be a rich source of data, some of it numerical. Then, too, there are national censuses. In the Paradise study, data provided by Statistics Canada were an important supplementary source, which sometimes served as a useful comparison with my own data on things such as ethnic composition and the proportion of residents who were commuters.

The main purpose of the ethnographic interview is to collect qualitative data. However, the interview is also potentially the most important source of quantitative data available to the researcher, although it is rarely fully exploited. When one does one to two hundred interviews, the normal number in a project, it simply makes sense to summarize the data across the cases in terms of the fundamental variables – age, sex, religion, ethnicity, and so on – and to place this material in tables. It is much more risky to attempt to lift a statistical portrait concerning people's attitudes from the interviews, such as the proportion of those who are tolerant or prejudiced, or who like or dislike commuting. However, if one's data are sound, it may be justifiable to do this, as long as the fieldworker cautions the reader that such data, despite being presented in numerical form, are only crude approximations at best.

EXAMPLES FROM THE LITERATURE

Some support for my arguments about the central importance of models and bursts of insights in ethnographic analysis can be found in the literature. Becker (1970) picked out model construction as one of the four basic steps involved in analysing qualitative data (the other three were selecting and defining problems and concepts, checking the distribution and frequency of phenomena, and deciding how to present the data and demonstrate their validity). Arensberg (1954) stressed that the fundamental goal of community studies is to build models. He also advocated comparing one's model with those in the literature based on other community studies. Then there is Foster's 1965 model of the limited good in peasant society. This model, Foster stated, is hopefully heuristic and illuminating, but it does not necessarily represent the conscious ideas of peasants themselves. In fact, he revealed that none of his informants in Mexico, on which he based his model, ever suggested that they thought in terms of the limited good. The model of the limited good, in other words, would seem to represent precisely the type of arrogant, outsider speculation that has drawn the ire of the postmodernists.

In my view, a model must be constructed out of the conscious and unconscious attitudes, values, and behaviour of the people studied. It must also be a micro model in the sense of being deliberately confined to the social universe under investigation. Finally, and most important of all, a model must make sense to the research subjects. For example, if the model which I built in the Paradise study does not ring true to residents of the community, and if they do not derive from it a deeper understanding of their community, the model has failed in its objectives.

My example from the literature of the burst of insight approach is

Vidich and Bensman's *Small Town in Mass Society* (1958). In many respects this is an unusual book. There is no discussion of general theory, virtually no review of the literature, no hypotheses, no footnotes – in fact, not even any references or bibliography. When I first read this book as a graduate student, I thought it was the work of amateurs.[3] After rereading it in preparation for the study of Paradise, I thought that it was just about the best community study in the business. The book is loaded with rich data and packed with deep insights. It also represents a style that is the polar opposite of some postmodernist works, in which we often learn as much about the author as we do about the research site.

Vidich and Bensman indicated that the topics on which they focused – class, power, and religion – were not what they had in mind when they began the project. Instead, the topics were dictated by what they learned in the field. In a subtle manner, the authors integrate the macro and the micro, showing how the outside bureaucracy penetrates the small community. The strength of the study, however, is the presentation of one insight after another. The authors do not test hypotheses; instead they attempt to provide a deep understanding of what life is like to the residents of the community.

As an example of their insights, consider what they have to say about gossip. The public arena, they state, is confined to expressions of the community ideals, such as the ideology that everyone is equal and harmony universally prevails. Gossip, however, exists as a separate and hidden layer in the community. Gossip is the vehicle for airing the negative aspects of the community and talking about people's foibles and failures. But because it is covert, unofficial, it rarely dislodges the public ideology, or adversely affects any individual. The authors go on to reflect about the great contradiction in the community between the public and private spheres of existence.

Vidich and Bensman also pointed out the deep-seated psychological ambivalence in the town regarding the urban world beyond it. People held scathing views about the frantic pace and dirty, dangerous environment of the city. Yet they also admired the power and wealth commanded by urban America. The insight that I personally found intriguing was that a prerequisite for public office in the town was incompetence. People did not like their elected officials to be too smart – an attitude that was well represented in Paradise.

3 Vidich and Bensman did publish conventional academic articles on the community elsewhere.

Small Town in Mass Society is not a theoretical work in a formal sense, such as Durkheim's *Suicide*, but it certainly is an analytic work. One finishes the book with a great understanding of the community. The authors obviously were successful in penetrating into the back stage, but this became the source of an extremely hostile reaction to the study among the residents of the community. People were angry about the authors' interpretations, such as their discussion of gossip, and the way in which it contradicted the public ideology.[4]

In a commentary on the hostility provoked by the book, Becker (1964) argued that consensus can never be achieved between researcher and research subjects. One reason is that they have different goals. The researcher wants to describe life as it actually is, which means getting into the back stage. The people who live in a community want a book to celebrate their ideals. A second reason, according to Becker, is that communities are always split into different factions. As he stated, 'Since one cannot achieve consensus with all factions simultaneously, the problem is not to avoid harming people but rather to decide which people to harm' (p. 273). This is a harsh judgment about ethnographic work, and once again we are confronted with the old bugbear. Is it justified to poke into the back stage because failure to do so will result in a superficial study? Or do we take the high moral ground occupied by the postmodernists and feminist methodologists and argue that a study is deficient, regardless of the validity of its findings and the depth of its understanding, if it does not empower the people who are investigated?

Writing

In setting out the steps involved in the analysis of qualitative data, I have highlighted the model and the burst of insight. There is, however, another feature of analysis that is even more significant: sheer writing.[5] To a very great degree, writing and analysing are one and the same thing. From the first day in the field, you will begin to write (in fact, even before that, if you produced a research proposal). Do not take notes on

---

4 The authors themselves reflected on the source and meaning of the hostility provoked by their study. See their chapter in Vidich, Bensman, and Stein (1964). For further reflections on the hostility, see Punch (1986:24).

5 I acknowledge the assistance in this section of the *Social Anthropology Handbook*, available in mimeo in the late 1960s at the University of Sussex. Although unpublished, Bailey's contribution on writing in the *Handbook* is as good as anything that exists in the literature.

individual leafs of paper. You will collect so much data that manipulation of these pages and retrieval of ideas and data contained in them will become difficult. Even if the notes are well organized, you will be constantly checking through them, and sheets of paper can become messy and torn. Many fieldworkers take their notes on a stenographer's pad. That isn't a bad idea. In fact, I do that myself! However, it is a mistake to leave things in that state. The notes should then be transferred to a more manageable format. Over the years I have used 5" × 8" index cards, but students nowadays may opt to put their notes on a disk. What is important is to have a system that enhances quick retrieval; otherwise the sheer volume of the data will become overwhelming.

The rule of thumb is to make at least two copies of one's field notes, one organized chronologically as the data were gathered, the other organized in terms of categories and themes. In my first research project I did this (and also made a third copy of the deck of cards arranged according to category and theme). However, I found that I rarely consulted the notes that were in chronological form and now, using carbon paper, I simply make two copies of my notes arranged by category and theme. Within a few weeks of research you should have settled on the basic organization of your notes. However, you should not hesitate to add new categories and modify old ones even after several months of fieldwork. If the organization of your notes has been well done, you leave the field with each category representing a potential chapter in your research report, thesis, or book.

Part of every day in the field should be set aside for writing. The best thing is to write up your observations and interviews at the end of each day. Yet because it is often important or unavoidable to do research during the evening, it is more feasible to put the writing off until the next morning. If this is done, however, a fairly detailed set of rough notes, if only in point form, should have been made the previous day. If one spends two or three hours observing or interviewing, it will take the same length of time to write up the data. Each set of observations or interviews should not simply be described. It should also be analysed, which means reflecting on the implications for previous observations and interviews, considering new directions of research which the data may suggest, and entertaining their broader theoretical significance. It also is relevant to comment on the methods used to gather the data. Was the interview a good one? If not, what went wrong, and how can it be done better next time? Was one a complete observer, or a highly involved participant, and how did one's role affect the data?

Some anthropologists, such as F.G. Bailey, my former teacher in England, have advocated writing papers periodically while still in the field. This is potentially a very important part of the analytic procedure. It forces the reader to pull chunks of data together, and to interpret them. There are, however, two related pitfalls here. The one is that you will fall in love with your own prose, and be reluctant to discard your ideas even if further research undermines them. The other is that it is extremely difficult to graft an obsolete framework of ideas onto a new one. Indeed, it sometimes is easier simply to throw away an old set of ideas and arguments and start afresh. Throughout the fieldwork phase you should constantly be trying to envisage what your thesis or book will look like. This can be done by summarizing your arguments, and composing alternative chapter outlines. Once again, however, these plans can only be tentative; not only will they change from one month to the next, but by the time you have left the field there will probably be little in common between your first chapter outline and your latest one.

Imagine that you are sitting in the library or in an office, fieldwork completed, ready to produce your magnus opus. How do you begin? The first rule is the old maxim: thought precedes action. Before you can put a word down on paper, except for jottings meant to be scrapped, you must think deeply about the overall picture: what are the central arguments, what will the final chapter outline look like? In a sense, the book-writing stage is simultaneously the most creative and dogmatic part of the research process. It is creative in that new ideas are always sparked off by the mere act of putting pen to paper. It is dogmatic in that one must finally take a stance on ambiguous issues, and one must cut off the inflow of data, otherwise the eventual book will lack consistency and coherence, if in fact it is ever completed.

Before beginning to write, you must thoroughly familiarize yourself with the entire body of data collected. This means reading and re-reading your field notes to the point where they are almost memorized. It also means thinking deeply as you read, striving for new interpretations, searching for relationships hitherto overlooked. If you have absorbed your field notes adequately, you will know where every datum is located, and be able to retrieve it in seconds – that is, if your field notes were well organized and are easily accessed. In some projects there will be such an enormous amount of data that the fieldworker will be daunted from the outset. My procedure in these cases is to make a précis of all of the data (reducing two or three thousand index cards to maybe one hundred cards), and then to make a précis of the précis (perhaps ten cards). If this is done well, the information in the ten cards rekindles one's memory about everything in the one hundred cards, and these cards in turn capture the central features of all the data in the project.

You are now ready to write your report, thesis, or book. In order to do so successfully, you must have sizable blocks of time. It is necessary to write for six or eight hours a day, five or six days each week. It is possible to tabulate, collate, and organize data if you only have one or two days available during the week. But creative work requires not just time, but sustained time. You will quite possibly discover that if you only write one or two days per week, each week when you start again you will spend most of your time merely familiarizing yourself with what you wrote during the previous week. Time also is required because to write with some profundity requires a certain degree of intellectual agitation. When one writes day after day, one reaches a level of nervous energy where one's brain hums, out of which emerge insights and interpretations that one never dreamed were in the data.

Do not try to make the first page perfect. Even if your field notes are superbly organized, and you have a marvellous outline, there are still too many choices about what to put down on the first page. The secret is to start with something, with the full realization that it will eventually be discarded. My own style is to write in very rough form an entire book in three or four months. The goal at this stage is to get everything down in each chapter from the various sources of data, such as field notes, documents, and references to the literature. I cannot emphasize too much how important it is to do this. When everything is down on paper, or on the computer screen, rather than scattered among various sources, you have reached a critical plateau; from that point on you will be working with a finite, manageable package, without having to look over your shoulder for possible additional material. In addition, after your data are written up in each chapter, you will be able to see that some themes fit better in other chapters. Often you end up keeping the bulk of the final chapters, but shifting and discarding much of the data and the ideas in the first ones.[6]

To write when one's brain is clear, and the words are flowing effort-

---

6 Becker (1986) is another useful source about writing. He advocates writing the introductory chapter last, because it is difficult to know what should go in it until the entire manuscript has been finished. Becker also has some interesting thoughts about 'classy' language – the tendency among sociologists to use big words and jargon, in order to impress the reader with one's erudition.

lessly, is a joyous experience. Not always does that happen. When you find yourself blocked and can't seem to make any headway, it may make sense to do one of two things. You can skip on to the next chapter, hoping it will go easier. Or you can just jot down in point form all the relevant data, ideas, and references; in my experience, it is rather amazing how these rough notes can be transformed quickly into finished prose when one returns to them with an unclouded mind.

I have suggested that a great deal of reflecting, planning, and organizing must precede writing. My own approach is not to write a word of the actual manuscript until I have worked out the entire thing in my head. Some people do not operate in this manner. They prefer to plunge into the first chapter, and to let their prose determine what the book will look like. In terms of the final outcome, this unstructured procedure is probably as sound as the one that I prefer, but it certainly is a great deal more time-consuming and frustrating. Even for those writers, like myself, who favour a more structured approach, the final product never will turn out as anticipated. One can begin a book with the best-organized notes possible, and with a detailed, powerful, explicit outline, and still there will emerge arguments and interpretations that will force a reorganization of the study. This is as it should be. The very act of writing is creative, an essential aspect of the analytic process. In this book, for example, I began with the plan of placing all the theory chapters in part one, and all the methods chapters in part two. It was only during the last couple of months of writing that I decided on the basis of the data and the arguments that it was more powerful to put theory and method together for each phase in the history of the discipline.

Let me conclude with a few words about style. Not everyone can write with grace and elegance, but all of us can write with clarity if we work at it. You should use the active rather than passive tense, and avoid long sentences and abstract nouns. You should also stay away from jargonistic, pretentious prose. I hesitate to make this last point, because it is often easier to get an article accepted for publication if it sounds professional than if it is written simply and clearly. I know, because that is how I wrote as a neophyte anthropologist. Max Weber, incidentally, commenting on his turgid prose, once quipped that since he found writing so difficult, why should readers have it any easier?

Most of us develop little rituals around our writing activity. Some people have to use paper of a particular colour. One anthropologist revealed that he always left the last sentence unfinished at the end of the day, which made it easier for him to continue the next day. Another man, a famous social scientist, told me that his trick was to begin each day by rewriting the last paragraph of the previous day's work. My advice is not to worry about your little rituals; if they work, stick to them.

Know your audience. Are you writing for a select number of specialists, for students, or for lay people such as the individuals in the community or institution that you investigated? Depending on your audience, your vocabulary and tone will vary. It may also be that the structure of your prose will change as well. In contrast to novels, where one conveys meaning indirectly – for example, indicating that it is raining by evoking the sound of running shoes squashing and smacking on the pavement – in social scientific writing one communicates more directly. In addition, in such writing the shadow of the framework of the study is usually more visible, and in some works it juts out, commanding our attention, often to the extent of distracting from the prose.

A decision also has to be made whether to provide separate chapters for the data and the analysis. In my West African project I did this, but now I agree with Hammersley and Atkinson (1983:222) that it was a mistake. One reason is that there is always the possibility in the analysis chapter that the writer will make theoretical claims far beyond what can be supported by the data. Another reason is that such a separation can give the misleading impression that the data chapters are the real thing, unanalysed raw data, devoid of the researcher's interpretations. The fact is, of course, that all data are interpreted data. As the postmodernists would say, the very act of writing is an interpretive venture. That is why I have argued that writing and analysis are one and the same thing.

Conclusion

I have argued that there are three key dimensions to the analysis of qualitative data: the model, the burst of insight, and the writing process. Not always, however, has the importance of these dimensions been recognized by ethnographers. In fact, in many research reports what often passes for analysis are two alternative procedures, each of them quite unsatisfactory. One is to employ a general perspective such as conflict theory or symbolic interaction as the explanatory framework. In my experience, undergraduate students, understandably desperate to hinge their data to something resembling theory, are particularly prone to presenting the basic features of an entire theoretical orientation in their research reports. In such an approach, the theory and the data are separate entities, the links between them tenuous. Sometimes students think their data can be 'proved' by such general theoretical orientations, but that is quite improbable. What the exercise amounts to is labelling, putting a well-known brand name on the ethnographic product.

I hasten to add that some of my colleagues proceed in a similar manner. The skeleton of an identifiable theoretical approach such as pluralism or cultural ecology is sketched out in an introductory chapter, then more often than not ignored in the rest of the book. It would make just as much sense, at least to a professional audience, if we assigned numbers to all of the known theoretical orientations, and merely mentioned the relevant number in our preface. This is because the point of the exercise appears to be little more than to convey to the reader the intellectual perspective in which the study has been set.

The other unsatisfactory approach is the review of the literature. It may be regarded as a type of theorizing, but if so it is an especially weak type. Even when done well, which amounts to identifying significant and relevant problems in the literature which then can be addressed by one's data, the literature review is analytically second-best when compared to the capacity of the model and the burst of insight to illuminate the inner workings of a community or institution. The tendency to present a review of the literature as the theoretical framework for a study is often apparent in the works of card-carrying anthropologists, and is particularly prevalent in graduate theses (and research proposals). Even when separate chapters in a thesis are devoted to the literature review and to the theoretical framework (or model), it is sometimes difficult to tell which is which.

The approach taken by graduate students in sociology, especially if they are doing a quantitative thesis, is quite intriguing from an ethnographer's point of view. Often a student will write a literature review chapter and a theory chapter before they even begin the task of analysing the data – at times even before the data have been collected. The impression is that the literature, the theory, the data, and the analysis are discrete sections, independent of each other. To some extent this is a reasonable procedure in sociology, because analysis does constitute a separate step in the research process if the data are numerical and if sophisticated statistical tests are employed. Besides, it could be argued that the thesis is only a learning vehicle in which the research process is broken down into its various steps in order to teach students more effectively how to conduct and present a study, and perhaps to make it easier for the instructor to evaluate their overall strengths and weaknesses.

This is not, let me stress, a reasonable procedure in ethnographic research, whether conducted by anthropologists or sociologists. First of all, the analysis of data begins with one's initial observation or interview, continues daily until fieldwork is completed, and extends through every step of the writing-up process. Second, the main goal of ethnography is (or should be) to provide an understanding of the community, institution, or category of people investigated, rather than to promote existing theory in the discipline.

In closing, let me speculate about how the fans of feminist methodology and postmodernism might react to this chapter. It is quite probable that they would find acceptable the argument that the model is restricted to the project under investigation, rather than drawn from general theory; but they would be unhappy with the attempt to craft a unified, coherent overview rather than being satisfied with fragmented sketches. They might also shudder at the idea of the burst of insight, especially if this implies that the fieldworker possesses a greater capacity to understand a community than the people who live in it; and there certainly would be misgivings about the slick scientific orientation, and about an analytical procedure which ignores the textual character of ethnography. But on one matter it would seem that conventional ethnographic analysis and the two recent intellectual revolutions would be on the same wavelength: the central importance of writing. Writing is what anthropologists do, and writing involves interpretation, and all that that implies about authority, distortion, empowerment, and explanation.

9

Taming the Anthropologist: The World Ahead

The imagery in the titles of the first and final chapters of this book – unleashing and taming the anthropologist – is meant to tell a story. The early anthropologists were set loose among the natives, armed with a sense of moral, cultural, and intellectual superiority, plus the authority of the Colonial Office. No doubt kind and compassionate feelings towards the natives often existed, not all of it paternalistic, but at the same time there were few constraints on the anthropologist's inquiries except for her or his own ethnocentrism and sense of decency. The world of the primitive, in other words, was a hunting ground stocked with a marvellous display of exotic species.[1] It might reasonably be argued that the anthropologist in the field, learning first-hand about pre-industrial peoples, was a marked improvement over the evolutionist in the armchair, filtering other cultures through Western lens. Some writers might even contend, as I would, that the ethnographic reports produced by individuals such as Franz Boas, Bronislaw Malinowski, and Audrey Richards have rarely been matched since then in terms of the quality of the data and the sophistication of the analysis. Yet it is hard to escape from the observation that early anthropology was an unequal clash between powerful outsiders and captive insiders (or between the hunter and the hunted).

That portrait of the anthropologist is barely recognizable today. In a whole range of ways, the anthropologist has been tamed. Tamed in the

---

1 In this context, it is relevant to quote from Malinowski's (1961:8) famous statement of method in *Argonauts*: 'the Ethnographer has not only to spread his nets in the right place, and wait for what will fall into them, he must be an active huntsman, and drive his quarry into them and follow it up to its most inaccessible lairs.'

sense that access to other cultures is no longer guaranteed. Tamed in the sense of being domesticated, reflected by the number of ethnographers who now practise their craft at home. Tamed by theory – the challenges of postmodernism and feminist methodology to the anthropologist's authority, scholarly goals, and ethics. Tamed, or at least cowed, by what Geertz has referred to as a loss of nerve. There was a time, not so long ago in fact, when the superiority of the fieldworker's perspective was taken for granted. Thus Gluckman could write: 'There is little doubt that the anthropologist, with his training and techniques and background of knowledge, can know far more about an unstudied area than the people who live in it' (1936:229). One would have to possess a pretty thick skin to make a similar claim in the 1990s. As Geertz has observed, 'The publication of Malinowski's *A Diary in the Strict Sense of the Term* ... pretty well exploded the notion that anthropologists obtained their results through some special ability, usually called "empathy," to "get inside the skins" of savages' (1983:9).

Finally, the anthropologist has been tamed by methodology. Qualitative methods may be more popular today in more disciplines than at any previous point in history. But this is qualitative investigation with a difference. Quickly disappearing is the image of the anthropologist, free in spirit, roaming the globe like an intrepid explorer, returning gloriously with the inside story of an exotic South Sea village, based on nothing more substantial than a few months' residence. One reason is that these exotic societies, in splendid isolation from the wider world, no longer exist. Another reason is that qualitative methods have been demystified, broken down into systematic steps that ethnographers are increasingly expected to follow. There even is a movement, as I indicated in an earlier chapter, to computerize the approach. Should it become the wave of the future, there no longer will be any doubt that anthropologists have been put on a leash.

Not all anthropologists have meekly accepted the taming influences on their discipline. Many established scholars still seem committed to fieldwork in other cultures, even if governments abroad are uncooperative and they have to make do with a short-term visitor's visa. Perhaps they can rationalize their intrusion by arguing that 'the people' want them even if political leaders don't, although that strikes me as arrogant. Some scholars would argue that their research interests are thoroughly up to date, revolving around political rhetoric, development, social change, and the impact of colonialism – the very topics, ironically, that Malinowski emphasized as far back as the late 1930s. Then, too, there is the assumption that the outsider's perspective is particularly powerful, and that the cross-cultural method lies at the very heart of the discipline. It could even be claimed that descriptions of customs and beliefs from around the globe have an important relativizing impact on citizens of the West, although it is equally possible that such accounts will reinforce the Western sense of superiority. Not to be overlooked is the romantic side of anthropology. If fieldwork in other cultures has little future, some students might wonder why they should bother becoming anthropologists at all.

Many anthropologists also have dug in their heels regarding the changes in method and theory. Fieldworkers today may be more willing to use a questionnaire or structured interview than in the past, but the lone participant observer in the company of informants continues to call the tune. As for theory, it is not unusual to hear anthropologists (and sociologists, geographers, and political scientists) complain about post-modernism, and declare that they have not devoted their entire careers to empirical social science only to give it up for an approach of dubious scholarly merit.

The changes in anthropology have had consequences for the concept of culture. In chapter one it was argued that culture is too general and vague to serve much use as an explanatory tool. In recent years there has been a new type of attack on the concept. Abu-Lughod (1991) urges anthropologists to write against culture, to undermine the concept. This is because culture, in her judgment, has become the contemporary equivalent of race. Like race, it separates people, arranges them into hierarchies, and freezes the system so that institutionalized inequality prevails. By brandishing the culture concept in their studies, anthropologists, she argues, have contributed to the tendency to treat difference and hierarchy as 'natural.'

Abu-Lughod recommends an alternative approach which she labels 'the ethnography of the particular.' Rather than describing Bedouin culture, for example, the ethnographer would provide a rounded account of the lives of particular Bedouins. 'By focusing closely on particular individuals and their changing relationships,' she wrote, 'one would necessarily subvert the most problematic connotations of culture: homogeneity, coherence, and timelessness' (p. 154).

In mounting this argument, Abu-Lughod has placed herself in good company. A couple of decades earlier Geertz advocated that anthropologists study not culture but a particular culture, not religion but a particular religion, not a particular culture or religion but a particular person in a culture or religion. In Geertz's words: 'the road to the general ... lies through a concern with the particular' (1973:53). He also offered a definition of culture that differed sharply from most others in the discipline: 'culture is best seen not as complexes of concrete behavior patterns – customs, images, traditions, habit clusters – as has, by and large, been the case up to now, but as a set of control mechanisms – plans, recipes, rules, instructions (what computer engineers call "programs") – for the governing of behavior.' Cultural patterns, he continued, are 'organized systems of significant symbols' (pp. 44, 46). The ideas of Abu-Lughod and Geertz, it will be apparent, overlap considerably with postmodernism and feminist methodology, where the life history and 'meaning' are emphasized.

With or without these changes (including the conception of culture), there are anthropologists who fear that the discipline is slated for extinction. As Ember and Ember have put it, 'Some of those who are worried about the future of cultural anthropology foresee the disappearance of their discipline because it has traditionally focused on cultural variation, and that variation is diminishing. Cultural anthropology, for these people, is synonymous with the ethnographic study of exotic, out-of-the-way cultures not previously described' (1988:338).' In this context, it is interesting that Lévi-Strauss once suggested that anthropology might be more appropriately renamed entropology – the study of the processes of disintegration (1974:414). Fabian has gone so far as to argue that anthropology 'should strive for its own liquidation' (1991:262). Whenever the conditions that produced anthropology, notably the imperialist age, wither away, anthropology, Fabian forecasts, will sink into oblivion. This will be a time to celebrate because it will be 'not just the end, but the overcoming ... of anthropology' (p. 261).

This is a bleak picture of the discipline's future, and I doubt that it is entirely accurate. Even if anthropology were to become a sort of cultural survival in Tylor's sense, an institution that continues to exist without function, academic vested interests will probably keep it afloat for a long time ahead. Besides, there have already been signs of adjustment, rendering the sole focus on other cultures obsolete – a trend, I predict, that will pick up speed as younger anthropologists replace their elders. If at the same time native and indigenous anthropology blossom and feminist anthropology continues to hold its own, thus overcoming past cultural, ethnic, racial, and gender biases, the prospects for the discipline are positive. Geertz, the most influential anthropologist today, has written 'it seems likely that whatever use ethnographic texts will have in the future, if in fact they actually have any, it will involve enabling conversation across social lines – of ethnicity, religion, class, gender, language, race – that have grown progressively more nuanced, more immediate, and more irregular' (1988:147). Any discipline capable of this accomplishment has too much to offer to be abandoned without a struggle.

Let me give the last word to theory and method. An eminent psychologist whom I once knew habitually argued with his dean that it was necessary to offer more money to new recruits in his department than in the hard sciences. His explanation was that psychology was so much more ambiguous and open-ended than biology or chemistry that only the best minds could make a contribution. In a sense, this accounts for the importance of theory and method in anthropology. Because the social world is ever-changing and difficult to grasp, much more attention must be paid to theory and method than in the natural and physical sciences. But the proliferation of theories and techniques, so characteristic of the social sciences, does not necessarily indicate explanatory progress. The social sciences have always been multi-paradigmatic, an inevitable product of their subject matter, which means experimentation in theory and method is the normal state of affairs.

For the student of anthropology, sophistication in theory and method is the measure of maturity. In this study I have attempted to provide a clear picture of the major theoretical orientations and techniques over time, and the relationships between them. What has stood out has been the growing gap between theory, method, and the fieldwork situation during the past couple of decades. If anthropology is indeed to have a future, this will in no small measure depend on the capacity of the next generation of ethnographers to bridge that gap.

Bibliography

Abu-Lughod, Lila. 1991. 'Writing Against Culture.' In Richard G. Fox, ed., *Recapturing Anthropology*, pp. 137–62. Sante Fe, NMex.: School of American Research Press.

Acker, Joan, et al. 1983. 'Objectivity and Truth: Problems in Doing Feminist Research.' *Women's Studies International Forum* 6:423–35.

– 1989. 'Making Gender Visible.' In Ruth A. Wallace, ed., *Feminism and Sociological Theory*, pp. 65–81. Newbury Park, Calif.: Sage Publications.

Ackerman, Robert. 1987. *J.G. Frazer. His Life and Work*. Cambridge: Cambridge University Press.

Adler, Patricia, et al. 1986. 'The Politics of Participation in Field Research.' *Urban Life* 14:363–76.

Agar, Michael H. 1980. *The Professional Stranger: An Informal Introduction to Ethnography*. Orlando, Fla: Academic Press.

Aguilar, John L. 1981. 'Inside Research: An Ethnography of a Debate.' In Donald A. Messerschmidt, ed., *Anthropologists at Home in North America: Methods and Issues in the Study of One's Own Society*, pp. 15–26. Cambridge: Cambridge University Press.

Albera, Dionigi. 1988. 'Open Systems and Closed Minds: The Limitations of Naivety in Social Anthropology – A Native's View.' *Man* 23:435–52.

Alcoff, Linda. 1988. 'Cultural Feminism Versus Post-Structuralism: The Identity Crisis in Feminist Theory.' *Signs* 13:405–36.

Allport, Gordon. 1942. *The Use of Personal Documents in Psychological Science*. New York: Social Sciences Research Council.

Althusser, L. 1969. *For Marx*. Trans. B. Brewster. London: Allen Lane, Penguin Press.

Anderson, Barbara Gallatin. 1990. *First Fieldwork: The Misadventures of an Anthropologist*. Prospect Heights, Ill.: Waveland Press.

Appadurai, Arjun. 1991. 'Global Ethnoscapes: Notes and Queries for a Transnational Anthropology.' In Richard G. Fox, ed., *Recapturing Anthropology*, pp. 191–210. Sante Fe, NMex.: School of American Research Press.

Arensberg, Conrad M. 1954. 'The Community-Study Method.' The *American Journal of Sociology* 60:109–24.

Asad, Talal, ed., 1973. *Anthropology and the Colonial Encounter*. London: Ithaca Press.

Atkinson, Jane Monnig. 1982. 'Anthropology.' *Signs* 8:236–58.

Babbie, Earl R. 1983. *The Practice of Social Research*. California: Wadsworth Publishing.

Bailey, F.G. 1969. *Stratagems and Spoils*. Oxford: Blackwell.

– 1991. *The Prevalence of Deceit*. Ithaca and London: Cornell University Press.

Banton, Michael. 1967. *Race Relations*. London: Tavistock Publications.

Barker, John. 1992. Review of *The Queen's People* in *Canadian Review of Sociology and Anthropology* 29:541–3.

Barnes, J.A. 1947. 'The Collection of Genealogies.' *Rhodes-Livingstone Journal* 5:48–55.

– 1967. 'Some Ethical Problems in Modern Field Work.' In D.G. Jongmans and P.C.W. Gutkind, eds., *Anthropologists in the Field*, pp. 193–213. Assen: Van Gorcum and Company.

– 1968. 'Networks and Political Process.' In Marc J. Swartz, ed., *Local-Level Politics*, pp. 107–33. Chicago: Aldine Publishing Company.

– 1969a. 'Graph Theory and Social Networks: A Technical Comment on Connectedness and Connectivity.' *Sociology* 3:215–32.

– 1969b. 'Networks and Political Process.' In James Clyde Mitchell, ed., *Social Networks in Urban Situations*, pp. 51–76. Manchester: Manchester University Press.

– 1972. *Social Networks*. Reading, Mass.: Addison-Wesley.

– 1990. *Models and Interpretations*. Cambridge: Cambridge University Press.

Barrett, Michele. 1986. 'The Soapbox.' *Network* (British Sociological Association newsletter) 35:20.

Barrett, Stanley R. 1974. *Two Villages on Stilts*. New York: Chandler.

– 1976. 'The Use of Models in Anthropological Fieldwork.' *Journal of Anthropological Research* 32:161–81.

– 1977. *The Rise and Fall of an African Utopia*. Waterloo, Ont.: Wilfrid Laurier University Press.

– 1984a. 'Racism, Ethics and the Subversive Nature of Anthropological Inquiry.' *Philosophy of the Social Sciences* 14:1–25.

– 1984b. *The Rebirth of Anthropological Theory*. Toronto: University of Toronto Press.

– 1987. *Is God a Racist? The Right Wing in Canada*. Toronto: University of Toronto Press.

– 1994. *Paradise: Class, Commuters, and Ethnicity in Rural Ontario*. Toronto: University of Toronto Press.

Barth, Fredrik. 1959. *Political Leadership among Swat Pathans*. London: Athlone Press.

– 1966. *Models of Social Organization*. London: Royal Anthropological Institute, Occasional Paper No. 23.

– ed. 1969. *Ethnic Groups and Boundaries*. Boston: Little, Brown.

Bartlett, F.G., et al., eds. 1939. *The Study of Society: Methods and Problems*. New York: The Macmillan Company.

Beals, Ralph L. 1967. 'Background Information on Problems of Anthropological Research and Ethics.' *Fellows Newspaper of the American Anthropological Association* 8:2–13.

Beals, Alan R., and Barnard J. Siegel. 1966. *Divisiveness and Social Conflict*. Stanford: Stanford University Press.

Beattie, John. 1964. *Other Cultures*. London: Cohen and West.

– 1965. *Understanding an African Kingdom: Bunyoro*. New York: Holt, Rinehart and Winston.

Becker, Ernest. 1971. *The Lost Science of Man*. New York: E. Braziller.

Becker, Howard S. 1958. 'Problems of Inference and Proof in Participant Observation.' *American Sociological Review* 23:652–60. Reprinted in 1970, William J. Filstead, ed., *Qualitative Methodology*. Chicago: Markham Publishing Company.

– 1964. 'Problems in the Publication of Field Studies.' In Arthur J. Vidich, Joseph Bensman, and Maurice R. Stein, eds., *Reflections on Community Studies*, pp. 267–84. New York: John Wiley and Sons.

– 1970. 'Problems of Inference and Proof in Participant Observation.' In William J. Filstead, ed., *Qualitative Methodology*, pp. 189–201. Chicago: Markham Publishing Company.

– 1986. *Writing for Social Scientists*. Chicago: University of Chicago Press.

Becker, Howard S., and Blanche Geer. 1960. 'Participant Observation: The Analysis of Qualitative Field Data.' In R.N. Adams and J. Preiss, eds., *Human Organization Research*, pp. 267–89. Homewood, Ill.: Dorsey Press.

Becker, Jean. 1993. The Implications of Post-Modern Theory for Aboriginal Studies., MA major paper. Department of Sociology and Anthropology, University of Guelph.

Benedict, Ruth. 1959 (orig. 1934). *Patterns of Culture*. Boston: Houghton Mifflin.

Bennett, John W. 1969. *Northern Plainsmen*. Chicago: Aldine Publishing Company.

– 1982. *Of Time and the Enterprise*. Minneapolis: University of Minnesota Press.

– 1993. *Human Ecology as Human Behavior*. New Brunswick: Transition.

Berg, Bruce L. 1989. *Qualitative Research Methods for the Social Sciences*. Needham Heights, Mass.: Allyn and Bacon.

Bernard, H.R., and M.J. Evans. 1983. 'New Microcomputer Techniques for Anthropologists.' *Human Organization* 42:182–5.

Berreman, Gerald D. 1962. 'Behind Many Masks.' Published by the Society for Applied Anthropology. Lexington, Ky: University of Kentucky.

– 1968. 'Is Anthropology Alive? Social Responsibility in Social Anthropology.' *Current Anthropology* 9:391–6.

Black-Michaud, Jacob. 1975. *Cohesive Force: Feud in the Mediterranean and the Middle East*. New York: St. Martin's Press.

Blumenbach, J.F. 1865 (orig. 1775). *The Anthropological Treatises of Johann Friedrich Blumenbach*. Trans. and ed. Thomas Bendyshe. London: Longman, Green, Longman, Roberts and Green.

Boas, Franz. 1897. *The Social Organization and the Secret Societies of the Kwakiutl Indians*. Washington: Report of the U.S. National Museum, 1895.

Boissevain, Jeremy. 1968. 'The Place of Non-Groups in the Social Sciences.' *Man* 3:542–56.

– 1971. 'Second Thoughts on Quasi-Groups, Categories and Coalitions.' *Man* 6:168–72.

– 1974. *Friends of Friends*. Oxford: Basil Blackwell.

Borman, K., and J. Taylor. 1986. 'Ethnographic and Qualitative Research and Why It Doesn't Work.' *American Behavioral Scientist* 30:42–57.

Boserup, Ester. 1970. *Women's Role in Economic Development*. London: Allen and Unwin.

Bott, Elizabeth. 1957. *Family and Social Network*. London: Tavistock Publications.

Bourguignon, E. 1979. *Psychological Anthropology*. New York: Holt, Rinehart and Winston.

Bowen, Elenore Smith. 1954. *Return to Laughter*. New York: Harper.

Brajuha, M., and L. Hallowell. 1986. 'Legal Instrusion and the Politics of Fieldwork.' *Urban Life* 14:454–79.

Brenner, M., et al., eds. 1985. *The Research Interview: Uses and Approaches*. London: Academic Press.

Brim, John A., and David H. Spain. 1974. *Research Design in Anthropology*. New York: Holt, Rinehart and Winston.

Bruyn, Severyn T. 1966. *The Human Prespective in Sociology: The Methodology of Participant Observation*. Englewood Cliffs, NJ: Prentice-Hall.

Bryman, Alan. 1984. 'The Debate About Quantitative and Qualitative Research: A Question of Method or Epistemology?' *British Journal of Sociology* 35:75–92.

Burgess, Robert G. 1982. *In the Field: An Introduction to Field Research*. London: George Allen and Unwin.

– ed. 1985. *Field Methods in the Study of Education*. London: Falmer Press.

Burling, R. 1964. 'Cognition and Anthropological Analysis: God's Truth or Hocus-pocus.' *American Anthropologist* 66:20–68.

Burridge, Kenelm. 1968. 'Lévi-Strauss and Myth.' In Edmund Leach, ed., *The Structural Study of Myth and Totemism*. Social Science Paperback, ASA Monograph 5.

Carstens, Peter. 1991. *The Queen's People: A Study of Hegemony, Coercion, and Accommodation among the Okanagan of Canada*. Toronto: University of Toronto Press.

Casagrande, Joseph B. ed., 1960. *In the Company of Man: Twenty Portraits of Anthropological Informants*. New York: Harper and Row.

Cebotarev, E.A. 1986. 'Women's Contribution to Agricultural Science and Technology.' *Resources for Feminist Research* 15:43–5.

Chagnon, Napoleon A. 1974. *Studying the Yanomamo*. New York: Holt, Rinehart and Winston.

Chirrey, G. Shawn. 1994. 'Medicine and the Postmodern Turn.' MA major paper. Department of Sociology and Anthropology, University of Guelph.

Chomsky, Noam. 1973. *Language and Mind*. 2nd ed. New York: Harcourt Brace Jovanovich.

Cicourel, Aaron V. 1964. *Method and Measurement in Sociology*. New York: The Free Press.

Clegg, Sue. 1985. 'Feminist Methodology – Fact or Fiction?' *Quality and Quantity* 19:83–97.

Clifford, James. 1980. 'Fieldwork, Reciprocity and the Making of Ethnographic Texts: The Example of Maurice Leenhardt.' *Man* 15:518–32.

– 1983. 'On Ethnographic Authority.' *Representations* 1:118–46.

– 1986. 'On Ethnographic Allegory.' In James Clifford and George E. Marcus, eds., *Writing Culture*, pp. 98–121. Berkeley: University of California Press.

Clifford, James, and George E. Marcus, eds. *Writing Culture*. Berkeley: University of California Press.

Codere, Helen. 1950. *Fighting with Property*. Monographs of the American Ethnological Society, vol. 18. New York: J.J. Augustin.

Cohen, Abner. 1969. *Custom and Conflict in Urban Africa*. London: Routledge and Kegan Paul.

Cohen, Eugene, and Edwin Eames. 1982. *Cultural Anthropology*. Boston, Toronto: Little, Brown and Company.

Cole, M. 1990. 'Cultural Psychology: A Once and Future Discipline?' In J.J. Berman, ed., *Cross-Cultural Perspectives*. Lincoln: University of Nebraska Press.

Collier, John, Jr. 1967. *Visual Anthropology: Photography as a Research Method*. New York: Holt, Rinehart and Winston.

Conrad, P., and S. Reinharz. 1984. 'Computers and Qualitative Data.' *Qualitative Sociology* 7:3–15.

Coser, Lewis. 1964 (orig. 1956). *The Functions of Social Conflict*. New York: The Free Press.

– 1967. *Continuities in the Study of Social Conflict*. New York: The Free Press.

Coser, Ruth Laub. 1989. 'Reflections on Feminist Theory.' In Ruth A. Wallace, ed., *Feminism and Sociological Theory*. pp. 200–7. Newbury Park, Calif.: Sage Publications.

Crane, Julia G., and Michael V. Angrosino. 1974. *Field Projects in Anthropology*. Morristown, New Jersey: General Learning Press.

Crapanzano, Vincent. 1980. *Tuhami: Portrait of a Moroccan*. Chicago: University of Chicago Press.

– 1986. 'Hermes' Dilemma: The Masking of Subversion in Ethnographic Description.' In Clifford, James, and George E. Marcus, eds., *Writing Culture*, pp. 51–76. Berkeley: University of California Press.

Cruikshank, Julie. 1990. *Life Lived Like a Story*. Vancouver, BC: University of British Columbia Press.

Culwick, A.T., and G.M. Culwick. 1938. 'Culture Contact on the Fringe of Civilization.' *Methods of Study of Culture Contact in Africa*, pp. 38–45. London: Oxford University Press.

Dahrendorf, Ralf. 1958. 'Out of Utopia: Towards a Reorientation of Sociological Analysis.' *American Journal of Sociology* 64:115–27.

– 1959. *Class and Class Conflict in Industrial Society*. Stanford: Stanford University Press.

Darnell, Regna, and Judith Irvine, eds. 1994. *The Collected Works of Edward Sapir* IV. Berlin and New York: Mouton de Gruyter.

David, Kingsley. 1959. 'The Myth of Functional Analysis as a Special Method in Sociology and Anthropology.' *American Sociological Review* 24:757–72.

Dean, John P. and William Foote Whyte. 1958. 'How Do You Know If the Informant Is Telling the Truth?' *Human Organization* 17:34–8.

Denzin, Norman K. 1970. *The Research Act*. Chicago.: Aldine Publishing Company.

Denzin, Norman K. and Yvonna S. Lincoln. 1994. *Handbook of Qualitative Research*. Thousand Oaks, Calif.: Sage Publications.

De Santis, G. 1980. 'Interviewing as Social Interaction.' *Qualitative Sociology* 2:72–98.

Diamond, Stanley. 1964. 'Nigerian Discovery: The Politics of Field Work.' In Arthur J. Vidich, Joseph Bensman, and Maurice R. Stein, eds., *Reflections on Community Studies*, pp. 119–54. New York: John Wiley and Sons.

Dietz, Mary Lorenz, et al. 1994. *Doing Everyday Life*. Mississauga, Ont.: Copp Clark Longman.

Dobbert, M. 1982. *Ethnographic Research: Theory and Application for Modern Schools and Societies*. New York: Praeger.

Dollard, John. 1935. *Criteria for the Life History*. New Haven: Yale University Press.

Douglas, Jack. 1985. *Creative Interviewing*. Newbury Park, Calif.: Sage Publications.

Driver, H.E. 1953. 'Statistics in Anthropology.' *American Anthropologist* 55:42–59.

Du Bois, Cora. 1970. 'Studies in an Indian Town.' In Peggy Golde, ed., *Women in the Field*, pp. 221–38. Chicago: Aldine Publishing Company.

Durkheim, Emile. 1933 (orig. 1893). *Division of Labor in Society*. New York: Macmillan.

– 1938 (orig. 1895). *The Rules of Sociological Method*. Chicago: University of Chicago Press.

– 1951 (orig. 1897). *Suicide*. Glencoe, Ill.: The Free Press.

Dwyer, Kevin. 1982. *Moroccan Dialogues*. Baltimore: Johns Hopkins University Press.

Eichler, Margrit. 1986. 'The Relationship Between Sexist, Nonsexist, Women-Centred, and Feminist Research.' *Studies in Communication* 3:37–74.

Ellen, R.F., ed., 1984. *Ethnographic Research: A Guide to General Conduct*. London: Academic Press.

Ember, Carol, and Melvin Ember. 1988 (orig. 1973). *Cultural Anthropology*. Englewood Cliffs, NJ: Prentice Hall.

Epstein, A.L., ed., 1967. *The Craft of Social Anthropology*. London: Tavistock Publications.

Erikson, Kai T. 1967. 'A Comment on Disguised Observation in Sociology.' *Social Problems* 14:366–73.

Evans-Pritchard, E.E. 1968 (orig. 1950). 'Social Anthropology: Past and Present.' In Robert Manners and David Kaplan, eds., *Theory in Anthropology*. Chicago: Aldine Publishing Company.

– 1969 (orig. 1940). *The Nuer*. Oxford: Oxford University Press.

Fabian, Johannes. 1971. 'On Professional Ethics and Epistemological Foundations.' *Current Anthropology* 12:230–1.

– 1991. *Time and the Work of Anthropology: Critical Essays, 1971–1991*. Reading: Harwood Academic Publishers.

Fallers, Lloyd. 1965. *Bantu Bureaucracy: A Century of Political Evolution among the Basoga of Uganda*. Chicago: University of Chicago Press.

Fielding, N., and R. Lee, eds. 1991. *Using Computers in Qualitative Analysis*. Newbury Park, Calif.: Sage Publications.

Filstead, William J., ed., 1970. *Qualitative Methodology*. Chicago: Markham Publishing Company.

Firth, Raymond. 1957 (orig. 1936). *We, the Tikopia*. London: George Allen and Unwin.

– 1964a. *Elements of Social Organization*. Boston: Beacon Press.

– 1964b. *Essays on Social Organization and Values*. London: The Athlone Press.

Fischer, Ann. 1970. 'Field Work in Five Cultures.' In Peggy Golde, ed., *Women in the Field*, pp. 267–92. Chicago: Aldine Publishing Company.

Fischer, J. 1958. 'The Classification of Residences in Censuses.' *American Anthropologist* 60:508–17.

Fortes, M. 1938. 'Culture Contact as a Dynamic Process.' *Methods of Study of Culture Contact in Africa*, pp. 60–91. London: Oxford University Press.

Fortes, M., et al. 1947. 'Ashanti Survey, 1945–46: An Experiment in Social Research.' *Geographical Journal* 110:149–79.

Foster, George. 1965. 'Peasant Society and the Image of the Limited Good.' *American Anthropologist* 67:293–310.

Frank, André Gunder. 1970. 'The Development of Underdevelopment.' In Robert I. Rhodes, ed., *Imperialism and Underdevelopment*. New York: Monthly Review Press.

Frazer, James. 1958 (orig. 1890). *The Golden Bough*. New York: Macmillan.

Freeman, Derek. 1983. *Margaret Mead and Samoa: The Making and Unmaking of an Anthropological Myth*. Cambridge, Mass.: Harvard University Press.

Fried, Morton H. 1972. *The Study of Anthropology*. New York: Thomas Y. Crowell Company.

Friedman, Jonathon. 1974. 'Marxism, Structuralism and Vulgar Materialism.' *Man* 9:444–69.

– 1988. 'Comments.' *Current Anthropology* 29:426–7.

Frielich, Morris, ed., 1970. *Marginal Natives: Anthropologists at Work*. New York: Harper and Row, Publishers.

Furnivall, J.S. 1939. *Netherlands India*. Cambridge: Cambridge University Press.

Gacs, Ute, et al. 1988. *Women Anthropologists: A Biographical Dictionary*. New York: Greenwood Press.

Geertz, Clifford. 1973. *The Interpretation of Cultures*. New York: Basic Books.

– 1983. *Local Knowledge*. New York: Basic Books, Inc.

– 1988. *Works and Lives*. Stanford, Calif.: Stanford University Press.

Gephart, Robert P., Jr. 1988. *Ethnostatistics: Qualitative Foundations for Quantitative Research*. Newbury Park, Calif.: Sage Publications.

Gerson, E. 1984. 'Qualitative Work and the Computer.' *Qualitative Sociology* 7:61–74.

Gilbert, J.P., and E.A. Hammel. 1966. 'Computer Simulation and Analysis of Problems in Kinship and Social Structure.' *American Anthropologist* 68:70–93.

Glaser, Barney G., and Anselm L. Strauss. 1967. *The Discovery of Grounded Theory: Strategies for Qualitative Research*. Chicago: Aldine Publishing Company.

Gluckman, Max. 1956. *Custom and Conflict in Africa*. Oxford: Basil Blackwell.

– 1963. *Order and Rebellion in Tribal Africa*. London: Cohen and West.

– 1968 (orig. 1944). 'The Difficulties, Achievements, and Limitations of Social Anthropology.' In Robert Manners and David Kaplan, eds., *Theory in Anthropology*. Chicago: Aldine Publishing Company.

Glucksmann, M. 1974. *Structural Analysis in Contemporary Social Thought*. London: Routledge and Kegan Paul.

Godelier, M. 1972 (orig. 1966). *Rationality and Irrationality in Economics*. London: Nlb.

Gold, Raymond L. 1958. 'Roles in Sociological Observations.' *Social Forces* 36:217–23.

Golde, Peggy, ed., 1970. *Women in the Field*. Chicago: Aldine Publishing Company.

Goodenough, Ward. 1956. 'Residence Rules.' *Southwestern Journal of Anthropology* 12:22–37.

Goody, Jack. 1969. *Comparative Studies in Kinship*. London: Routledge and Kegan Paul.

– 1976. *Family and Inheritance: Rural Society in Western Europe, 1200–1800*. Cambridge: Cambridge University Press.

– 1983. *The Development of the Family and Marriage in Europe*. Cambridge: Cambridge University Press.

Gough, Kathleen. 1968. 'New Proposals for Anthropologists.' *Current Anthropology* 5:403–7.

Gramsci, Antonio. 1976. *Selections from the Prison Notebooks*. ed., and trans. Quinton Hoare and Geoffrey Nowell-Smith. New York: International Publishers.

Greenhouse, C.J. 1985. 'Anthropology at Home: Whose Home?' *Human Organization* 44:261–4.

Gubrian, Jaber. 1988. *Analyzing Field Reality*. Newbury Park, Calif.: Sage Publications.

Gudschinsky, Sarah C. 1967. *How to Learn an Unwritten Language*. New York: Holt, Rinehart and Winston.

Gwaltney, John L. 1981. 'Common Sense and Science: Urban Core Black Observations.' In Donald A. Messerschmidt, ed., *Anthropology at Home in North America: Methods and Issues in the Study of One's Own Society*, pp. 46–61. Cambridge: Cambridge University Press.

Hall, John R., and Mary Jo Neitz. 1993. *Culture: Sociological Perspectives*. Englewood Cliffs, N J: Prentice Hall.

Hammersley, Martyn. 1992. *What's Wrong with Ethnography?* London and New York: Routledge.

Hammersley, Martyn, and Paul Atkinson. 1983. *Ethnography: Principles in Practice*. London and New York: Tavistock Publications.

Harding, Sandra. 1992. 'Subjectivity, Experience and Knowledge: An Epistemology from/for Rainbow Coalition Politics.' *Development and Change* 23:175–93.

Harris, Marvin. 1966. 'The Cultural Ecology of India's Sacred Cattle.' *Current Anthropology* 7:51–66.

– 1968. *The Rise of Anthropological Theory*. New York: Thomas Y. Crowell Company.

– 1971. *Culture, Man, and Nature*. New York: Thomas Y. Crowell Company.

– 1975. *Cows, Pigs, Wars and Witches*. New York: Vintage Books.

– 1991. *Cultural Anthropology*. New York: Harper Collins Publishers.

– 1993. 'Post-Modern Anti-Scientism.' Paper presented at the annual meeting of the American Association for the Advancement of Science, February 1993.

Harris, Rosemary. 'Women and Anthropological Fieldwork.' In *Social Anthropology Handbook*, University of Sussex. Undated, in mimeo.

Harvey, David. 1989. *The Condition of Postmodernity*. Cambridge, Mass.: Basil Blackwell.

Harvey, S. 1938. 'A Preliminary Investigation of the Interview.' *British Journal of Psychology* 28:263–87.

Hatch, E. 1973. *Theories of Man and Culture*. New York: Columbia University Press.

Held, D. 1980. *Introduction to Critical Theory*. Berkeley and Los Angeles: University of California Press.

Henry, Frances, and Satish Saberwal, eds. 1969. *Stress and Response in Fieldwork*. New York: Holt, Rinehart and Winston.

Henry, Jules. 1940. 'A Method for Learning to Talk Primitive Languages.' *American Anthropologist* 43:635–41.

Henry, Jules, and Melford E. Spiro. 1953. 'Psychological Techniques: Projective Tests in Field Work.' In A.L. Kroeber, ed., *Anthropology Today*, pp. 417–29. Chicago: University of Chicago Press.

Hill, Jonathan, ed., 1988. *Rethinking History and Myth*. Chicago: University of Illinois Press.

Honigmann, John J. 1982. 'Sampling in Ethnographic Fieldwork.' In R. Burgess, ed., *Field Research: A Sourcebook and Field Manual*, pp. 79–90. London: George Allen and Unwin.

Honigmann, John J., and Irma Honigmann. 1955. 'Sampling Reliability in Ethnographic Field Work.' *Southwestern Journal of Anthropology* 11:282–7.

Hunter, Monica. 1934. 'Methods of Study of Culture Contact.' *Africa* 7:335–50.

Hymes, Dell. ed., 1964. *Language in Culture and Society*. New York: Harper and Row, Publishers.

– ed. 1965. *The Use of Computers in Anthropology*. The Hague: Mouton and Company.

Jackson, P. 1989. *Maps of Meaning*. London: Unwin Hyman.

Jameson, Frederic. 1984. 'Postmodernism or the Cultural Logic of Late Capitalism.' *New Left Review* 146:53–93.

Jarvie, I.C. 1969. 'The Problem of Ethical Integrity in Participant Observations.' *Current Anthropology* 10:505–8.

– 1986. *Thinking About Society: Theory and Practice*. Dordrecht: D. Reidel Publishing Company.

– 1988. 'Comments.' *Current Anthropology* 29:427–9.

– 1989. 'Recent Work in the History of Anthropology and Its Historiographic Problems.' *Philosophy of Social Science* 19:345–75.

Jay, M. 1974. *The Dialectical Imagination*. London: Heinemann.

Johnson, A. 1978. *Quantification in Cultural Anthropology*. Stanford, Calif.: Stanford University Press.

Johnson, John M. 1975. *Doing Field Research*. New York: The Free Press.

Jones, Delmos J. 1982. 'Towards a Native Anthropology.' In Johnnetta B. Cole, ed., *Anthropology for the Eighties*, pp. 471–82. New York: The Free Press.

Jongmans, D.G., and P.C.W. Gutkind, eds. 1967. *Anthropologists in the Field*. Assen: Van Gorcum and Company.

Junker, Buford H. 1960. *Field Work*. Chicago: University of Chicago Press.

Kahn, R., and C. Cannell. 1957. *The Dynamics of Interviewing*. New York: John Wiley and Sons.

Kaplan, David, and Robert Manners. 1972. *Culture Theory*. Englewood Ciffs, NJ: Prentice-Hall.

Kay, Paul. 1971. *Explorations in Mathematical Anthropology*. Cambridge, Mass.: MIT Press.

Keesing, Roger M. 1976. *Cultural Anthropology: A Contemporary Perspective*. New York: Holt, Rinehart and Winston.

Kent, Stephen A. 1989. 'The Sage Qualitative Research Methods Series.' *Canadian Review of Sociology and Anthropology* 26:848–52.

Killworth, P., and H. Russell. 1976. 'Informant Accuracy in Social Network Data.' *Human Organization* 35:269–86.

Kirby, Vicki. 1991. 'Comment on Mascia-Lees, Sharpe, and Cohen's "The Postmodernist Turn in Anthropology: Cautions from a Feminist Perspective".' *Signs* 16:394–400.

Kirk, Jerome, and Marc L. Miller. 1986. *Reliability and Validity in Qualitative Research*. Newbury Park, Calif.: Sage Publications.

Kluckhohn, Florence. 1940. 'The Participant Observer Technique in Small Communities.' *American Journal of Sociology* 46:331–43.

Krauss, Irving. 1976. *Stratification, Class, and Conflict.* New York: The Free Press.

Kroeber, A.L., ed., 1953. *Anthropology Today.* Chicago: University of Chicago Press.

– 1963. *Anthropology.* Harbinger Books.

Kroeber, A.L., and H.E. Driver. 1932. 'Quantitative Expression of Cultural Relationships.' University of California, Publications in American Archaeology and Ethnology 9:253–423.

Kroeber, A.L., and J. Richardson. 1940. 'Three Centuries of Women's Dress Fashions: A Quantitative Analysis.' *University of California Anthropological Records* 5:111–54.

Kuhn, Thomas S. 1962. *The Structure of Scientific Revolutions.* Chicago: University of Chicago Press.

Kuper, Adam. 1975 (orig. 1973). *Anthropologists and Anthropology.* London: Peregrine Books.

Kuper, Hilda. 1947. *An African Aristocracy.* London: Oxford University Press.

Lamphere, Louise. 1977. 'Anthropology.' *Signs* 2:612–27.

Langness, L.L. 1965. *The Life History in Anthropological Science.* New York: Holt, Rinehart and Winston.

Lanoue, Guy. 1991. Review of *The Queen's People.* In *Canadian Journal of Native Studies* 11:355–63.

Leach, Edmund R. 1958. 'An Anthropologist's Reflections on a Social Survey.' *Ceylon Journal of Historical and Social Studies* 1:9–20.

– 1961a. 'Lévi-Strauss in the Garden of Eden: An Examination of Some Recent Developments in the Analysis of Myth.' *Transactions of the New York Academy of Sciences.* Series 2:386–96.

– 1961b. *Rethinking Anthropology.* London: Athlone Press.

– 1962. 'Genesis as Myth.' *Discovery,* May: 30–5.

– 1965. *Political Systems of Highland Burma.* Boston: Beacon Press.

– 1966. 'The Legitimacy of Solomon: Some Structural Aspects of Old Testament History.' *European Journal of Sociology* 7:58–101.

– ed. 1968. *The Structural Study of Myth and Totemism.* London: Tavistock Publications.

– 1973. 'Structuralism in Social Anthropology.' In David Robey, ed., *Structuralism: An Introduction.* Oxford: Clarendon Press.

– 1974. *Lévi-Strauss.* London: Fontana.

Leacock, Eleanor. 1977. 'Women in Egalitarian Societies.' In Renate Bridenthal and Claudia Koonz, eds., *Becoming Visible: Women in European History.* Boston: Houghton Mifflin Company.

Lee, Richard B. 1979. *The !Kung San: Men, Women, and Work in a Foraging Society.* New York: Cambridge University Press.

Lee, Richard B., and Irven Devore. 1976. *Kalahari Hunter-Gatherers.* Cambridge, Mass.: Harvard University Press.

Lenski, G. 1966. *Power and Privilege*. New York: McGraw-Hill.

Lévi-Strauss, Claude. 1963 (orig. 1962). *Totemism*. Boston: Beacon Press.

– 1966 (orig. 1962). *The Savage Mind*. London: Weidenfeld and Nicolson.

– 1967a (orig. 1958). *Structural Anthropology*. New York: Anchor Books.

– 1967b. *The Scope of Anthropology*. London: Jonathan Cape.

– 1969 (orig. 1949). *The Elementary Structures of Kinship*. Boston: Beacon Press.

– 1974 (orig. 1955). *Tristes Tropiques*. New York: Atheneum.

– 1975 (orig. 1964). *The Raw and the Cooked*. Vol. 1. New York: Harper Colophon.

– 1978. *Myth and Meaning*. Toronto: University of Toronto Press.

Lewis, I.M. 1985 (orig. 1976). *Social Anthropology in Perspective*. Cambridge: Cambridge University Press.

Lewis, Oscar. 1951. *Life in a Mexican Village, Tepoztlan Restudied*. Urbana, Ill.: University of Illinois Press.

– 1960. *Tepoztlan, Village in Mexico*. New York: Holt, Rinehart and Winston.

Lloyd, P.C. 1968. 'Conflict Theory and Yoruba Kingdoms.' In Michael Banton, ed., *History and Social Anthropology*, pp. 25–61. London: Tavistock Publications.

Lofland, John. 1971. *Analyzing Social Settings*. Belmont, Calif.: Wadsworth Publishing Company.

Lowie, Robert H. 1937. *The History of Ethnological Theory*. New York: Holt, Rinehart and Winston.

– 1940. 'Native Languages as Ethnographic Tools.' *American Anthropologist* 42:81–9.

Lucacs, G. 1971 (orig. 1923). *History and Class Consciousness: Studies in Marxist Dialectics*. Trans. R. Livingstone. London: Merlin Press.

MacFarlane, Alan. 1979. *The Origins of English Individualism*. New York: Cambridge University Press.

MacKinnon, Catherine A. 1982. 'Feminism, Marxism, Method, and the State: An Agenda for Theory.' *Signs* 7:515–44.

– 1983. 'Feminism, Marxism, Method, and the State: Toward Feminist Jurisprudence.' *Signs* 8:635–58.

MacKinnon, Neil J. 1994. *Symbolic Interactionism as Affect Control*. Albany, NY: State University of New York Press.

Madge, John. 1953. *The Tools of Social Science*. Longman, Green and Company. Republished in Anchor Books 1965.

Mair, L. 1972. *An Introduction to Social Anthropology*. Oxford: Clarendon Press.

Malinowski, Bronislaw. 1938. 'Introductory Essay: The Anthropology of Changing African Cultures.' In *Methods of Study of Culture Contact in Africa*, pp. vii–xxxviii. London: Oxford University Press.

– 1941. 'An Anthropological Analysis of War.' *American Journal of Sociology* 46:521–50.

- 1944. *A Scientific Theory of Culture*. Chapel Hill, NC: University of North Carolina Press.
- 1945. *The Dynamics of Culture Change: An Inquiry into Race Relations in Africa*. P. Kaberry, ed., New Haven: Yale University Press.
- 1961 (orig. 1922). *Argonauts of the Western Pacific*. New York: E.P. Dutton and Company.
- 1967. *A Diary in the Strict Sense of the Term*. London: Routledge and Kegan Paul.
Manning, Peter K. 1987. *Semiotics and Fieldwork*. Newbury Park, Calif.: Sage Publications.
Marcus, George E., and Michael M.J. Fischer. 1986. *Anthropology as Cultural Critique*. Chicago: University of Chicago Press.
Marshall, Gloria. 1970. 'In a World of Women: Field Work in a Yoruba Community.' In Peggy Golde, ed., *Women in the Field*, pp. 167–91. Chicago: Aldine Publishing Company.
Marwick, M.G. 1956. 'An Experiment in Public-Opinion Polling Among Preliterate People.' *Africa* 26:149–59.
Mascia-Lees, Frances E., et al. 1989. 'The Postmodernist Turn in Anthropology: Cautions from a Feminist Perspective.' *Signs* 15:7–33.
- 1991. 'Reply to Kirby.' *Signs* 16:401–8.
Maybury-Lewis, David. 1965. *The Savage and the Innocent*. Boston: Beacon Press.
- 1970. 'Science as Bricolage?' In E. Hayes and T. Hayes, eds., *Claude Lévi-Strauss: The Anthropologist as Hero*. Cambridge, Mass: MIT Press.
Mayer, Adrian. 1966. 'The Significance of Quasi-Groups in the Study of Complex Societies.' In Michael Banton, ed., *The Social Anthropology of Complex Societies*, pp. 97–122. London: Tavistock Publications.
McClelland, David. 1967. *The Achieving Society*. New York: The Free Press.
McClintock, C., et al. 1979. 'Applying the Logic of Sample Surveys to Qualitative Case Studies: The Case Cluster Method.' *Admin. Sci. Q.* 24:612–29.
McCormack, Thelma. 1989. 'Feminism and the New Crisis in Methodology.' In Winnie Tomm, ed., *The Effects of Feminist Approaches on Research Methodologies*, pp. 13–30. Waterloo, Ont: Wilfrid Laurier University Press.
McCracken, Grant. 1988. *The Long Interview*. Newbury Park, Calif.: Sage Publications.
McDonald, Lynn. 1993. *The Early Origins of the Social Sciences*. Montreal and Kingston: McGill-Queen's University Press.
McEwen, W. 1963. 'Forms and Problems of Validation in Social Anthropology.' *Current Anthropology* 4:155–83.
Mead, Margaret. 1928. *Coming of Age in Samoa*. New York: Morrow.
- 1930. *Growing Up in New Guinea*. New York: Morrow.

– 1933. 'More Comprehensive Field Methods.' *American Anthropologist* 35:1–15.

– 1935. *Sex and Temperament in Three Primitive Societies.* New York: Morrow.

– 1938. Anthropological Papers on the American Museum of Natural History, Vol. xxxvi, Part III. 'The Mountain Arapesh 1. An Importing Culture,' pp. 138–349. New York: the American Museum of Natural History.

– 1939. 'Native Languages as Field-Work Tools.' *American Anthropologist* 41:189–205.

– 1970. 'Field Work in the Pacific Islands, 1925–1967.' In Peggy Golde, ed., *Women in the Field,* pp. 293–332. Chicago: Aldine Publishing Company.

Mead, Margaret, et al. 1949. 'Report of the Committee on Ethics.' *Human Organization* 8:20–1.

Meillassoux, C. 1964. *Anthropologie Économique des Gouro de Côte d'Ivoire.* Paris: Mouton et Cie.

Menzies, Ken. 1982. *Sociological Theory in Use.* London: Routledge and Kegan Paul.

Meis, Maria. 1983. 'Towards a Methodology for Feminist Research.' In Gloria Bowles and Renate Duelli Klein, eds., *Theories of Women's Studies,* pp. 117–39. London: Routledge and Kegan Paul.

Mepham, John. 1973. 'The Structural Sciences and Philosophy.' In David Robey, ed., *Structuralism,* pp. 104–37. Oxford: Clarendon Press.

Merton, R.K. 1949. *Social Theory and Social Structure.* New York: The Free Press.

Merton, R.K., and P. Kendall. 1946. 'The Focused Interview.' *American Journal of Sociology* 51:541–57.

Methods of Study of Culture Contact in Africa. 1938. London: Oxford University Press; reprinted from *Africa,* vols. 7, 8, and 9.

Messerschmidt, Donald A., ed., 1981. *Anthropology at Home in North America: Methods and Issues in the Study of One's Own Society.* Cambridge: Cambridge University Press.

Middleton, John. 1970. *The Study of the Lugbara: Expectation and Paradox in Anthropological Research.* New York: Holt, Rinehart and Winston.

Mitchell, J. Clyde, ed., 1969. *Social Networks in Urban Situations.* Manchester: Manchester University Press.

Mitchell, William E. 1978. *The Bamboo Fire: Field Work with the New Guinea Wape.* Prospects Heights, Ill.: Waveland Press.

Moore, Frank W., ed., 1961. *Readings in Cross-Cultural Methodology.* New Haven: HRAF Press.

Morgan, Louis H. 1877. *Ancient Society.* New York: Holt.

Murdock, George Peter. 1949. *Social Structure.* New York: Macmillan.

Murphy, Robert. 1971. *The Dialectics of Social Life.* New York and London: Basic Books.

– 1986 (orig. 1979). *Culture and Social Anthropology: an Overture*. Englewood Cliffs, NJ: Prentice Hall.

Myers, V. 1977. 'Towards a Synthesis of Ethnographic and Survey Methods.' *Human Organization* 36:244–51.

Nadel, S.F. 1939. 'The Interview Technique in Social Anthropology.' In F.C. Bartlett et al., eds. *The Study of Society: Methods and Problems*, pp. 317–27. New York: Macmillan Company.

– 1951. *The Foundations of Social Anthropology*. Glencoe, Ill.: The Free Press.

Nader, Laura. 1970. 'From Anguish to Exultation.' In Peggy Golde, ed., *Women in the Field*, pp. 97–118. Chicago: Aldine Publishing Company.

– 1972. 'Up the Anthropologist – Perspectives Gained from Studying Up.' In Dell Hymes, ed., *Reinventing Anthropology*. New York: Pantheon Books.

– 1988. 'Post-Interpretive Anthropology.' *Anthropological Quarterly* 61:149–59.

Narayan, Kirin. 1993. 'How Native Is a "Native" Anthropologist?' *American Anthropologist* 93:671–86.

Naroll, Raoul, and Ronald Cohen, eds. 1970. *A Handbook of Method in Cultural Anthropology*. Garden City, NY: Natural History Press.

Notes and Queries in Anthropology. 1967 (orig. 1874). Royal Anthropological Institute of Great Britain and Ireland. London: Routledge and Kegan Paul. 6th ed.

Oakley, Ann. 1981. 'Interviewing Women: A Contradiction in Terms.' In Helen Roberts, ed., *Doing Feminist Research*. London: Routledge and Kegan Paul.

O'Barr, William M., et al., eds. 1973. *Survey Research in Africa*. Evanston: Northwestern University Press.

Opie, Anne. 1992. 'Qualitative Research, Appropriation of the "Other" and Empowerment.' *Feminist Review* 40:52–69.

Ortner, Sherry B. 1991. 'Reading America: Preliminary Notes on Class and Culture.' In Richard G. Fox, ed., *Recapturing Anthropology*, pp. 163–89. Santa Fe, NMex.: School of American Research Press.

Oxall, I., et al., eds. 1975. *Beyond the Sociology of Development*. London: Routledge and Kegan Paul.

Paul, Benjamin D. 1953. 'Interview Techniques and Field Relationships.' In A.L. Kroeber, ed., *Anthropology Today*, pp. 430–51. Chicago: University of Chicago Press.

Peacock, James, and A. Thomas Kirsch. 1980. *The Human Direction; An Evolutionary Approach to Social and Cultural Anthropology*. New York: Appleton-Century-Crofts.

Pelto, Pertti J. 1970. *Anthropological Research: The Structure of Inquiry*. New York: Harper and Row.

Penniman, T.K. 1965. *A Hundred Years of Anthropology*. London: Gerald Duckworth and Company.

Pfaffenberger, Bryan. 1988. *Microcomputer Applications in Qualitative Research.* Newbury Park, Calif.: Sage Publications.

Phillips, Derek. 1971. *Knowledge from What?* Chicago: Rand McNally.

Pincus, Fred L. 1982. 'Academic Marxists: A Study in Contradictions.' *The Insurgent Sociologist* 11:85–8.

Pitt, David C. 1972. *Using Historical Sources in Anthropology and Sociology.* New York: Holt, Rinehart and Winston.

Podelefsky, A., and C. McCarty. 1983. 'Topical Sorting: a Technique for Computer Assisted Qualitative Data Analysis.' *American Anthropologist* 85:886–9.

Powdermaker, Hortense. 1966. *Stranger and Friend.* New York: W.W. Norton and Company.

Pratt, Mary Louise. 1986. 'Fieldwork in Common Places.' In James Clifford and George E. Marcus, eds., *Writing Culture*, pp. 27–50. Berkeley, Calif.: University of California Press.

Price, John. 1973. 'A Holism through Team Ethnography.' *Human Relations* 26:155–70.

Punch, Maurice. 1986. *The Politics and Ethics of Fieldwork.* Newbury Park, Calif.: Sage Publications.

Rabinow, Paul. 1977. *Reflections on Fieldwork in Morocco.* Berkeley, Calif.: University of California Press.

– 1986. 'Representations Are Social Facts: Modernity and Post-Modernity in Anthropology.' In James Clifford and George E. Marcus, eds., *Writing Culture*, pp. 234–61. Berkeley, Calif.: University of California Press.

– 1991. 'For Hire: Resolutely Late Modern.' In Richard Fox, ed., *Recapturing Anthropology*, pp. 59–71. Santa Fe, NMex.: School of American Research Press.

Radcliffe-Brown, A. 1952. *Structure and Function in Primitive Society.* London: Cohen and West.

Rappaport, Roy. 1967. *Pigs for the Ancestors.* New Haven: Yale University Press.

Redfield, Robert. 1930. *Tepoztlan: A Mexican Village.* Chicago: University of Chicago Press.

– 1960. *The Little Community.* Chicago: Phoenix Books.

Rex, John. 1970. *Race Relations in Sociological Theory.* New York: Schocken Books.

Rhodes, Robert I., ed., 1970. *Imperialism and Underdevelopment.* New York: Monthly Review Press.

Richards, Audrey. 1938. 'The Village Census in the Study of Culture Contact.' *Methods of Study of Culture Contact in Africa*, pp. 46–59. London: Oxford University Press.

– 1939. 'The Development of Field Work Methods in Social Anthropology.' In F.C. Bartlett et al., eds. *The Study of Society: Methods and Problems*, pp. 272–316. New York: Macmillan Company.

Richards, Tom, and Lyn Richards. 1987. 'Qualitative Data Analysis: Can Computers Do It?' *Australian and New Zealand Journal of Sociology* 23:23–35.

– 1989. 'The Impact of Computer Techniques for Qualitative Data Analysis.' La Trobe University, Department of Computer Science, Technical Report 6/89.

– 1991. 'The NUDIST Qualitative Data Analysis System.' *Qualitative Sociology* 14:307–24.

Richer, Stephen. 1988. 'Fieldwork and the Commodification of Culture: Why the Natives Are Restless.' *Canadian Review of Sociology and Anthropology* 25:406–20.

Rivers, W.H.R. 1900. 'A Genealogical Method of Collecting Social and Vital Statistics.' *Journal of the Royal Anthropological Institute* 30:74–82.

– 1910. 'The Genealogical Method of Anthropological Inquiry.' *Sociological Review* 3:1–12.

Rodney, Walter. 1972. *How Europe Underdeveloped Africa*. Washington: Howard University Press.

Roe, A. 1952. 'A Psychological Study of Eminent Psychologists and Anthropologists and a Comparison with Biologists and Physical Scientists.' *Psychological Monographs* 67:1–55.

Sacks, Karen. 1979. *Sisters and Wives: The Past and Future of Social Equality*. Westport, Conn.: Greenwood Press.

Sahlins, Marshall. 1960. 'Evolution: Specific and General.' In M. Sahlins and E. Service, eds. *Evolution and Culture*. Ann Arbor: University of Michigan Press.

– 1981. *Historical Metaphors and Mythical Realities*. Ann Arbor: University of Michigan Press.

Said, Edward W. 1979. *Orientalism*. New York: Vintage Books.

Salamone, Frank A. 1977. 'The Methodological Significance of the Lying Informant.' *Anthropological Quarterly* 50:117–24.

Sangren, P. Steven. 1988. 'Rhetoric and the Authority of Ethnography.' *Current Anthropology* 29:405–24.

Schapera, Isaac. 1935. 'Field Methods in the Study of Modern Culture Contacts.' *Africa* 8:315–28.

Schatzman, L., and A. Strauss. 1973. *Field Research*. Englewood Cliffs, NJ: Prentice-Hall.

Schusky, Ernest L. 1965. *Manual for Kinship Analysis*. New York: Holt, Rinehart and Winston.

Seidel, J.V., and J.A. Clark. 1984. 'THE ETHNOGRAPH: A Computer Program for the Analysis of Qualitative Data.' *Qualitative Sociology* 7:110–25.

Seidel, J.V., R. Kjolseth, and J.A. Clark. 1985. *The Ethnograph: A User's Guide* (Version 2.0). Littleton, Colo.: Qualis Research Associates.

Seidel, J.V., R. Kjolseth, and E. Seymour. 1988. *The Ethnograph: A User's Guide* (Version 3.0). Littleton, Colo.: Qualis Research Associates.

Selltiz, Claire, et al. 1959 (orig. 1951). *Research Methods in Social Relations*. Revised ed. New York: Holt, Rinehart and Winston.

Shaffir, William, et al., eds. 1980. *Fieldwork Experience: Qualitative Approaches to Social Research*. New York: St. Martin's.

Shankman, Paul. 1984. 'The Thick and the Thin: On the Interpretive Theoretical Program of Clifford Geertz.' *Current Anthropology* 25:261–70.

Shields, Vickie Rutledge, and Brenda Dervin. 1993. 'Sense-Making in Feminist Social Science Research.' *Women's Studies Int. Forum* 16:65–81.

Shostak, Marjorie. 1981. *Nisa: The Life and Words of a !Kung Woman*. Cambridge, Mass.: Harvard University Press.

Shweder, Richard A. 1990. 'Cultural Psychology: What Is It?' In J. Stigler, et al., eds., *Cultural Psychology*. New York: Cambridge University Press.

– 1993. '"Why Do Men Barbeque?" and Other Postmodern Ironies of Growing Up in the Decade of Ethnicity.' *Daedelus* 122:279–308.

Siegel, Sidney. 1956. *Nonparametric Statistics for the Behavioral Sciences*. New York: McGraw-Hill.

Silverman, S. 1966. 'An Ethnocentric Approach to Social Stratification: Prestige in a Central Italian Community.' *American Anthropologist* 68:899–921.

– 1974–5. 'Bailey's Politics.' *Journal of Peasant Studies* 2:111–20.

Singer, Merrill. 1993. 'Knowledge for Use: Anthropology and Community-Centered Substance Abuse Research.' *Soc. Sci. Med.* 37:15–25.

Smith, Dorothy. 1986. 'Institutional Ethnography: A Feminist Method.' *Resources for Feminist Research* 15:6–13.

– 1987. *The Everyday World as Problematic: A Feminist Perspective*. Boston, Mass.: Northeastern University Press.

Smith, Gavin. 1991. *Livelihood and Resistance*. Berkeley and Los Angeles: University of California Press.

Social Anthropology Handbook. University of Sussex. Undated, available in mimeo 1970.

Soja, E.W. 1989. *Postmodern Geographies*. London: Verso.

Spencer, Herbert. 1876. *Principles of Sociology*. New York: D. Appleton. Reprinted 1896.

Spencer, Jonathan. 1989. 'Anthropology as a Kind of Writing.' *Man* 24:145–64.

Spindler, G., ed., 1970. *Being an Anthropologist: Fieldwork in Eleven Cultures*. New York: Holt, Rinehart and Winston.

Spindler, G., and W. Goldschmidt. 1952. 'Experimental Design in the Study of Culture Change.' *Southwestern Journal of Anthropology* 8:68–83.

Spradley, James P. 1979. *The Ethnographic Interview*. New York: Holt, Rinehart and Winston.

– 1980. *Participant Observation*. New York: Holt, Rinehart and Winston.

Stacey, Judith. 1988. 'Can There Be a Feminist Methodology?' *Women's Studies Int. Forum* 11:21–7.

Stanley, Liz, and Sue Wise. 1990. 'Method, Methodology and Epistemology in Feminist Research Processes.' In Liz Stanley, ed., *Feminist Praxis: Research, Theory and Epistemology in Feminist Sociology*, pp. 20–60: London: Routledge.

Stephenson, Peter. 1986. 'On Ethnographic Genre and the Experience of Communal Work with the Hutterian People,' *Culture* 6: 93–100.

Steward, Julian. 1955. *Theory of Culture Change*. Urbana: University of Illinois Press.

Stocking, George W., ed., 1983. *Observers Observed: Essays on Ethnographic Fieldwork*. History of Anthropology, Volume 1. Madison, Wis.: The University of Wisconsin Press.

– 1987. *Victorian Anthropology*. New York: The Free Press.

Strathern, Marilyn. 1987a. 'An Awkward Relationship: The Case of Feminism and Anthropology.' *Signs* 12:276–92.

– 1987b. 'Out of Context: The Persuasive Fictions of Anthropology.' *Current Anthropology* 28:251–70.

Strauss, A. 1987. *Qualitative Analysis for Social Scientists*. Cambridge: Cambridge University Press.

Strauss, A., and J. Corbin. 1990. *Basics of Qualitative Research (Grounded Theory Procedures and Techniques)*. Newbury Park, Calif.: Sage Publications.

Strieb, G.F. 1952. 'The Use of Survey Methods among the Navaho.' *American Anthropologist* 54:30–40.

Sturtevant, William C. 1959. 'A Technique for Ethnographic Note-Taking.' *American Anthropologist* 61:677–8.

Tallerico, Marilyn. 1991. 'Applications of Qualitative Analysis Software: A View from the Field.' *Qualitative Sociology* 14:275–85.

Terray, E. 1969. *Le Marxisme devant des Sociétés Primitives: Deux Études*. Paris: Maspero.

Tesch, Renata. 1991. 'Introduction.' *Qualitative Sociology* 14:225–43.

Thomas, David H. 1976. *Figuring Anthropology*. New York: Holt, Rinehart and Winston.

Thornton, Robert J., and Peter, Skalnik, eds. 1993. *Bronislaw Malinowski*. Cambridge: Cambridge University Press.

Tiffany, Sharon W. 1978. 'Models and the Social Anthropology of Woman: A Preliminary Assessment.' *Man* 13:34–51.

Trautman, Thomas R. 1987. *Louis Henry Morgan and the Invention of Kinship*. Berkeley and Los Angeles: University of California Press.

Tremblay, Marc-Adélard. 1957. 'The Key Informant Technique: A Non-Ethnographic Application.' *American Anthropologist* 59:688–701.

Trigger, Bruce G. 1968. *Beyond History: The Methods of Prehistory*. New York: Holt, Rinehart and Winston.

Trouillot, Michel-Rolph. 1991. 'Anthropology and the Savage Slot: The Poetics and Politics of Otherness.' In Richard Fox, ed., *Recapturing Anthropology*, pp. 17–44. Santa Fe, NMex.: School of American Research Press.

Turner, Victor. 1957. *Schism and Continuity in an African Society*. Manchester: Manchester University Press.

– 1967. *The Forest of Symbols: Studies in Ndembu Ritual*. Ithaca, NY: Cornell University Press.

– 1969. *The Ritual Process: Structure and Anti-Structure*. Chicago: Aldine Publishing Company.

– 1974. *Drama, Fields, and Metaphors: Symbolic Action in Human Society*. Ithaca, NY: Cornell University Press.

Tyler, Stephen A., ed. 1969. *Cognitive Anthropology*. New York: Holt, Rinehart and Winston.

– 1986. 'Post-Modern Ethnography: From Document of the Occult to Occult Document.' In James Clifford and George E. Marcus, eds., *Writing Culture*, pp. 122–40. Berkeley: University of California Press.

Tylor, E.B. 1871. *Primitive Culture*. London: John Murray.

– 1889. 'On a Method of Investigating the Development of Institutions; Applied to Laws of Marriage and Descent.' *Journal of the Royal Anthropological Institute* 18:245–69.

Udy, Stanley. 1959. *The Organization of Work: A Comparative Analysis of Production among Nonindustrial Peoples*. New Haven: HRAF Press.

Van den Berghe, Pierre. 1965. *South Africa, a Study in Conflict*. Middletown, Conn.: Wesleyan University Press.

Van Maanen, J. ed., 1983. *Qualitative Methodology*. Newbury Park, Calif.: Sage Publications.

Vidich, A. 1955. 'Participant Observation and the Collection and Interpretation of Data.' *American Journal of Sociology* 60:354–60.

Vidich, A., and J. Bensman. 1954. 'The Validity of Field Work Data.' *Human Organization* 13:20–7.

– 1958. *Small Town in Mass Society: Class, Power and Religion in a Rural Community*. Princeton: Princeton University Press.

Vidich, A., J. Bensman, and M. Stein, eds. 1964. *Reflections on Community Studies*. New York: John Wiley and Sons.

Vidich, A., and G. Shapiro, G. 1955. 'A Comparison of Participant Observation and Survey Data.' *American Sociological Review* 20:28–33.

Wagner, P.L., and M.W. Mikesell. eds. 1962. *Readings in Cultural Geography*. Chicago: University of Chicago Press.

Ward, Martha C. 1989. *Nest in the Wind: Adventures in Anthropology on a Tropical Island*. Prospect Heights, Ill.: Waveland Press.

Warner, W. 1949. *Social Class in America: A Manual of Procedure for the Measurement of Social Status*. Chicago: Science Research Associates.

Warren, Carol A.B. 1988. *Gender Issues in Field Research*. Newbury Park, Calif.: Sage Publications.

Wax, Murray. 1977. 'On Fieldworkers and Those Exposed to Fieldwork.' *Human Organization* 36:321–8.

Wax, Rosalie. 1971. *Doing Fieldwork: Warnings and Advice*. Chicago, Ill.: University of Chicago Press.

Webb, Eugene J., et al. 1966. *Unobtrusive Measures*. Chicago: Rand McNally and Company.

Weber, Max. 1958. *The Protestant Ethic and the Spirit of Capitalism*. Trans. Talcott Parsons. New York: Charles Scribner's Sons.

Weiner, Annette. 1976. *Women of Value, Men of Renown*. Austin, Tex.: University of Texas Press.

Werner, Dennis. 1984. *Amazon Journey*. New York: Simon and Schuster.

White, Leslie. 1949. *The Science of Culture*. New York: Grove Press.

– 1959. *The Evolution of Culture*. New York: McGraw-Hill.

Whittaker, Elvi. 1986. *The Mainland Haole*. New York: Columbia University Press.

– 1994. 'Decolonizing Knowledge: Towards a Feminist Ethic and Methodology.' In J.S. Grewal and Hugh Johnston, eds., *The India-Canada Relationship*, pp. 347–65. New Delhi: Sage Publications.

Wickwire, Wendy, and Michael McGonigle. 1991. 'The Queen's People: Ethnography or Appropriation?' *Native Studies Review*: 7:97–113.

Williams, Thomas Rhys. 1967. *Field Methods in the Study of Culture*. New York: Holt, Rinehart and Winston.

Willis, W.S. 1972. 'Skeletons in the Anthropological Closet.' In Dell Hymes, ed., *Reinventing Anthropology*. New York: Pantheon Books.

Wilson, Stephen. 1988. *Feuding, Conflict and Banditry in Nineteenth-Century Corsica*. Cambridge: Cambridge University Press.

Wilson, E.O. 1978. *Sociobiology – The New Synthesis*. Cambridge, Mass.: Harvard University Press.

Wolcott, Harry F. 1981. 'Home and Away: Personal Contrasts in Ethnographic Style.' In Donald A. Messerschmidt, ed., *Anthropologists at Home in North America: Methods and Issues in the Study of One's Own Society*, pp. 255–65. Cambridge: Cambridge University Press.

Wolf, Eric. 1969. *Peasant Wars of the Twentieth Century*. New York: Harper and Row, Publishers.

– 1982. *Europe and the People without History*. Berkeley and Los Angeles: University of California Press.

Worsley, Peter. 1964. *The Third World*. London: Weidenfeld and Nicolson.

Young, F., and R. Young. 1961. 'Key Informant Reliability.' *Human Organization* 20:141–8.

Zimmerman, Kate B. 1993. 'In Search of the Myth in History: The Narrative of the Quest from Sacred to Secular.' MA thesis, Department of Anthropology and Sociology, University of British Columbia.

Index